T0244483

The Hidden Order
of Intimacy

The Hidden Order
of Intimacy

REFLECTIONS ON
THE BOOK OF LEVITICUS

Avivah Gottlieb Zornberg

Schocken Books, New York

All rights reserved. Published in the United States by Schocken Books,
a division of Penguin Random House LLC, New York, and distributed in
Canada by Penguin Random House Canada Limited, Toronto.

Schocken Books and colophon are registered trademarks of
Penguin Random House LLC.

Library of Congress Cataloging-in-Publication Data
Name: Zornberg, Avivah Gottlieb, author.
Title: The hidden order of intimacy: reflections on the Book of Leviticus /
Avivah Gottlieb Zornberg.
Description: First edition. | New York: Schocken Books, 2022. |
Includes bibliographical references and index.
Identifiers: LCCN 2021030990 (print). | LCCN 2021030991 (ebook). |
ISBN 9780805243574 (hardcover). | ISBN 9780805243581 (ebook).
Subjects: LCSH: Bible. Leviticus—Criticism, interpretation, etc.
Golden calf (Bible).
Classification: LCC BS1255.52 .Z67 2022 (print) |
LCC BS1255.52 (ebook) | DDC 222/.1306—dc23
LC record available at https://lccn.loc.gov/2021030990
LC ebook record available at https://lccn.loc.gov/2021030991

www.schocken.com

Jacket art © 2021 Yoram Raanan/Raanan Art
Jacket design by Emily Mahon

Printed in the United States of America
First Edition
2 4 6 8 9 7 5 3 1

O the mind, mind has mountains; cliffs of fall.

—Gerard Manley Hopkins

The tears of the living . . . are themselves far from having a meaning opposite to joy. Far from being sorrowful, the tears are the expression of a keen awareness of shared life grasped in its intimacy. It is true that this awareness is never keener than at the moment when absence suddenly replaces presence, as in death or mere separation. . . . [I]t is precisely the disappearance of duration, and of the neutral behaviors associated with it, that uncovers a ground of things that is dazzlingly bright.

—Georges Bataille, Theory of Religion

Let them make for Me a holy place and I shall dwell within them.

—Exodus 25:8

CONTENTS

ACKNOWLEDGMENTS

Since Leviticus is not, for the most part, a narrative book, I had originally assumed that I would not be writing about it. This changed once I entered into the realm of midrashic readings of this largely legalistic text. What I discovered was a wealth of transformative narrative. The two worlds—one formalistic, factual, objective; the other intimate, ambiguous, and fraught with imagination—entered into a conversation that rang with a strange truth for me. The hidden theme of the Golden Calf organized the material in a powerful way. And the closing down of the public and the social world in the year of Corona gave me time to sit and write.

I am grateful, as always, for my ongoing exposure to lively students and for their ways of listening and responding. In this year of Corona, however, I have been teaching largely through the wizardry of Zoom—a technology that at first seemed forbiddingly alienating but that, unpredictably, began to open up a different kind of intimacy. My thanks to Matan Women's Institute for Torah Studies for hosting my classes, as part of a rich and varied program for learners, women and men, across continents. Beit Avi Chai, too, has always been hospitable to my classes and this year widened its hospitality to include learners in the United States. When I had to cancel my regular lecture tour in the United States, many of my hosts there worked with me to organize wonderful Zoom events.

What makes this book different from its predecessors, however, is that it is not based on lectures and live teaching. Because of my travel calendar, Leviticus has not been on my teaching schedule for many years. In this sense, this book was a more purely *literary* project, conceived and written in the seclusion of the Corona reality.

I want to acknowledge the gifts offered, especially in this Corona time, by two very different teachers: Professor Arthur Green and Yishai Mevorach. Art gave a weekly class in Hebrew for a group of Jerusalem scholars and creative thinkers in the period leading up to the Corona outbreak, when the class continued on Zoom. I was moved by Art's teaching and captivated by the minds and souls in conversation during these meetings. Yishai has been recording his weekly classes in Hebrew for many years. His passionate and highly original thinking about a core group of Jewish texts has challenged me in profound ways. The privilege of learning from these great teachers is not diminished by the fact that both come from worlds very different from mine, and from each other.

Special thanks to Altie Karper, my editor and source of encouragement at Schocken, together with her devoted team. And to Sharon Friedman, my friend and agent, here in Jerusalem. My warmest thanks to my dear friends: Betsy Rosenberg, who read my chapters as they arrived in the world, delivering back to me resonances and an alternative perspective; and Linda Zisquit, whose enthusiasm kept me going at insecure times.

This year, I lost a dear friend, the eminent psychoanalyst Dr. Anna Antonovsky, with whom I had an unusual relationship over the course of many years. We first met when I gave some lectures at the William Alanson White Institute, where she was a leading figure. A longtime secularist, skeptical about religion in the style of her generation, significantly older than I: worlds, one might say, divided us. And yet, perhaps because of her origins—Vienna, Galicia, an Orthodox background, an intense, implicit Jewishness—we recognized each other and cherished a unique encounter that deepened over the years. My annual lecture tour in the United States always included visits to her home and good conversations. May her memory be blessed.

To my husband, Eric, I hold the deepest gratitude and appreciation for building with me the home in which, among other things, I am able to write. It can't be easy to live with the storm cloud that is a writing wife! The miracle of family, children, and grandchildren has, perforce, been held at arm's length in this Corona year. But Eric was that miracle of home in my life and, I hope, I was that for him. To paraphrase Rabbi Akiva, "What is mine and what is yours is his."

INTRODUCTION

HAUNTED BY THE GOLDEN CALF

One day as I was reflecting on the book of Leviticus, I had a sudden intuition regarding the pervasive presence of the Golden Calf, an image that haunts the midrashic narratives that thread through this biblical text. In meaning and in fantasy, that catastrophic episode gives depth and resonance to the entire book of Leviticus. Later on, it occurred to me that the idea might be rooted in my own preoccupation with post-traumatic memory. "Post" words—like postmodernism and postcolonialism—tend to evoke the troubling continuity of the past. Although the post-traumatic effects of the Golden Calf episode are apparently overcome, they continue to call out like unlaid ghosts.

The central subject of Leviticus is the functioning of the *Mishkan*, the Holy Tabernacle, with its sacrifices, its pollution taboos, its priesthood with its powers and limitations. Other subjects are covered, such as bodily impurity, leprosy, the *Shmittah* and the *Yovel* (the seventh and the fiftieth year of the cycle), as well as the violent narratives of Nadav and Avihu, who are burned in fire on the day of the consecration of the *Mishkan*, and of the blasphemer who, without obvious cause, curses the divine Name. But the earlier sections of the book are focused on the question of God's presence, coming to rest in the *Mishkan*. This divine Presence, devoutly to be wished, has its counterpart in the spectral presence of the Golden Calf. God-in-your-midst[1] will signify people's successful repentance for "that deed," as the midrash names it.[2] The *Mishkan* will intimate full forgiveness.

The midrashic literature goes farther. The *Mishkan* does not merely represent forgiveness; it becomes a therapeutic device for healing the national disorder that is called the Golden Calf. Beginning with the inventory for its building, we find the recurrent theme: "Let the gold of the *Mishkan* atone for the gold they brought toward the making of the Golden Calf."[3] The work with the materials of the *Mishkan* homeopathically counteracts that sin. The image becomes medicalized in some texts: Bezalel, for instance, as the chief craftsman, is credited both as a goldsmith and as a divinely inspired medical student who "applies a plaster to the wound."[4] God, as Bezalel's teacher, prides Himself on His student's uncanny knowledge, his *da'at:* "It was I who created and taught him!"

Here, the question of chronological order becomes interesting. The instructions for the *Mishkan* are first laid out in Exodus 25, and the Golden Calf narrative follows several chapters later, in chapter 32. The usual reading (the *p'shat*) of the sequence describes the project of the Tabernacle as primary, with the Calf incident as an interruption in the happy narrative of Revelation and divine Presence.

Against this "straightforward" reading, many midrashic sources recast the chronology.[5] The narrative now holds profound spiritual tension. Far from being an interruption, the Golden Calf is the story itself. The *Mishkan* is the divine, therapeutic *response* to what is, in a sense, a necessary story. Without the sin of the Golden Calf, there would have been no *Mishkan:* in reality, though not in the text, the sin must have preceded its cure.

Beyond this, however, an even more radical midrashic claim returns us to the obvious chronological order of events. The instructions for the *Mishkan* are given first, by way of *preempting* the disease with the cure.[6]

In one midrash,[7] both sequences appear in tension with each other. In the biblical text, the people first donate gold for the Golden Calf and then for the *Mishkan,* while in the midrashic parable, the generous young man gives money to charity and then to "theater" (a licentious project). The sequence of sin and penitence is reversed and thus subverted. The normal structure of atonement is upended. What happens to our understanding when the virtuous act (charity) comes *before* the deplorable one (theater)? The gold of the *Mishkan* comes to atone for a future act, one that has not yet been committed. Perhaps our generous young man is simply indiscriminate in his projects? How is narrative meaning to be found in this case? In what sense can the cure heal a sickness that has not yet manifested? The midrash challenges the reader to discover more radical ways of reading.

NO MERE EPISODE

The book of Leviticus begins after the construction of the *Mishkan* is completed. It is primarily concerned with the proper functioning of the Tabernacle, its rituals and taboos. Purity and impurity are the poles of its ongoing drama. It is within this text that the midrashic tradition has detected the continuing traumatic presence of the Golden Calf. If the *Mishkan* gives the people a possibility of translating the Revelation at Sinai into a different and more intimate[8] ritual language, it also gives them the opportunity to confront the pathology of the Golden Calf and its implications. One of these implications is that the Revelation and the Golden Calf are, in a strange sense, inherent in each other.

On the face of it, the episode of idolatry is dealt with rather summarily. Three thousand dead, Moses's prayers, his ascents and descents of the mountain—and, it seems, that event has been brought to closure. However, an important tradition claims that the effects of this sin will remain to ferment throughout the generations. "On the day when I make an accounting (*pokdi*), I will bring them to account (*u-fakadti*) for their sins" (Exod. 32:34). The root *pakad* has both ominous and vital meanings, variously referring to both death and birth. In the wake of midrashic sources, Rashi reads: "Now, I accede to your prayers not to destroy them. But *always, always,* when I make an accounting of their sins, then I will bring them to account for a *little of this sin,* together with their other sins. No punishment ever comes upon Israel that does not contain a *little punishment* for the sin of the Golden Calf."

This notion, that the effects of the sin, as well as its punishments, will be diffused over many generations, may imply a kind of suspension of the full gravity of the law. Or it may suggest that a residue of that failure will linger forever. It is somehow endemic in human nature, even if only in the quasi-scientific measure of an *onki*, an alchemically minute quantity of Calf-substance that ferments in all generations.[9]

The ambiguous effect of these Talmudic readings—Is this diffusion an act of divine charity or of endless doom?—is augmented by Rashi's unusual repetition, "always, always," to express the inescapable remainders of the Golden Calf throughout history. The concrete, historical meaning of idolatry is fragmented by this device; margins of metaphorical meaning demand to be taken up.

Here, the Golden Calf is no mere episode. Its implications and effects have revealed something about human beings in the world. Rather than excising this pathology with the surgeon's knife, God offers a possibility of living with it. This will mean bearing the brunt of the challenge it offers to wishful thinking. A sobering truth is also a revelation of a kind.

DOUBLE REVELATION

Perhaps the two revelations are bound up with each other. Perhaps, beyond the narrative of the Golden Calf as a disruptive *aftermath* of Sinai, there exists another narrative in which the Golden Calf makes its appearance at the very heart of Revelation. In constructing the *Mishkan,* therefore, the people would be seeking relief from the tensions implicit within the experience of Revelation. On this reading, there is a single, complex story with Revelation at its heart:

> Said Ulla: Shameless is the bride who plays the harlot while still under her wedding canopy! Said R. Mari the son of Samuel's daughter: What verse refers to this? "While the king still sat at his banquet, my spikenard gave forth its fragrance" (Songs 1:12).[10]

The bride plays the harlot in the *middle* of the wedding ceremony, *under* the wedding canopy, *while* the King is celebrating, *even as* the fire of Revelation still burns at Sinai.[11] A grotesque synchronicity links the moments of revelation and idolatry. This affects the reader like a blow; the physical image makes one flinch.

But the image intimates an inner reality, a moment of emotional recoil from the very intensity of the sublime experience. A laser beam is directed at the strange ways of the human heart, what Kant called its "crooked timber." The Hebrew expression *me-zanah* covers the whole range of *waywardness,* from mental to physical adultery.[12] The heart is the theater of betrayal. The surrealistic image of the wayward bride makes its impact but then resolves into an emotional rather than a physical claim. The bride inwardly turns aside from her commitment to the King. Some other erotic interest arouses her, shamefully, in the very midst of the wedding.

In a similar vein, another midrash minimizes the forty days that officially separate the two moments of Revelation and the Golden Calf. A mere forty days becomes in this challenging midrash: "Not even one day were they *with God;* [after that] they were [already] calculating how to make the Calf!"[13] The inability to be *with God* is worked out by gradually whittling away at the numbers, from forty to "not even one day." Like one who departs on a journey and without any delay at all goes off on the wrong track: "R. Meir said: They stood at Sinai and said with their mouth, We shall do and we shall hear, while their hearts were turned, attuned (*mechuvan*) to idolatry: 'They seduced Him with their mouth . . . but their heart was not steadfast (*nachon*) with Him' (Ps. 78:36–37)."

Focusing on the core utterance of commitment to God, *"Na'aseh ve-nishma*—We shall do and we shall hear!" R. Meir declares that this was a moment of "seduction"; heart and mouth are at odds, inner experience pulling away from language. Or, more strongly, language being used by the wayward in order to beguile God.

This midrash is, in its way, as shocking as the imagery of the bride under the wedding canopy. Effectively, it undermines the one good moment in a history of backslidings and rebellions. In general, midrashic literature builds on this moment to spell out the people's commitment to *doing* even before *hearing;* to fulfilling the commandments even before trying to understand them. "We shall do and we shall hear" has become the blazon of Israel's true faith.[14] Here, strangely, *na'aseh ve-nishma* becomes mere lip service. So powerful is the people's inner resistance to the Revelation that, even as they mouth the words of faith, they are already creating the Golden Calf.

LISTENING FOR GOD

In a powerful teaching, R. Yehuda Aryeh Leib Alter (known as the Sefat Emet) works against the grain of the usual understanding of *na'aseh ve-nishma.* He reads *hearing* as the spiritual horizon of *doing.* For him, this great faith moment is one in which the people declare their readiness to *listen for* intimations of God's will, beyond the mini-mum of the law. This involves a constant attunement, a readiness to respond to the demand of the godly whenever it becomes audible. This posture of aspiration is what will characterize the Jewish spiri-tual genius. Obedience to the law is not the final goal; that is why it is written first, as preamble to the larger demand.[15]

For Sefat Emet, the purpose of the Exodus and the Revelation at Sinai is to acquire this position of *listening.* When the people desire to return to Egypt, to the condition of slavery, they resist this divine demand. To return to Egypt is the easy option, falling back on habit, on the constricted life of the slave for whom obedience is all. Free-dom means a turning toward the future and its possibilities, its dif-ficult demands. Always hoping to hear *more* from God, one realizes the exodus project in its fullness.[16]

For this reason, he explains, the Hebrew slave who "freely" opts for continued slavery ("I love my master—I will not go out to free-dom!") has to undergo the ritual of having his earlobe pierced against the door lintel (Exod. 21:5–6). He has sinned against that passion for *hearing more* that is to inform spiritual life. "The *ear* that heard at Sinai, 'Unto Me shall the Israelites be slaves, and not slaves of slaves,' and then he went and acquired a master for himself, that ear shall be pierced."[17] To opt for slavery is to betray, to immobilize, one's "ear" for the sacred, for freedom and responsibility.

For Sefat Emet, then, listening is the posture of aspiration. It rep-resents a mode beyond that of action or obedience. We may think of the many biblical texts that place listening at the center: whether it is in the credo—the call to attention, uttered twice daily—of "Hear O Israel, God, our God, God is one!" or in the preamble to Revelation, "If you will indeed listen to My voice and keep My covenant, you shall be to Me a treasure among the nations" (Exod. 19:5).

A certain quality of attention (tension, desire) is invoked in this listening. Perhaps the *na'aseh ve-nishma* response conceals a reserva-tion about the larger aspiration of listening. By putting obedience before listening, one may be reserving the option of *making do* with mere performance. Even as one commits oneself in words that carry the vitality of aspiration, one is flinching from the radical demand of those very words.

RECEIVING TORAH

That flinching—that backward and forward movement—is, I suggest, inherent in the drama of Revelation. The sublime comes with overwhelming force. It is experienced as impinging on the mind of the listener who, in the same gesture, both accepts and resists. "If we continue to *listen for* the voice of God, our God, any longer, we shall die. For who that is entirely flesh has heard the voice of the living God speaking from the midst of the fire as we have—and has lived?" (Deut. 5:22–23). The impact of God's voice on human flesh is corrosive; its very vitality is excessive. So ambivalence, flinching, makes the receiver of Torah unreceptive. All that is being given is both desired and reflexively warded off.

The expressions used in the Scriptures for the moment of receptivity, when the Speaker leaves His mark on the surface of consciousness, include *hearing* (*sh'miah*), having one's heart inscribed or engraved, and *remembering* (*zechirah*). One may be susceptible to this impact, or one may be resistant to it. The language of Revelation may be effective or ineffective—it may affect or fail to affect. The listener may remain unmarked, may be ambivalent, or may even have strategies to nullify the impact of what is being revealed.

GEORGE ELIOT ON ETHICAL HEARING

By way of analogy, it is interesting to notice the ways in which such complex moments characterize the work of the nineteenth-century English novelist George Eliot. On many occasions, Eliot analyzes spiritual confrontations of this kind. There is a passionate speaker who seeks to inscribe a moral message on the consciousness of the weaker, morally endangered character. Imagery of burning and biting and branding marks these passages. Implicit in these scenes is a kind of violence of ethical passion. But the power of this moral utterance is met by a resistance that deprives it of all its power.

At the end of *Daniel Deronda*, Ezra (Mordecai) reproaches his gambler father, who responds with hysterical tears that somehow serve to suspend the force of his son's attack: "and his [Ezra's] words had the heart eaten out of them."[18]

The force of words is met by a counterforce, a tissue of fantasy, which neutralizes or nullifies it. Such moments of spiritual impulse and repression recur throughout George Eliot's fiction. In a similar way, Freud describes the death drive as a "silent, colorless something that both *sustains and erodes* the erotic drives."[19] The numbing effect both receives and corrodes, accepts and invalidates whatever tries to enliven. George Eliot precedes Freud in her interest in the primal struggle between life wishes and death wishes.

Often, in her fiction, as well as in her own letters, the theme recurs. Its origin in her writing lies in her own experience, which she struggles to understand and master. "Quickness of hearing," "a fine ear," "a roar of sound" become metaphors for the enlivened sensibility that does not yield to the spell of numbness. Her most famous passage in this vein is one in which she admonishes the reader to become aware of her own "stupidity":

> If we had a keen vision and a feeling for all ordinary human life, it would be like hearing the grass grow and the squirrel's heart beat, and we should die of that roar which lies on the other side of silence. As it is, the quickest of us walk about well wadded in stupidity.[20]

In this acerbic passage, the reader's limited moral perception is figured through the metaphor of hearing. Although the narrator, by contrast with her reader, at least *aspires,* she, too, knows the dangers of a too intensive imagination. In the end, she, too, ("the quickest of us") is included in the general human condition of "stupidity."

"We are all of us born in moral stupidity, taking the world as an udder to feed our supreme selves: Dorothea had early begun to emerge from that stupidity."[21] The pain of *emerging* in this way can be viewed as a gift or as a curse, but it is a necessary movement if one is to grow at all.

THE EGYPTIAN IDOL

The alternative is the numbing, neutralizing space that the midrashic imagination has called *mitzrayim/m'eitzarim.* This is Egypt, in Hebrew letters that mean constriction, a hindered life. *Emerging* from that space is called Exodus—*yetziat mitzrayim*. The presiding image of that space, its deity, is the calf, which the Egyptologist Jan Assmann identifies with the Egyptian bull, Apis.[22] As he describes its history, the engraved representation of this animal indicates an early stage in the history of idolatry, in which animal figures "are just signs which stand for some tutelary gods or deified hero-kings."[23] This was followed by the "worst form of idolatry"—brute worship, the worship of the animal itself.

So that when the Golden Calf leaps out of the fire of Sinai, something primal to the people's experience is suddenly revealed. Aaron apologizes in a rather bemused tone for his role in the narrative: "Behold, this calf emerged!"[24] As though to say, "I thought we had left that behind in Egypt"? The Calf is the unconscious residue of that hindered life of Egypt. It casts an imperious spell, emanating an apparent vitality that stupefies its worshippers. The people's joy as they dance around the Calf brings Moses to despair: they are now incapable of hearing anything new.[25]

Aaron's numbed astonishment is carried over, according to a surrealistic midrash, into the guilt and shame that fill him when he begins to officiate in the *Mishkan:* "Some say that Aaron saw the altar in the form of an ox and he was afraid of it."[26] Shame becomes fear that threatens to paralyze him in his role as High Priest. Moses encourages him to confront his fear, not to allow it to hinder him from his work of atoning for the deadening impact of the Calf.[27]

EGYPTOMANIA AND EXODUS

The Golden Calf, then, is an image for the neutralizing counterforce that erodes the impact of Sinai. In a sense, as the French philosopher Gaston Bachelard argues, the stable and completed image always has this effect: it clips the wings of the imagination.[28] Paradoxically, he defines imagination as the "faculty of *deforming* the images formed by perception." These images represent unchanging present reality. "If there is not a changing of images, an unexpected union of images, there is no imagination. . . . Soon, instead of making us dream and speak, [the image] makes us act."

The spiritual imagination is characterized by the experience of *opening* and *newness.* "Undoubtedly, the imaginary lays down images during its prodigious life, but it always appears to exist beyond its images, it is always a little more than its images. The poem is essentially an *aspiration to new images.*" Their verbal force makes us ask, "[H]ow do we pull it loose from the too stable bedrock of our familiar memories?"

Bachelard's language itself pulls loose from familiar uses, as he attempts to describe the indescribable. How does the erotic force make its way despite the inertia of the rigid image? The Golden Calf, as the quintessential unchanging image, carries this inertia with it. As soon as the power of God's words is felt, the Calf is summoned up to neutralize it. The force of life encounters the numbing counterforce of the Egyptian idol that both sustains and erodes it. On one level, this is precisely the paradox of Sinai: "We shall do and we shall listen!" affirms obedience while in some way warding off the larger inspirations of Revelation. "Soon, instead of making us dream and speak, it makes us act."

One clue to the meaning of the Golden Calf is the language that is later used to describe its effects. "My people have *forgotten* Me days without number" (Jer. 2:32); "They speedily *forgot* His works. . . . They made a calf in Horev and worshipped a molten image. Thus they exchanged their glory for the likeness of an ox that eats grass. They *forgot* God their savior" (Ps. 106:13). Forgetting God is an effect of the unreceptive surface, the counterforce that resists being inscribed, engraved, inspired by the divine word.

In the midrashic imagination, when Moses wants to defend his people against the charge of idolatry, he claims that the Calf was made *unwittingly—be-shogeg.*[29] The people are, he implies, ruled by their unconscious lives, by the compulsive repetitions that blur the impact of Revelation. They act without full intentionality, out of that moral stupidity that is related to stupor.[30]

Mei Ha-Shilo'ach develops the notion of inertia. The Golden Calf, he suggests, represents a desire for an untroubled spiritual existence, with no need for prayer. The very word *egel* (calf) is read as spiritual impatience. This world is "still incomplete," requiring time and development to come to fullness. Calf worshippers lust for frozen time, for the stable and completed image. Aspiration, breath after breath, requires imagination, a *listening-out* for what is still absent.

Even the expression "a *stiff-necked* people," which makes its first biblical appearance in God's rejection of the Calf worshippers, conveys this willful, rigid quality of consciousness. In Rashi's paraphrase, it indicates an inability to *turn one's head to hear something new.*

The German literary critic Eric Santner writes of Egyptomania—the Egyptian madness: its cure is "indeed a kind of 'exodus,' only not one out of Egypt; it offers, rather, an exodus out of the various forms of Egyptomania that so profoundly constrain our lives and, while sustaining a level of adaptation, keep us from opening to the midst of life."[31] In order to achieve exodus, this psychic rigidity needs to be engaged.

Drawing on Freud and Franz Rosenzweig, Santner argues that being in the midst of life means being with an Other precisely in his or her "Egyptomania." "It means exposure to the . . . way in which the Other is disoriented in the world."[32] The ethical relation to the Other means that "the Other to whom I am answerable *has an unconscious,* is the bearer of an irreducible and internal otherness." Unconscious fantasy constrains human life; defensive, it bars us from answering to the reality of the Other's presence. Revelation seeks to suspend the thrall of repetition compulsions that permeate our being.

BREAKING THE SPELL

In the book of Leviticus, the problem of Egyptomania—of the Golden Calf—manifests itself time after time. Often veiled in the text and revealed in the midrash, the Calf haunts incidents as various as the induction of the *Mishkan,* the difficulties and failures involved in the process of God's bringing His presence to dwell in the work of the *Mishkan;* in the Yom Kippur ritual of the goat to Azazel; in the isolation of the leper, who has alienated others from one another. The aspirational reach of commandments like "Love your neighbor like yourself" and "Be Holy, as I your God am holy" emerges from this inertia. A people enthralled by the image of the Calf are challenged to listen better, to mobilize a larger imagination.

The theme of aspiration emerges from this text that appears so thickly encrusted in law. Without the acute experience of inertia, without the Calf, would the *Mishkan* ever have been built? Without the experience of "nothing happens," would the force of God's desire—"Let them make Me a *Mishkan,* and I will dwell in their midst"—ever have come alive in the mind and heart? *"Sometimes, the annulling of*

Torah is its fulfillment" (*Bitulah shel torah zeh hu kiyumah*).[33] Words like "Exodus" and "Revelation" find their proof in the live possibility of God dwelling in one's midst. Only after the Calf nullifies that aspiration does the desire for it become real.

This is a matter of intimate *experience,* as the philosopher Franz Rosenzweig describes it:

> What we can thus state—or even prove—about God is related to our possible "experience" in the same way that the empty announcement that two persons have married, or the showing of the marriage certificate, is related to the daily and hourly reality of this marriage. . . . And so even the bare fact of marriage does not become real save where it leaves the sphere of what can objectively be stated and enters the secret pale of the festive days and anniversaries of private life.[34]

The secret pale of married life is the realm evoked by Leviticus, the Book of Holiness. Within its rituals, practices, and procedures, a certain *everyday-ness*—a sense of sacred housekeeping—is conveyed. In the intimate rituals of marriage, an otherwise inexpressible excess of experience is worked through in the midst of life.

The intensity of such an experience emerges from the encounter with otherness, with the resistance offered by the Calf. In a similar vein, R. Nahman teaches the paradox embodied in the work of charity.[35] Giving to the poor is a spiritual exercise; it works to break one's natural cruelty and to convert it into compassion. This natural cruelty is the dark side of "natural compassion," which surges spontaneously toward hopeful objects—the worthy poor, for instance, who offer the possibility of redemption. The problem with this primal form of compassion is that the *unworthy* poor, those who cannot be saved, arouse an equally primal form of cruelty. In confronting the despair of the unredeemable Other, one confronts one's own fear. Precisely in this case, *tzedakah* (charity) becomes a commandment: *You shall surely open your hand to him* (the poor man) (Deut. 15:8). Here, the act of *tzedakah* opens up the clenched hand of unconscious cruelty, and true compassion is born. Like all births, especially first births, that first opening is the difficult breakthrough of the new. That is the meaning of the intensified commandment: You shall *open, open* your hand.

R. Nahman's teaching about *tzedakah* (charity) as the secondary movement from cruelty to compassion represents a larger vision of the ethical life. It is precisely through a crisis in the habitual, through a sharp experience of the Other and his human despair, that reality breaks through a fantasy world. The break can become a happy break if it softens and enlarges the opening; if it breaks a spell.

THE SECONDARY MOVEMENT

Such moments of crisis, writes the American poet and essayist Louise Glück, can at first feel like an impoverishment:

> Realize, then, that impoverishment is also a teacher, unique in its capacity to renew, and that its yield, when it ends, is a passionate openness that in turn reinvests the world with meaning. . . . [An intensity of awareness] is impoverishment's aftermath, and blessing.[36]

Such periods of impoverishment as the crisis of the Golden Calf, then, allow the people to encounter their own depths. Here, at the moment of breakdown, work can be done and something new may be born. In relinquishing an omnipotent self, the old callosities drop away. One has, in a sense, engineered one's own defeat. Something may soften and open.

The Talmudic Sages have a powerful expression for this idea: "One does not understand (lit., stand upon) the words of Torah until one has stumbled over them."[37] The stumbling, the failure is the process by which Torah becomes real: inherent in the spiritual work of reading, studying, and living Torah is the experience of losing the ground under one's feet.[38] Remotely related to *flinching*, the metaphor of stumbling evokes both the burlesque and the tragic. There is the moment when human dignity is upended by the banana peel; there is also the graver moment of ruin, perhaps of irredeemable failure. In a *kishalon,* a stumble, a slippage, saving oneself in mid-fall is not always possible. The business has failed, bankruptcy is declared. It is from despair that standing, understanding arises.

In our narrative of the Golden Calf, then, the disruption is the heart of the story. The Calf does not represent an episode followed by a return to the main plot. Rather, it remains for all generations to confront us with the inertia that was always inherent in the moments of highest aspiration. A slip, a jolt, a shock, a knowledge of failure, of *not yet*—the Tablets inscribed by the finger of God are shattered. Unthinking compassion is recognized as cruelty; moral stupidity gives birth to a keener vision. One's neighbor is revealed in all her out-of-joint reality and is to be loved. In this movement, God is implicated: a new intimacy with God and neighbor is revealed.

This secondary movement of the soul is the subject of the book of Leviticus. On one level, the original revelation contains the seeds of its own erosion. It is neutralized by the banality of the Calf. Out of this despair, the *Mishkan* emerges. The work of building the structure, creating the sacred objects, has a therapeutic effect. But only in Leviticus do we read of the crises that accompany the process by which the *Mishkan,* and therefore the people, deeply encounter the divine. Here, the need to wait, to live a life that is used by time, cannot be evaded. Fear and shame gather around the obsession that is the Golden Calf. These, too, must be lived through.

In this book, I read Leviticus through the prism of midrashic narratives that connect the surface with the depths of this text. Following my original intuition that the Golden Calf pervades that space, I find, sometimes to my own surprise, how often the Calf, as the moment of slippage in human life, does make its appearance. As in dreams, the details of law and ritual turn out to be haunted by something repetitious, a sense of nameless loss; and by a secondary revelation of a different kind, which involves time and work and the birth of compassion.

The Hidden Order
of Intimacy

Vayikra

Hearing the Grass Grow:
Guilt, Atonement, Intimacy

THE UNNAMED SUBJECT OF REVELATION

The opening word of Leviticus: *"Vayikra—And He called* to Moses" (Lev. 1:1). Who is the one who calls? Presumably, it is God who calls Moses's name. But He is unnamed. Strangely, the new book begins with an unnamed subject of revelation. God's name follows only in the next clause, "And God spoke to him." Only after the anonymous call does *God* speak to Moses, revealing the laws of sacrifice and other laws relating to the newly constructed Tabernacle.

There is, of course, no real mystery about who is calling. Nevertheless, why, at the very beginning of the book is His identity somewhat awkwardly obscured ("He called . . . and God spoke")?

The classic medieval commentator Ramban sets this anomalous opening in the context of the conclusion of the previous book, Exodus: "Moses was unable to enter the Tent of Assembly, for the Cloud rested upon it and God's glory filled the Tabernacle" (Exod. 40:35). Exodus ends with Moses excluded from the sacred space he has so faithfully constructed. The Cloud and the fire that represent God's presence in the Tabernacle make it impossible for him to enter that space. Until, that is, God calls his name, inviting him, as it were, to enter into the Cloud. Only with this call is a human path opened up for him into the mysterium tremendum.

In Ramban's narrative, the two books are joined across a formal gap. God's glory is the subject of the closing sentence of Exodus; God remains the subject of the opening sentence of Leviticus. Moses's situation outside the Tabernacle, excluded by God's presence, is resolved by His call of invitation. In this situation, the divine call overcomes Moses's exclusion. At the same time, however, a new consciousness of *inside* and *outside* comes into existence. One book ends with alienation, while the new book begins with closure.

Rashi reads the opening word, *vayikra,* in order to raise a different question: What is the function of the act of *calling*?

> Every time God *spoke* or *said,* or *commanded,* He prefaced these terms by *calling,* in a tone of affection—*chibah*—and encouragement—in the tone that the ministering angels use, as it is said, "They call to one another, saying *Holy, Holy, Holy is the God of Hosts*" (Isa. 6:3).

Before *every* divine revelation (and not only in this particular situation) there is a *calling.* Rashi (and his midrashic forebears, as we shall see) is interested in the phenomenon of revelation that is glimpsed in the *Call-Speech* nexus. The question of the subject of the call is not overtly addressed.

In Rashi's proof text from Isaiah, the angels call to one another, even before they begin praising God. Rashi shifts the scene, from the call of God to a human being to a mutual calling between equals. To illustrate God's particular relation to Moses, Rashi focuses on the tonal resonance of the word *kara,* calling; affection and encouragement set the key for the heavenly choir; it is the essential preliminary—like the sounding of the tuning fork—to their harmony. An intimate calling to attention. For Rashi, this tone always characterizes God's calls to Moses. In a sense, it bridges the gap that exists even between equals.

The Talmudic Sages shift the scene yet again, from angelic choir to the human etiquette of address: "Why did God preface *speaking* with *calling*? The Torah teaches polite behavior: that one should not say anything to one's friend without *calling* his name first."[1]

The Talmud teaches a norm of polite behavior: to address the other by name before beginning to speak. To start speaking abruptly without calling by name is a kind of aggression, an entry into private space. Similarly, "God hates one who enters his friend's house suddenly (i.e., without warning)."[2] The door knocker protects privacy. This can be learned from God's behavior when He enters the Garden of Eden in order to rebuke Adam: "And God called out to Adam and said: 'Where are you?'" (Gen. 3:9). God observes the same decorum in addressing

Moses, even though Moses is described as "faithful (i.e., a familiar presence) in all My household" (Num. 12:7). He calls his name before speaking to him—that is, before entering his domain.

Calling before speaking, then, is a matter of propriety shared by God, angels, and human beings. It is a matter of respecting boundaries. When God calls out, however, this can signify two different situations: when He gives permission to Moses to enter the sacred interior, and when He *asks* permission to address him. In both cases, there is a real gap between self and other that requires bridging, a sense of delicacy in difference. Breaking through the gap could be considered threatening, or rude—an act of aggression. But in the one case, it is Moses who is in awe of the boundary and awaits God's invitation. In the other case, it is God who, in calling Moses's name, models sensitivity around thresholds. In the first situation, it is God who is inside, Moses who is outside. In the second, God is outside, addressing Moses: Moses is the object of God's desire.

Who, then, is the subject of desire in our text? The one who calls is presumably God. But perhaps the fact that God's name is not used at the moment of calling evokes the tension of such moments—moments of revelation, of incipient intimacy. Whose is the desire? Perhaps Moses, the object of the divine call, is also in some sense its subject?

THE DESIRE FOR DESIRE

Here are some midrashic narratives that explore this *vayikra* moment:

> "And God called to Moses": When God said to Moses, "Make Me a Tabernacle" (Exod. 25:8), he (Moses) inscribed on everything he made, "even as God commanded Moses." God said, "Moses has done Me all this honor, and I am inside while he is outside! Call him, that he may enter the innermost sanctum." Therefore it is said, "And God called to Moses."[3]

Explicitly linking the books of Exodus and Leviticus, the midrash describes the divine discomfort at excluding Moses from the structure he himself had so devotedly built for God. The appropriate separation between the work-overseer and the owner of the building suddenly seems strangely inappropriate. A conventional decorum is swept aside by a finer divine sensibility. In light of this, the very dedication of the overseer comes to suggest an underlying desire: to join his employer, in greater intimacy, here in his new "residence." For in His original command to Moses, God had said, "I shall encounter you there and I shall speak to you from above the Ark cover" (Exod. 25:22). "There" had referred to the innermost sanctum, equivalent to the owner's private chamber.

This house was designed for encounter, for intimate speech between God and Moses. Moses thus belongs inside. But in conventional terms, as an employee, he belongs outside. God resolves the matter by disregarding the more banal sense of boundaries and responding to Moses's desire:

> R. Zereka said, "Can you imagine that Moses left God and went elsewhere, since the text says, 'And He *called* to Moses . . .'? The text wants to convey Moses's humility and diffidence. Usually, the king's confidant, who has the king's ear at all times, will enter the palace and leave it without asking permission, since he has become over-familiar with the king. But Moses was different. Even though God spoke to him often, face-to-face, he stood trembling with all due ceremony before God, as though He had never spoken with him. Because of this, he merited what no other human being had ever merited: that whenever he entered, God would immediately speak with him, as it is said, 'And whenever Moses entered the Tent of Assembly he heard the Voice speaking to him' (Num. 7:89)."[4]

"Familiarity," according to the adage, "breeds contempt." Moses, however, remains sensitive to God's otherness, "as though He had never spoken with him." Precisely because of this, God acts freely on His affection, turning aside from affairs of state to speak exclusively with His friend. Moses's deference arouses in God a responsive desire for intimacy. Here, the moment of *calling* is not addressed, obscuring the pivoting point between Moses's decorum and God's affection.

In *Midrash Vayikra Rabbah*, however, Moses's modesty becomes a theme that arouses God's response. In one midrash, for instance, this modesty is traced back to the Burning Bush, when he hides his face from the divine revelation. *Because of this,* God commissions him to speak to Pharaoh. A similar dynamic occurs at the Red Sea, at Sinai, and now at the Tabernacle. On this occasion, God addresses him with some ambivalence: "How long will you humble yourself? The hour awaits none but you!" God singles out Moses, time and time again; but on this last occasion there is a note of criticism in God's reproach, even as He calls out to Moses alone.[5]

Here, the situation is intensified: God chooses to address Moses alone precisely in the new context of the Tabernacle and its sacrifices. Here, Moses might well have been justified in lowering his profile: his brother Aaron is properly the man of the hour, as High Priest and chief officiant in the Tabernacle rituals. But, precisely now, God places Moses front and center, even suggesting that Moses's diffidence is excessive.

Similarly, in another passage in *Vayikra Rabbah,* Moses bewails the fact that he donated no precious objects to the Tabernacle. God responds: "As you live, your conversation (lit., your *speaking*) is more precious, beloved (*chaviv*) to Me than all else."[6] The evidence of this singular love is the divine call that overrides all conventions.

The word *vayikra* comes to evoke an intimate, paradoxical affection. The words *chibah* and *chaviv* convey the tone of the call. It is this tone, rather than the content of God's speech—the commandments of the sacrifices—that becomes the subject of midrashic interest.

God's tenderness comes to close the gap between Moses outside and God inside. From this point onward, God's relations with Moses are played out under the sign of *chibah,* of a newly tender tone of revelation. And under this sign, it is Moses's *conversation* that endears him: "Your speaking is dear to me" can be read, simply, "I love the way you speak." Something indefinable but essential in Moses's way of speaking is precious to God.

Perhaps the nucleus of his language is his hidden desire? God calls Moses's name because He knows that Moses is filled with a barely recognized yearning. God's call arouses that yearning, which was already there before the call.

At this juncture, a new intensity enters the relationship. In the past, God always *called,* subverting the natural boundaries of *inside* and *outside.* From the Burning Bush onward, this has been the pattern: Moses resists, God insists—a dance of decorum. This time, as several midrashic texts suggest, God is particularly loving in His invitation:

"The hour belongs to none but you!" "Your conversation is more precious to me than all else."

Another midrash specifies Moses's particular mission from this time onward. After Moses has repeatedly fled from power only to have leadership repeatedly thrust upon him, he finally protests, with increased conviction: "From now on (after the Tabernacle has been constructed), what do I have to do?" And God answers, "As you live, you have a greater task now than ever! To teach My children about impurity and purity, and to prepare them to offer sacrifices before Me."[7]

"As you live!" Here is the tone of impassioned divine eros: "I want you now more than ever!" Now begins Moses's most significant role—to teach his people the laws of the Book of Holiness. Just at the moment when Moses is sure that his time is over, God reverses his expectations. Or is it that God responds to Moses's incipient desire? Even as he withdraws from positions of power, Moses yearns for *dibbur*, for ongoing communication with God. Even as he acknowledges boundaries, yielding his place to Aaron, barely recognizing his own yearning, God has responded to his desire.[8]

Such a scenario ultimately blurs the difference between lover and beloved. One is both inside and outside, subject and object; the decorums of the social world are transcended. The angels call and are called to; one who enters his friend's house, calling the owner's name, hopes for the desire of the other. The friend who is called responds and converts the aggression of abrupt speech into intimacy. The spaces of sacredness, of proper difference, become spaces inhabited by the desire for desire.

HAUNTED BY THE GOLDEN CALF

This new period of the Tabernacle is marked by the trauma of the Golden Calf. The event itself leaves behind it a complex sense of distance and alienation on the one hand, and yearning for a different connection on the other. Now, with the Tabernacle in place, Moses's energies will be focused on teaching the laws of sacrifice and of purity and impurity. His teaching role will be rooted in a new *chibah,* an affectionate closeness between Moses and God. The world of sacrifices, the material world of animals and other physical objects, will form the subject matter of his teaching. But the midrashic tradition is interested, for the most part, in the emotional tone of his newly intimate connection with God.[9]

Within this tradition, the world of sacrifices and of a retuned relation between Moses and God comes to atone for the sin of the Golden Calf. That catastrophe is not easily healed. Even after God has formally forgiven the people, the rupture in the "marriage" of God and Israel is still palpable. Particularly as refracted in midrashic literature, the book of Leviticus remains haunted by the Calf.

Midrashic narratives tell how the pathology of idolatry is "healed" by the Tabernacle and its rituals. The fire and the gold of the Tabernacle, for example, provide an antidote for the fire and gold of the Calf. The idolatrous fantasy is in some sense worked through in the practices of worship in the Tabernacle.[10]

In many sources, moreover, the command to build the Tabernacle— "If they make Me a sanctuary, I shall dwell in their midst" (Exod. 25:8)— is in itself understood as a sign of forgiveness for the sin of the Calf. In one classic view, this forgiveness allows this original Tabernacle command to be reinstated after the rupture. In another view, this command is to be read as consequent upon the sin; effectively, it is only *because* of the sin that the Tabernacle is projected in the first place—as sign and as process of atonement.[11]

The latter part of Exodus, then, is structured as an enactment of the turbulence created by the sin. God's instructions for the Tabernacle (chapters 25–31) are followed by the account of the Golden Calf (chapters 32–34), and then by the narration of the artisans' execution of the building instructions (chapters 35–40). The pivotal role of the Calf in the building narrative is quite clear. The two classic readings I have just described affect how we read the chronology. One possible reading sees the Golden Calf as the sin that blocks the execution of the divine building instructions; these can be implemented only after Moses finally returns from the mountain, bearing the second set of Tablets in his arms. On the second reading, the original commandments are to be read as "out of order," as in a flashback, they are issued to the people only in the post-Calf period.

On the second reading, revelation is not simply reinstated; rather, it enters a new phase. God will speak to Moses from within the interior of a "tent" rather than from the clouds ringing the mountaintop.

In this new theater of revelation, the Golden Calf haunts the narrative. It has been forgiven, but the impact of the trauma lingers. One of its effects, strangely, is the Tabernacle itself, the site of continuing revelation. "If I had not committed that deed," Israel says, "You would not have brought Your presence to dwell within me."[12]

The Sages view the apparently discrete crisis of the Golden Calf as returning in repressed form throughout the generations. "There is no generation that does not carry a vestige (lit., a tiny amount) of the Golden Calf."[13] A toxin persists to trouble the fantasy life of human beings. Such a statement presumably refers to the vestigial impact of idol worship. Some resistant strain remains in the blood, breaking out anew in every generation.

RECONCILIATION AND ALIENATION

One early enactment in this post-Calf history is the compelling scene in Exodus 33:7–11. Moses pitches his personal tent—also called the Tent of Meeting—*outside* the camp. Those of the people who "seek God" make a sort of pilgrimage out to that tent to learn God's word from Moses. Within that tent, Moses and God meet and speak, "face to face, as one speaks to one's friend" (v. 11).

But the most haunting moment of this account is recounted from the people's perspective. The people stand at the entrance to their tents and follow Moses with their eyes as he leaves the camp and enters his own tent. A Cloud then descends over the entrance to Moses's tent and "it speaks with Moses" (v. 9). The entire people see this; they rise up and bow down at the entrance of their own tents.

Here, the people act out their alienation, which is represented in Moses's external position in relation to them. His movement back and forth from tent to camp, with repeated idioms of externality, culminates in the description of the people's gaze as they imagine the interior encounter within Moses's tent. Only in imagination, in yearning, can they participate in the scene of revelation.

It is the Cloud, however, that strangely seems to "speak with Moses." *Ve-dibber im Moshe:* Rashi reads this as *middaber* and cites the Targum's translation: The Voice spoke *to itself* in Moses's hearing.[14] Through this reflexive reading, Rashi suggests the distance between the speaker and the listener, even when they are both imagined as human—a man speaking with his friend. In all acts of communication, we might say, there is a dimension of "speaking to oneself," with the other "overhearing" and translating into another language.

This scene of alienation takes place, it seems, after Moses has returned from the mountain, after the people have been forgiven. Why, then, the demonstrative drama of distance? And why the repeated movement between two spaces: the private but external space of meeting with God and the public space of the Israelite camp?

Maharal raises this question and formulates an enigmatic distinction. God may be reconciled with the people (*be-ratzon*), but the people are still "as though alienated from God" (*ke-menudin lo*). This obscure state will be resolved only once they have offered the specific sacrifices commanded as *Sin Offerings*. Meantime, they are suspended in an alienated state, even though God has been appeased. This situation represents asymmetry: God is reconciled with them, but the people's work of atonement is still incomplete. Only after they have made the appropriate sacrifices will atonement be achieved.

This twilight period suggests that the impact of the Golden Calf still haunts the people. Moses daily paces the distance between the people and his private tent, which he himself names the Tent of Meeting. There, he has meetings of great intimacy with God. ("God spoke to Moses face-to-face, as one speaks to one's friend.") The eyes of all the people follow him on this trajectory; at the imagined moment of meeting, the people rise up and prostrate themselves. At the entrance to their own tents, between inside and outside, they gaze at the Cloud-covered entrance to his tent and bow low. Rashi quotes a midrash: "[What are they thinking?] Happy is the man born of woman who is so assured that God's Presence will enter after him into his tent!"[15]

After the Tabernacle is completed, the site of meeting is moved inward, into the Israelite camp, at its center. From this new position—"I will inhabit your *midst*"—new laws about the functioning of the Tabernacle are given, and the rituals of sacrifice begin. It is only at this point, Maharal suggests, that the people can fully atone for, and in a sense resolve, the trauma of the Golden Calf.

It is at this juncture that Moses has to be summoned by name to enter the new sacred space that now directly serves the people. As we have seen, midrashic narratives mark this moment not as the end of Moses's encounters with God but as the beginning of the most intense period of his life with God. What is the nature of this new phase? What is suggested by the new tone of *chibah,* of intimacy?

VIOLENT ADVOCACY

We remember the traumatic crisis on the mountain, when God—in the midst of transmitting the Torah—reveals to Moses what has been happening at the base of the mountain. He proposes to annihilate the people: "Let My anger burn against them and I will consume them and make you into a great nation!" (Exod. 32:10). Moses's response is classic; he appeases God: "Why should Your anger burn against Your people?" He speaks of a shared history, of divine energy invested in "*Your* people" and of promises made to their ancestors. His speech of intercession is effective. God's fiery anger abates, and the disaster is averted.

We turn now to a startling midrashic account of the same moment of intercession. Here, Moses's strategy is to meet anger with anger. I quote at length:

"And Moses besought the presence of God his God": R. Tanchuma b. Abba began thus: "Therefore He said that He would destroy them, had not Moses His chosen stood before Him in the breach, to turn back his anger" (Ps. 106:23). R. Hama b. Chanina said: The good advocate knows to present his case clearly before the tribunal (lit., to present the best face). . . . [He] set his face against the attribute of strict justice in order to plead for mercy on Israel's behalf.

Rabbenu said: It can be compared to a king, who was sitting in judgment on his son, while the accuser was indicting him. When the prince's tutor saw that his charge was being condemned, he thrust the accuser outside the court and put himself in his place in order to plead on the prince's behalf. Similarly, when Israel made the Golden Calf, Satan stood inside [before God] accusing them, while Moses remained outside. What then did Moses do? He arose and thrust Satan away and placed himself in his stead, as it says, "Had not Moses His chosen stood before Him in the breach"; that is, he put himself in the place of the one who was causing the breach.

R. Samuel b. Nahman said: It is rather difficult to say that he "stood before Him in the breach." It can be explained by the case of a king who was angry with his son and took his place on the tribunal and tried him and pronounced him guilty. As he was about to take up his pen to sign the verdict of the court, his associate snatched the pen from his hand in order to appease his wrath. Similarly, when Israel committed that act, God sat in judgment upon them to condemn them, for it says, "Let Me alone that I may destroy them!" (Deut. 9:14). He had not yet done so, but was about to seal their decree, as it says, "He that sacrifices to the gods, except to God alone, shall be utterly destroyed" (Exod. 22:19). So what did Moses do? He took the Tablets from God's hands in order to appease His wrath.

This is like a king who sent a marriage broker to betroth a wife for him, but while the broker was on his way, the woman corrupted herself with another man. What did the broker, who was entirely innocent, do? He took the marriage document that the king had given him to betroth her with, and tore it up, saying "Better that she be judged as an unmarried woman than as a married woman." This is what Moses did. When Israel did that act, he took the Tablets and shattered them, as if to imply that had Israel known their punishment ahead of time, they would not have sinned in this way.

Moses moreover said: *"Better they should be judged as doing it unintentionally than as if they did it willfully."* Because in the Decalogue it says, "I am God, your God"; and the punishment for breaking this commandment is: "He that sacrifices to the gods, except to God alone, shall be utterly destroyed." So he broke the Tablets.

"And He thought to destroy them." Immediately, Moses girded himself for prayer. That is the meaning of "Moses besought the Presence of God, his God." He placed himself before God with scant respect in order to request Israel's needs. Hence, "And Moses besought the Presence of God, his God."[16]

In this text, Moses's posture is described as disrespectful in both words and actions. Across several readings, different Sages convey their understanding of the proof text: "And Moses besought—

Vayichal—before the face of God, his God." *Vayichal* is read as deriving from the root *chol*—profane, violent. The Sages pursue several avenues of association with the notion of Moses as a defense counsel who takes his stand "in the breach," in the very place of the crime and of the breach it has made in the world order. Moses's intervention, in all these parables, holds an inherent violence. He pushes the prosecutor off the dais and *takes his place*—the very place where the prosecution is making its case against the king's son. From that vulnerable place—the breach—the defense counsel makes his case, presenting a face to meet the angry face of God. At first he stands *outside* the court, ineffective: then he leaps *inside,* into the all-too-effective position of the prosecutor, the *poretz,* the one who has made the breach. In some sense, he assumes the adversary face of Satan.

Here, R. Samuel takes over with an alternative story about Moses's advocacy. Violent imagery intensifies as the text moves from one Sage to the next. In this version, Moses is the king's associate. He snatches the king's pen before he can sign the verdict. Though this move might have backfired, we are assured that it is intended to avert the king's wrath. Moses snatches the Tablets away, perhaps to distract the king from the incriminating law against idolatry.

In the final courtroom drama, the king's anger is now turned against his unfaithful wife rather than his disobedient son. Even more fraught, this scene has the marriage broker tear up the marriage document before handing it to the unfaithful wife. Moses smashes the Tablets, thus retroactively destroying the covenant and construing the people as having sinned *unintentionally* (since they never actually encountered the incriminating text, "One who sacrifices to idols shall be proscribed" [Exod. 22:19]). In the biblical text, this happened later, after Moses had descended the mountain and witnessed the rites of idol worship. In the midrashic narrative, the smashing of the Tablets becomes a violent dimension of his prayer of intercession.

In these scenarios, a prayer of entreaty becomes an occasion for acts of rupture, violating space and time. The rituals of due process are interrupted. The face that Moses presents to God is aggressive: "he stood with scant respect—lit., in light-headedness—before God's face."

In this situation, the midrash understands Moses's *face-to-face* relationship with the divine as including a provocative and adversary posture *against* God's "face" of strict justice. A prayer becomes an act of war (girding himself for prayer). How does this way of speaking relate to the intimacy we have encountered in the midrashic literature?

Perhaps it is precisely the *chibah* relationship that allows for such a display of passion—and even creates a situation in which God finds Moses's *way of speaking* more lovable than all else? What connects this *way of speaking* with Moses's legendary humility, his habit of standing aside, of fleeing positions of authority? The Golden Calf apparently brings out a different facet of his being—anger breaks out when he sees the fate of his people hanging in the balance. This is an emergency outrage, a boundless passion in which entreaty comes to sound very much like peremptory demand.

Only within an intimate relationship can such unceremonious behavior be understood as a plea for compassion. In order better to understand this dynamic between Moses and God, we will need to look more closely at the problem of the Golden Calf itself, the catalyst of this new phase in the narrative.

EGYPTOMANIA AND THE GOLDEN CALF

The Golden Calf signifies a moment of collapse in the religious order that has just been instituted at Sinai. Midrashic sources offer the analogy of an act of adultery committed shortly after the marriage ceremony. The fantasy of the Calf induces an adulterous ecstasy that is characterized, at the same time, by a strange *deadness*. In its fixation on the object, it seeks to flee from the agitation and turbulence that are part of the marriage relationship. This idolatrous/adulterous moment is a breakdown in the ability to live in intimacy in the *midst of life.*

In *On the Psychotheology of Everyday Life,* Eric Santner writes:

> What psychoanalysis ultimately tells us is that . . . our bodies are always haunted by nameless loss, by an ontological incompleteness against which we *defend* . . . by our specific form of "Egyptomania." If there is a "Jewish" dimension to psychoanalytic thought, it is this: the cure is indeed a kind of "exodus," only not one out of Egypt; it offers, rather, an exodus out of the various forms of Egyptomania that so profoundly constrain our lives and . . . keep us from opening to the midst of life.[17]

Santner's "Egyptomania" refers to the compulsive defense mechanisms by which we attempt to escape the "out-of-jointness" of our own experience; truly entering *the midst of life* will become possible only when we acknowledge our own inner strangeness, as well as the equivalent "internal alienness of the Other."

The Golden Calf, I suggest, is one form of Egyptomania. It represents the idealizing fantasy—the investment of transcendent power in an object. A kind of rigid energy animates the fantasy, which acts as a defense against aliveness. The cure for this form of pressure "will involve a labor of traversing, of working through the fantasies that in one way or another close us off from the midst of life."[18]

Santner generates a conversation between Freud and Rosenzweig on this question. Against the metaphysical questions of the philosophers, Rosenzweig declares: "Only from the center does there arise a bounded home in the unbounded world, a patch of ground between four tent pegs that can be posted further and further out."[19] Describing his own personal history, Rosenzweig speaks of a "dark drive" that had emerged in the context of a breakdown; this "drive" now bound him to the patch of ground between four tent pegs (i.e., the Tabernacle *in the midst* of the people). He is now drawn to the intimacy of his repressed Jewish identity. Only by working through this drive can it come to be experienced as a new source of vitality and humanity.[20] Stripping himself of his fantasy defenses, he passes through and beyond these to a world of real questions, in the midst of time and space.

Santner uses Freudian language to convey Rosenzweig's understanding of his paradoxical situation. In doing this, he connects with Rosenzweig's own use of Freud's vision. The fantasy of escape from the struggle of existence must be deeply addressed if one is to find the vital center of one's being.

Moses's behavior in our midrash represents a "working through" of the fantasy of the Golden Calf. Relinquishing binary positions—prosecution/defense, strict judgment/compassion, unintentional sin/willful sin, inside/outside—Moses enters into the very place of the adversary, of the dark drive, in order to arouse God's compassion.

In disrupting the civilized rituals of the law court—and of courtship—Moses is engaging with the uncanny dimension of any

relation with the Other. The new religious language of Sinai has col-
lapsed back into chaos. The irony is that, in fantasy, the Golden Calf
had offered to hold the always-collapsing world together. This was its
ecstatic promise, at the center of the dancing circle of worshippers.
But truly being "in the midst of life" means "being with another," as
Santner puts it. It involves exposure "to the Other's touch of madness,
to the way in which the Other is disoriented in the world. . . . The
Other to whom I am answerable *has an unconscious,* is the bearer of
an irreducible and internal otherness."[21] Recognizing one's own disorder, one may acknowledge the disorder of the other. Unconscious
impulses can be neither acted out nor overridden.

This is the difficulty of the commandment that stands at the very
heart of the book of Leviticus: "You shall love your neighbor as yourself" (Lev. 19:18). The religious world order is centered on a concrete
obligation to the human other. This, in itself, becomes revelation,
knowledge of a God who remains irreducibly other. Rosenzweig cites
the example of a marriage. The daily and hourly reality of a marriage becomes real only "when it leaves the sphere of what can be
objectively stated and enters the secret pale of the festive days and
anniversaries of private life."[22] In this "secret pale," singular practices,
irrational to the outsider, form the essential reality of the marriage
experience. In the "marriage" of God and Israel, too, practices of
everyday life maintain the idiosyncratic reality of intimacy.

Love of the neighbor, who may be husband, or colleague, or God,
involves an acceptance of an irreducible *strangeness.* The Other makes
demands by his very presence. *What do you want of me?* There is disappointment and anger—"Let My anger burn against them!" And
Moses asks, "Why, O God, should Your anger burn against Your people?" (Exod. 32:11). A classic midrash elaborates, spinning out the logic
of Moses's argument:

> This is like a king who came home to find his wife caressing a
> wooden object, and he was angry. His matchmaker said to him,
> "If that wooden thing were potent [lit., could impregnate her],
> you would be right to be angry." The king answered, "It has no
> power of that kind, but just to teach her not to do such things!"
> So God said, "I know that there is no real power in this object,

but just so they should not even think of making a real idol!"
His friend then answered him, "But if it has no real power, why
are You angry at Your children?"[23]

What is the point of being angry at one's wife's passion for an
inanimate object? Idols are impotent, mere blocks of matter. Moses
is trying to catch God on the horns of formal logic: Since the idol is
impotent, what could the rationale for jealousy be? And since there
is no rationale, why should God be angry? The neat logic of the argument only points up the irrationality of human anger, of the ways in
which human beings love—haunted by fantasy, driven to anger.

This audacious parable extends the commonplace of comparing
human marriage to the relationship of God and Israel. Here is the
"touch of madness," the unconscious of human erotic love and infidelity. God's passion for Israel is nothing if not exclusive. And the
wife's offense lies precisely in her inability to find satisfaction in her
husband's love. Moses's plea for compassion here reaches into the
dark places of human desire, where a woman's passion for a piece of
wood may well arouse jealousy in her husband's heart. "Why are You
angry?" translates into a plea for God's acceptance of the analogy in
its fullness.

"WE ARE ALWAYS A THREESOME"

Emmanuel Levinas frames the larger issue this way: "Is morality possible without God? . . . As Jews, we are always a threesome: I and you
and the Third who is in our midst. And only as a Third does He reveal
himself."[24]

Or again: "Revelation, which is from the start linked in its *con-
creteness* to obligations toward humans—the idea of God as love of
the neighbor—is 'knowledge' of a God who, offering himself in this
'opening,' would also remain absolutely other or transcendent."[25]

This "paradoxical knot" haunts the Golden Calf narrative. The obligation, central to the book of Leviticus,[26] to "love your neighbor as
yourself," lies at the very heart of divine Revelation. In the thick of
the specific obligations that embody this commandment,[27] one finds
"the Third who is in our midst." At our most turbulent, when we have

to deal with the "touch of madness" inherent in the Other, we are in the midst of life, where God in His otherness makes His demands.

That God is subject to anger, then, is all too plausible to the human imagination. Like a father with a wayward son, or a husband with a restless wife, He is enraged by the dark drives that alienate the objects of His love. In our midrashic narrative, Moses engages with God's anger by engaging with his own rage. The process that Freud calls "working through" is played out in these violent, often bizarre parables. Instead of smoothing things over, Moses attempts to "turn aside His anger" by snatching and tearing, by smashing the Tablets; by entering deep into the innermost places in himself. As though, at such moments of terrible intimacy, the only way out is through.

The dangerous moment passes. God turns away, He "relents." Moses turns away, descends the mountain, sees the Calf, and in an explosion of anger smashes the Tablets.

How strange that the anger that now should find its natural target—the people's idolatry—is doubly displaced: in the text, from the people or the Calf to the Tablets; and in the midrash, from the base of the mountain to the earlier moment on the mountain when it was turned against God's anger. Under the rubric of *vayichal* Moshe—of a prayer of intercession—all that violence finds expression. Only *after* that scene with God can Moses play out his role as representative of God and castigator of his people. But even the scene of outraged authority at the base of the mountain is haunted by the demonic imagery of his prayer, in its midrashic enactment. What he shatters in his rage are the Tablets that embody his life with God.

In rage as in entreaty, Moses plays his role in the "threesome" of "I and you and the Third who is in our midst." Even in Moses's most intense moments of dialogue with God—at the top of the mountain, in the crevice in the rock (*not-seeing* God's face), the people remain at the heart of their mutual concern. Even in Moses's violence, God finds the quality of *chibah*—that loving familiarity that freely improvises relationship. Even in God's apparent harshness, Moses reads the same quality of love for the people.

"Lech red"—"Go on down the mountain!" (Exod. 32:7), God tells Moses. The midrash intensifies this harsh rejection: "Why did I give you greatness if not for the sake of your people? Now that they have

sinned, *what do I need you for?*"[28]—emphasizing the harshness of divine
repudiation. Moses's strength fails but is revived when he rereads this
repudiation as a divine demand that Moses use his strength to inter-
cede. The divine-human intimacy at its most intense is haunted by its
other pole, love of the people.

The story is told in the Talmud of the High Priest, R. Ishmael ben
Elisha, who entered the awesome intimacy (*lifnai u-lifnim*—lit., the
innermost of the innermost) of the Holy of Holies on Yom Kippur,
the Day of Atonement, and saw the ineffable presence of God, seated
on His lofty throne:

> He said to me, Ishmael, My son, bless Me! I replied, May it be
> Your will that Your compassion may prevail over Your other
> attributes, so that You may deal with Your children according to
> the attribute of compassion and You may stop short, for their
> sake, of the limit of strict justice! And He nodded His head to
> me. Here we learn that the blessing of an ordinary man should
> not seem light in your eyes.[29]

The High Priest knows God's most intimate wish. The Talmudic
passage in fact begins with the questions: "How do we know that
God prays? And what does He pray?" Word for word, His prayer for
Himself to Himself appears in the formula that the High Priest proceeds to use in blessing God: "May it be My will that My compassion . . ." Quietly, the proprieties are reversed—son is to bless father,
priest is to bless the ineffable divine. But the divine has many contrary
facets—largely, compassion and anger. So R. Ishmael blesses God that
His deepest prayer be fulfilled. In blessing God, he is of course concerned with his people, the children of God. At its climax, his blessing
is that God *enter into,* be contained by, *stop short* of the extremity of
strict justice. Essentially, he is blessing God to contain Himself within
His compassion. May the internal pressure of anger be kept at bay. . . .
   "And He nodded His head to me." The poignant nod signifies a kind
of gratification. The blessing has done its work in this most intimate

dialogue, where all the forms are reversed. The knowledge of God that R. Ishmael demonstrates is founded on his knowledge of the dynamics of human prayer. Created in God's image, the human being possesses a valuable key to the workings of the divine economy. However, the impact of the narrative is, at least in part, ironic. R. Ishmael is aware of both the power of his story and its limitations.

He focuses on the *intimacy* of his experience, of the way in which the mysterium tremendum has become a familial encounter that has reversed the conventions of family authority. The majestic otherness of God is drawn inward, clothing itself in the human polarities of anger and compassion. God's mute nod of the head intimates assent, even a kind of relief, which is not without its own ironic awareness.

Such a language of encounter remains fraught with memories of divine otherness. God as the transcendent creator and inscrutable ruler of the world withdraws into the shadows; He becomes an intimate God who asks his "son" for a blessing. But the shadows, the anxiety about saying the wrong thing, of angering the King, of overstepping the bounds, still trouble the intimate scene.

Irony would, then, be the mode in which R. Ishmael tells his story. The confidence with which he responds to God's invitation to bless holds at its heart a knowledge of God's threatening otherness: "May Your compassion prevail over Your anger!" The blessing acknowledges the uncanny, the violent, the inscrutable in the divine persona. *What do You really want of me?* God seems well pleased with R. Ishmael's daring obedience; the father's nod sponsors future acts of playful intimacy.

However unceremoniously he speaks to God, however disruptive the roles he plays in engaging with God's anger, Moses knows well the anxiety about meeting the desire of such a God. In infancy, his life was set adrift in the Egyptian river of death. At the Burning Bush, he was confronted by a consuming fire that was not itself consumed; and by an unfathomable demand to speak for God and save His people. In resisting this call, He knew God's anger (Exod. 4:14). Then, as a young father, he experienced a sudden attack by God in a mysterious "hotel," as he made his way back from Midian to Egypt. "God sought to kill him"—a stark narrative, telling of an encounter that is an attack (*va-yifgeshehu*); of his wife cutting off her son's foreskin, throwing it at Moses's feet, declaring, "You are a bridegroom of blood to me!" (Exod. 4:25). Violent and enigmatic, the story assails the reader with its mystery.

These experiences with the God whose meanings lie beyond human grasp might well have made Moses wary of provoking such a God, of being too familiar, too knowing. From where, then, did the midrashic Sages draw their parables for a Moses who could respond to the crisis of the Golden Calf with such abrasive enactments—with an intuitive freedom, finding a voice and a face with which to meet the face of God's anger?

The midrashic theme of *chibah,* intimate affection between God and Moses, seems to originate in a strange scene in Exodus 33:12–17:

> And Moses said to God: "See, You say to me, Take this people up [to the Land], but You have not let me *know* whom You will send with me. You did say, I have *known you by name* and you have moreover *found favor in My eyes.* So now, if I have really *found favor in Your eyes,* please give me *knowledge* of Your ways that I may *know* You, in order that I shall *find favor in Your eyes.* For see, this nation is Your people! . . . How then should I *know* that I have *found favor in Your eyes,* I and Your people? Only if You accompany us and differentiate us, I and Your people, from all other nations on the face of the earth? And God said to Moses: Even this thing that you have spoken I will do; for you *have found favor in My eyes* and I *will know you by name.*

Repeatedly, both Moses and God use the expression *find favor in Your/My eyes,* together with the other key phrase, *to know You by name.* Moses appeals to God to accompany the people on their journey, in spite of God's recent declaration: "I will not go up among you! For you are a stiff-necked people!" (Exod. 33:3). Moses bases his appeal on the fact that God has told him that *he has found favor in His eyes.* This idiom can be simply translated: God *likes* Moses. But the Hebrew idiom is eloquent. Moses sees into God's eyes and finds there *chen*—grace, favor, relationship. This is the intimate dynamic of two friends or two lovers. As though *chen* waits for the right partner to elicit it from one's depths. An enlivening movement runs between the two pairs of eyes.

Like other anthropomorphisms in the Torah—but perhaps even

more stirring than most—this physical image evokes deep relationship. Faces and eyes act on one another, even as they mirror one another. The other expression, "I will know you by name," also refers to this kind of knowing, in which self and Other lose subject/object difference.

These phrases, repeated throughout the passage, form the basis for Moses's plea that God will not, after all, distance Himself from His people. Moses moves swiftly from his personal relationship with God to I *and Your people.* He pleads for his people as an extension of himself: How can they be excluded from God's favor? His desire for this quality of relationship must, in some measure, be theirs.

This passage, focused on *finding favor* and *knowing by name,* may well lie behind the midrashic emphasis on the *chaviv* nature of Moses in God's eyes. Translating the biblical expressions into more colloquial language, the Sages pinpoint the basis of the special relationship between God and Moses (and, ultimately, God and Israel). The nub of the matter is that Moses's intimacy with God encompasses an unceremonious, intuitive, performative way of speaking. Asking for compassion can sometimes mean setting oneself against God's stern face, snatching and tearing and smashing, in the knowledge that this is what God really wants of him.

In the biblical text, God acknowledges this intimacy and even accepts the practical conclusions that Moses draws from it. Meantime, however, Moses speaks to God *outside* the camp, far from the camp. As far as the people are concerned, during these months leading up to the completion of the Tabernacle, God may hold them in favor, but they are still, in Maharal's words, "as though alienated from Him." The Golden Calf remains, in some real way, an alienating force in their lives. The betrayed husband may be reconciled but the wife is preoccupied with her betrayal. She is not at one with herself or with her husband. The past inhabits the present. Atonement is necessary. For Maharal, this means offering the necessary Sin Offerings, which would be the ritual means of such atonement.

In the meantime, until the Tabernacle is completed and the sacrifices are inaugurated, the public world acknowledges distance, boundaries, otherness; while in Moses's personal world, there is the face-to-face intimacy with the divine. At this point, the gap between Moses and the people is still palpable.

IRONIC DISRUPTION AS A FORM OF LOYALTY

So we return to the *Vayikra* moment. The Tabernacle is filled with God's glory and Moses, like his people, is excluded. For him, too, the irreducible Otherness of God leaves no space for the human. Moses hangs back; he is well trained in awe, in anxiety about impinging on private space. As the midrash portrays it, this modesty is praiseworthy; and yet on occasion one hears a note of exasperation in God's invitation: "Moses! Moses![30] How long will you go on belittling yourself? . . . As you live, this is your finest hour! . . . Your speech is more dear to Me than all else!" Moses's hesitation begins to seem compulsive; he fails to understand the intimacy of God's love for him. God's call is all tone, drawing him across the gap.

The paradox was there from the beginning. God's glory will inhabit the Tabernacle; but precisely from that most intimate site (in the Holy of Holies, between the Cherubs) He "will meet you there and speak with you there" (Exod. 25:22). It emerges that God loves what is singular about Moses's way of speaking: his "familiarity" with God that uses his own anger to defuse God's anger.

Ironically, the Golden Calf is responsible for Moses's spontaneity in prayer. But the larger paradox remains. When the Tabernacle is completed, God has to "call" Moses out of his respectful posture, to remind him of the depth of intimacy. Constantly, Moses reverts to a formal mode. Perhaps he has presumed too far? Perhaps there is now no room for him within the divine space?

What is played out in many midrashic scenes is a tension within language itself. Between candid speech and the etiquettes of distance, the language of conversation opens up a multitude of possibilities. What God values in His conversation with Moses is its quotidian, informal quality. The king who turns aside from all his royal preoccupations when his friend (the governor of a province) turns up feels a secret pleasure in discussing the prosaic details of running the country. The content of the conversation is overshadowed by the way language itself functions in generating *chibah*—that loving intimacy that holds tensions in play.

However, here, too, the language of the midrash is disrupted by irony. The experience of irony, as Jonathan Lear understands the term, occurs when a gap opens between pretense and aspiration.[31] One becomes suddenly aware of a gap between normal social practice and an ideal. This is a moment of disorientation, a disruption of social practice. Lear speaks of ironic uncanniness, a state in which the familiar reality shifts in the reminder of a larger aspiration.

Lear offers the example of teaching: the sudden question about the radical meaning of what one is doing as a teacher. This is a moment of utter seriousness and commitment to the meaning of teaching. It is "radically first-personal, present tense."[32] The ironic moment brings about a breakdown in one's practical identity as a teacher, making one aware of the larger implications of one's practice. "Developing a capacity for ironic disruption may be a manifestation of seriousness about practical identity. It is not merely a disruption of one's practical identity. It is a form of loyalty to it."[33] The breakdown is in the service of more authentic practice.

In this sense, the midrash is not shy about using the language of social practice to describe God's relations with Moses: diffidence about entering the Other's domain, pleasure in inviting the friend to enter, pleasure in the friend's way of discussing immediate issues. This kind of religious language falls ironically short of encompassing the fullness of what it aspires to convey.

"As one speaks to one's friend," for instance, is a striking but ironic analogy for a relationship with the divine. It expresses a certain truth only to disrupt it. For the conversation between friends is in itself subject to ironic disruption. In the course of such a conversation, there may be a moment when one's conscious ease breaks up in a sudden awareness of all that is, and is not, being expressed. Beyond the ease, there is danger, desire, memory, hope. Religious language, for all its efficacy, gaps open under internal pressure.

In the metaphors that figure in the midrash about Moses's outrageous response to God's anger, for instance, the father-son image quickly reveals the internal pressure that it carries. Father and son are, on the one hand, intimate; they identify with each other; they represent continuity. But on the other hand, this relationship is also a site of danger, of power, provocation, and punishment. The closeness generates difference and distance.

These midrashic analogies evoke what is at stake in the Golden

Calf crisis. The father-son relation and the husband-wife relation are both highly charged. It is Moses, as mediator, as defense counsel, as the prince's tutor, the King's associate, the marriage broker, who grounds the current running between polarities.

His role is to bear the ironic uncanniness of his position. Between the exclusive demand of the divine and the fantasy-ridden drivenness of the human, Moses stands *in the midst:* open to the strangeness of the Other and to the dimension in himself where words fail. This experience of incompleteness, ironically, makes him the quintessential *speaker.*

INADVERTENT SIN AND RESPONSIBILITY

His greatest task begins only now, in the traumatic aftermath of the Golden Calf. His will be the double work of teaching his people the laws of sacrifice and of representing them to God as *unintentional* rather than *willful* sinners.

With this unexpected legal formula, the Sages represent the meaning of Moses's project—to reframe the charge against his people to one of *unintentional* sin. By tearing up the marriage document, the broker retroactively annuls the marriage. This legal fiction is reflected in the smashing of the Tablets of the Covenant, which contain the punishment for infidelity.

Moses goes to the very heart of the human relation with God. At the critical point where the relation collapses, he finds a way to continue it. We might say that this is Moses's strongest act of *interpretation.* Paul Ricoeur expresses the paradox: "Interpretation is the attempt to make estrangement, distanciation productive."[34]

In the imagination of the rabbinic Sages, *Moshe rabbenu*—Moses our Teacher—reinterprets the catastrophic estrangement between God and His people. The Golden Calf is described in the book of Psalms as a crisis of *forgetting:* "They forgot God their Savior" (Ps. 106:21). The whole wondrous saga of the Exodus, says the Psalmist, has simply dropped from their minds—a process that began right after the crossing of the Red Sea: "They speedily forgot His deeds." A strange amnesia brings them to the crisis of the Golden Calf and to Moses's reaction: "God was about to destroy them, if Moses had not stood in the breach against Him."

What are we to make of this motif of alienation as *forgetting*? Rephrasing Ricoeur, we might say that Moses's active interpretation of the crisis as *unwitting* sin is an attempt to make this very crisis productive. Distance between father and son, husband and wife, Israelites and God can be reframed as a loss of awareness. If the legal category of *shogeg* (unintentional sin) can be conjured up in their defense, this makes their sin atonable. The Sin Offering, one of the central operations of the Tabernacle, becomes an effective mode of atonement. For only when a sin is committed *be-shogeg*, unwittingly, can it be cleansed with a Sin Offering (*chattat*). Once there is a Tabernacle, a new option opens up for dealing with that enigmatic category of human actions called unintentional sins. This Sin Offering becomes one of the main raisons d'être of the Tabernacle.

The laws of the *chattat* are given in Leviticus, chapters 3 and 4, along with the *asham* (the Guilt Offering), a related category. I suggest that we consider these laws in the context of the Golden Calf—in relation to the quality of *unconsciousness* that, in Moses's midrashic reframing, inhabits that crisis.

But first, we must ask, Why do unwitting sins need atonement at all? This basic question is answered by Ramban, who lays out a theological rationale. He cites the verse that initiates these laws ("When a person [*nefesh*—lit., a soul] sins unwittingly"), in order to explain that since sins of consciousness occur in the *nefesh*, they require atonement for the taint they leave on the *nefesh*, even if they are committed unawares.[35] Only a pure *nefesh* may approach God in the Holy Tabernacle. A *korban* (sacrifice = *bringing close*) is needed precisely for that purpose of coming close to God.

This is a radical claim: consciousness includes what is obscured in consciousness. Even if the sin is committed out of ignorance, or obliviousness, one remains responsible. In Talmudic discussions, a complex set of possibilities is analyzed. For example, if one forgets a law of Shabbat observance, or alternatively if one somehow forgets one's reality—that today is Shabbat—these slips of mind, once one becomes aware of them, can be atoned by a Sin Offering. This category covers serious sins that would be gravely punished[36] if they had been committed willfully.

These are sins of commission, not omission (i.e., one has violated a negative commandment). They may be committed by an individual, or by the Sanhedrin (the High Court) that has made a mistaken ruling, or by the king. And the sin must have been committed totally, "from beginning to end," within a state of unconsciousness (*be-shegagah*)—as with throwing a stone on Shabbat, where the act cannot be termed inadvertent if one realizes one's mistake in mid-flight!

The state of *shogeg* can be understood as one of inattention, carelessness, unconsciousness, inadvertence, or obliviousness.[37] The return to awareness is an internal movement; it cannot, for instance, be enforced by external evidence. Only if one becomes aware of one's sin—that is, one recognizes one's own mistake—does the Sin Offering become an obligation.[38]

The dramatic situation of *yecheta v'ashem*—unconsciousness followed by consciousness, or, as we might say, the moment of *insight*—is repeatedly described as "sinning in error" and "becoming/feeling guilty."[39] The meaning of the second term, *v'ashem,* is clarified by Rashi: "when he comes to a *recognition of himself* to repent of his sin and makes up his mind to confess that he has sinned and has incurred guilt." *V'ashem* refers to an internal act of *accepting responsibility* for an act of which he had previously had no awareness. It is this intimate moment of recognition that generates repentance and the concrete act of sacrifice. It is only the sinner himself who can affirm or deny his own error.[40]

Intentionality, or its absence, then, is a matter of conscience. In line with this, Jacob Milgrom translates *v'ashem*—"experiences contrition" or "feels guilt." He comments: "I deliberately chose the noun 'guilt' over the common adverb 'guilty' in order to convey its substantive nature. It is not a metaphor or mental abstraction, but a physical reality, felt in pain or illness—literal pangs of conscience."[41] The topic here is actually a *willful* crime—denying an act under oath. But "voluntary contrition (*ashem*) has the power to *correct retroactively his advertent sin into an inadvertent offense,* which is expiable by sacrifice" [my emphasis].

Milgrom speaks of the pang of conscience that accepts responsibility for the sin. This pang constitutes the *asham* experience, which leads to verbal confession, payment of a fine,[42] and bringing a reparation offering (the *asham*).

Voluntary contrition, I suggest, maps onto the notion of accepting responsibility. Jonathan Lear distinguishes between two ideas: *holding oneself responsible* and *accepting responsibility* for one's inner world. "In *holding oneself responsible* one is essentially taking a third-personal stance with respect to oneself and deciding whether one's character, actions, thoughts or feelings are worthy of praise or blame. . . . But as she is able to cease *holding* herself responsible for her emotions, she is able to *accept* responsibility for them: that is, she is able to acknowledge them as hers. Accepting responsibility is essentially a first-person relation. In accepting responsibility I acknowledge who or what I am."[43]

The ability to speak in the first person is to acknowledge without blame that one's emotions are part of one's own functioning. Holding oneself responsible, on the other hand, is the position of hysteria, which is "in its essence a disclaimer of responsibility for the unconscious." Ironically, achieving the first-person position entails a shift of perspective. It is an active position, but also one that entails a relaxation of the muscles, a new relation to repressed emotion. Rather than feeling crippled by an alien force, one recognizes the alienness as one's own.

BLIND SPOTS

We return to the issue of the inadvertent sin. The point at which one feels guilt is the intimate moment of remorse. This is in accord with Rashi's reading of Leviticus 5:23. The text describes not simply the behavioral response of the sinner—restitution (*v'heishiv*) of money owed—but the cognitive shift that precedes restitution.[44]

For what exactly does one accept responsibility? For the fact that something has slipped one's mind, been forgotten, and is now remembered? The act committed could be the involuntary swallowing of a piece of forbidden fat—the operation of a reflex.[45] A moment of absence, of absentmindedness, non-mindedness, followed by the retroactive experience of what was not experienced at the time. A disruptive recollection of distraction. Or, better, a sudden lucidity about *my* loss, when *I* lost *myself*, when *I* was lost. An awareness of *my* blind spot.

Related to the biblical *shogeg* is the root *shogeh*—go astray, err, swerve, meander, reel, roll—which serves as the Aramaic translation in Targum Onkelos for the Hebrew *nifkad*—missed, lacking, empty.[46]

To accept one's guilt, to find oneself *ashem,* then, is to accept the unconscious into one's realm of responsibility. Unknowable, uncontrollable, the stranger within is acknowledged as mine; I identify with my own points of failure, my deadlocks. King David is preoccupied with this dimension of the mind. When he begins Psalm 7 with the words *Shigayon le-David,* the midrash elaborates: "Lord of the world, do not judge me a willful sinner but an unwitting sinner!" Clearly, David is invoking the less serious diagnosis, but at the same time, he is not rejecting all responsibility: he is acknowledging a constitutive blind spot.

Or when David cries out in Psalm 19, "Who can be aware of errors (*shigyonot*)? Clear me of hidden things!" he expresses the same sense of ownership over that which cannot be owned. Rashi conveys the paradox: "I have been wary of errors, but it is impossible to be so wary that one never errs; Clear me of things that I am blind to."

David accepts responsibility for the blind spot that is in any case inevitable. Error, unconsciousness, deadlock—these become constitutive of being human. One is inside, not outside; implicated in this unfathomable humanity.

Dostoyevsky noted that "[i]t is not by locking up one's neighbor that one can convince oneself of one's own soundness of mind." Jacques Lacan wittily assays a similar notion: *Les non-dupes errent*— a wordplay on *le nom du père.* Those who most confidently set themselves against error err nonetheless—or perhaps all the more.

The paradox of engaging with a blind spot appears in one of the most dramatic moments of recognition in Genesis. Joseph, in the role of Egyptian viceroy, demands of his brothers that they leave their brother Simeon behind as a hostage. They respond by turning to one another: "Indeed, we are guilty for our brother, whose anguish we saw as he begged for his life, and we would not hear him!" (Gen. 42:21). Their sudden pang of guilt—apparently the first they have experienced in twenty years—retrieves an ancient trauma. In acknowledging guilt, they are not simply noting a wrong: they are accepting responsibility for that long-ago scene by the pit, when they *saw* without *hearing* their brother's cry. Now, they experience, for the first time, the "blind spot" of that moment.

This is a crisis of intimacy, when an inner deadness must be entered anew. The trauma of the past returns to implicate them. Now, they live that scene as they did not (could not) live it then. With its return, it opens up the question of the future.

> Our Rabbis taught: One good deed draws another in its wake; one sin draws another in its wake. So one should not suffer over a sin committed in error but rather over the fact that this opens up more possibilities for sin, whether intentional or unintentional. And one should not rejoice over a good deed that came to hand but over the many good deeds that will in future come to hand. So if one sinned inadvertently, this is not a good sign.[47]

Both inadvertent sins and happy opportunities for good deeds open up a flow of similar future deeds. The midrash looks at the larger shifts that a single act can catalyze, even if it is "accidental," or unwitting in nature. Acts reshape the world of possibility; in a sense, they reshape the self. A crack, that can henceforth widen, is made in the walls of the ego.

What is striking here is the emphasis on *happenstance.* The sin *be-shogeg,* committed unwittingly, and the good deed that "comes to one's hand," both tell of a hidden world that finds an opportunity to erupt. The world of the unconscious finds a moment of what Jonathan Lear calls "possibilities for new possibilities." Such moments are, as he puts it, "breaking out all the time."[48]

Lear discusses "happy" moments that "happen" in psychoanalysis. The very meaning of "happiness" is bound up, in English, with chance, "lucky breaks." The Tanchuma passage we have just seen complicates the issue by emphasizing that such breakthrough moments can work in opposite ethical directions. For good or ill, such moments arouse a certain anxiety. Anything can happen. One's act can disrupt a preconceived structure. But by accepting responsibility for such moments and the acts they generate, one actively determines "the shape of the soul," as Lear puts it.[49]

However, we notice that the thrust of the Tanchuma passage is less masterful. Acts, whether good or bad, may have a generative power. The structure of the soul may be affected by the work of one's hand, even if unconscious. But the soul itself is implicated in the uncanny nature of those acts, the sense that they are both ours and not ours.

THE SENSITIVE CONSCIENCE

Here arises one more aspect of the laws of sacrifice. In discussing the Sin Offering, the Talmudic Sages disagree on the issue of *asham talui*—the "suspended" Guilt Offering that constitutes a separate category: the case of one who is *unsure* whether he did or did not in fact commit the act. This sacrifice is a temporary measure, effective until the situation becomes clear.[50] In this case, the uncertainty is doubled: there is doubt whether in fact one sinned inadvertently. How commonly would this dilemma occur? R. Eliezer says: "One may offer a Suspended Guilt Offering every day, and at any time that one wishes. This is called the Guilt Offering of the Pious."[51] An example is brought of Baba ben Buti, who did actually offer such a sacrifice every day except the day after Yom Kippur (the Day of Atonement).

As against this practice, the Sages declared: "Wait until you are in a situation of real doubt." One offers the sacrifice only for acts that are punishable, when done deliberately, by excommunication, and, when done inadvertently, by a Sin Offering.

A controversy arises between the Rabbis who hold to the notion of a specific sinful act and those who relate to the issue of guilt as a diffuse sensibility, a sense of perpetual sinfulness. R. Eliezer and Baba ben Buti go against the general trend of Sages who insist that the sacrifice can be offered only in cases of uncertainty about concrete sinful acts. For these two Sages, as Rashi explains, "[e]very day one stands in doubt whether one has sinned, and one's heart troubles one that one has sinned."[52] This is a subjective state, the sensitive conscience suffering pangs that demand sacrificial expiation.

Both positions respect the power of the unconscious to infiltrate the practical order of things. In general, the Rabbis insist that law deals only with the conscious realm. If the inadvertent—and even doubt about the inadvertent—must be acknowledged, at any rate the sin must be specific, a particular act of commission. The other position makes room for a pervasive sin awareness, like a Geiger counter that is set on "high." Rashi interprets this as a sensitive rather than a pathological position. It creates turbulence and disrupts a sane, practical life such as the Rabbis in general advocate. But the sense of constant permeability is nevertheless an authentic human experience.

Over this question, the Rabbis are divided. How to relate to the accidents, blind spots, dark drives, as Rosenzweig refers to them? R. Eliezer and Baba ben Buti regard these phenomena, in their most intrusive form, as a part of their human reality. To acknowledge how much of life eludes one's grasp is, for them, to inhabit the midst of life.

These two Sages speak for the normalcy of forgetting. In our context, the sacrifices that acknowledge the unwitting elements, the dimensions of doubt, chance, and error in human life, are a direct response to the sin of the Golden Calf. As a sin of forgetting, the Golden Calf represents the loss of attention that is in some way inherent in the people's originally rapt attention to the revelation at Sinai. In the relation of son and father, the son moves between poles of closeness and alienation, merging with the father and separating from him.

VIRTUES OF FORGETTING

When Moses wishes to reframe the charge against the people, he tears up the marriage document, which represents the clear inscription of consciousness, and declares that "it is better that they be judged as *shogegin*—as unwitting sinners!" To be *shogeg* is to have forgotten, to have become unaware, to have lost the thread of meaning. To recognize oneself as belonging in this category is to reimagine the dynamics of the inner world.

So, the people *mourn* on hearing that God has responded to the Golden Calf by distancing Himself from them ("I will no longer go up in your midst" [Exod. 33:3]). They enact mourning by "stripping themselves of their ornaments." According to Rashi, these ornaments represent the sublime moment in which they had declared, "We shall do and we shall hear!" (24:7). They relinquish an omnipotent fantasy. They accept responsibility for forgetting God.

Philosophers and Sages have mused on the paradoxical virtues of forgetting. Montaigne, for instance: "Experience teaches that a good memory is generally joined to a weak judgment." Or Nietzsche: "Many a man fails to become a thinker for the sole reason that his memory is too good." "Life in any true sense is absolutely impossible without forgetfulness." "Error is the condition of life—the knowledge that one errs does not eliminate the error." Adam Phillips: "Conscious memory is a saboteur." As though error and forgetting may potentially be a ground for blessing.

In his classic literary fiction, Jorge Luis Borges tells the story of Funes, a young man who falls from his horse and suffers a kind of stroke: in his case, his brain is jolted into perfect memory. Now over-responsive to the details of a constantly changing world of phenomena, he cannot move past particulars in order to arrive at generalizations. How can one use the word "dog," when the dog changes so radically with every second? He can learn languages, but, says Borges omi-nously, "I suspect however that he was not very capable of thought. To think is to forget differences." Like Montaigne and Nietzsche, Borges understands thought as what grows in the crevices of conscious-ness. Sleep, too, becomes impossible for the "memorious" sufferer; as Borges puts it, "[T]o sleep is to turn one's mind from the world." He is unable to lose consciousness, to escape the "heat and pressure of reality." Hyperaware, he cannot perform the essential human tasks of dreaming, representing, thinking. He dies of congestion of the lungs.[53]

On the other hand, as Borges says at the close of his melancholy case history, before his stroke Funes had been "what all human beings are: blind, deaf, addle-brained, absentminded." As in science fiction, Borges's story jolts our sanely moderate perspectives. Too much mem-ory, too little memory—the reader is not offered a choice but rather two narratives, one a nightmare scenario of excess, the other a passing reference to quotidian insufficiency. Neither is this a dialectical per-spective; instead, we are suspended between two helpless conditions, as though there is no other way to reveal an irreducible dilemma, for which the solution is not simply "the right amount."

In a sense, George Eliot offers us a related paradox in her well-known passage in *Middlemarch*:

If we had a keen vision and a feeling for all ordinary human life, it would be like hearing the grass grow and the squirrel's heart beat, and we should die of that roar which lies on the other side of silence. As it is, the quickest of us walk about well wadded in stupidity.[54]

The hypothetical syntax of Eliot's vision of extreme sensitivity— "the squirrel's heart beat" induces in the reader the pulse of the unbearable—is balanced by a brief, forceful description of a damningly commonplace reality. She will not allow us to opt for one or the other. Rather, she exposes us to a radical blind spot, the alternative to which is madness. The illusion of mastery is swept away.

This is the power of literature. Freud often emphasizes the fact that the reader is "rhetorically placed *within* the madness, that there is no place from which that madness can be judged *from the outside.*"[55] The space of reading literature does not allow the reader to situate herself outside the madness portrayed within it.

"CONGRATULATIONS THAT YOU SMASHED THEM!"

We read in the Talmud: "Three hundred laws were forgotten in Israel during the mourning period for Moses. They were restored by Otniel ben Kenaz in his *pilpul* (ingenious interpretations)."[56] After Moses dies, an epidemic of forgetting sweeps over the people. His lifework is apparently lost. That, for the people, is the meaning of his death and the mourning that follows it. An act of *interpretation,* of *thinking,* saves the day. Otniel ben Kenaz (one of the Judges in the period following Moses's death) performs a redemptive act of *pilpul*—a playful but earnest exercise in recuperating lost knowledge.

The remarkable aspect of this midrashic narrative is that it is Moses himself who is elsewhere credited with initiating this process of interpretation. The Sages read his smashing of the Tablets as an inspired response to the fixities of idolatry: " 'The Tablets which you smashed' (Exod. 34:1)—congratulations that you smashed them!"[57] His ultimate greatness is that this act performed "before the eyes of Israel" is acknowledged by God, in all its audacity, as a signally inspired act.[58] "Congratulations that you smashed them!"

"Sometimes the suspension of Torah constitutes its fulfillment."[59] The Talmud links the smashing of the Tablets with the suspension of Torah. "If the Tablets had not been smashed, the Torah would not have been forgotten from Israel."[60] The idea emerges that it is possible for the Torah to thrive by being forgotten. The three hundred forgotten laws are creatively reconstructed. And the lively disagreements and differences of opinion among the Sages, which result from forgetting the Torah, become the fertile ground for amplifying the body of law.

What is shattered with the Tablets? Fetishizing memory, extreme awareness that allows nothing to slip. So God assents to Moses's instinct to break the Tablets—to make space for the human modality of absence, loss, fragmentation, error, of the "blind, deaf, addle-brained, absentminded" human reality. But, as with the Borges story, and as with George Eliot's meditation on awareness and stupidity, the two modalities both remain vital. Clearly, the Rabbis have a large investment in learning and remembering—as, indeed, does the Torah itself: "Beware and be highly watchful lest you forget the things that your eyes have seen and lest they move away from your heart all the days you live" (Deut. 4:9). "Remember, do not forget, how you made God angry in the wilderness" (9:7).

This is not simply about a proper balance between the values of memory and those of forgetting. A constant dynamic keeps the two modalities in motion. Here is another such polarity: "There is no human being, righteous person in the world, who does good without ever sinning/erring" (Eccles. 7:20). There is doing good, and there is erring. Ba'al Shem Tov invites us to read differently: "There is no human being, righteous person in the world, who does not err *in doing good.*" Again, a perspective on the inevitability of error. There is an uncanny irony even in the righteous human existence. Something out of joint that skews even good acts. The blind spot inhabits every insight.

Such spotted insight may even yield wisdom of its own. So much attention paid to the *shogeg,* the inadvertent act, the slip of mind—and to the sacrifice that atones for it—focuses us on one of the main dynamics of the Tabernacle.

The Sin Offering acts as atonement for the trauma of the Golden Calf, which is perpetually repeated, in moments of absentmindedness, of not being fully witted. By reframing the Golden Calf as a lapse of this kind, as a regression into fantasy life, Moses can represent his people as constitutively prone to such lapses—complex states in which conscious and unconscious life interweave. In this, they are simply human. More than that, such a state may bear the good fruits of dream life, of reverie; of creative thinking and interpretation. For this, it will be necessary to process, to *work through* the fantasy. The Sin Offering represents such a cathartic process, prefaced as it is by the inner work of self-recognition.

PROSAIC INTIMACY

Moses's way of speaking after the Golden Calf crisis is precious to God because it is intimate, informal, responsive to the immediate demands of relationship. Instead of emphasizing fully grasped, conscious meaning, Moses enacts the movement of process and activity.[61] He is taking a risk, one might say: a diffident, modest person, he breaks out of type. Perhaps God finds this manner of speaking lovable precisely because Moses knows how *not* to be true to type. Although God is omniscient, He apparently loves the unexpected, the human gleam of improvisation that speaks of live presence. This, in some way, frees Him, too, to be unexpected, to be capable of *other thoughts.*[62]

Error, improvisation—the work of making estrangement productive—are aspects of the way Moses now listens and speaks, so that the King turns aside from His majestic preoccupations and speaks only to him. In a deeply anthropomorphic movement, the biblical description of Moses "finding favor in God's eyes" is translated in the midrash into a mode of familiarity, emotional intimacy.

Failure and loss, the smashed Tablets, the familiar strangeness of the unconscious—these drive the process of the human/divine relationship from now on. Even the religious language of the midrash adopts this register. Within this language, human beings and God accept responsibility for the otherness that inhabits them:

> "Speak to the children of Israel": (Lev. 1:2) Said R. Judah in the name of R. Samuel b. Nahman: This may be compared to the case of a king who had an undergarment concerning which he instructed his servant, telling him: "Fold it and shake it out and

pay close attention to it." His servant asked him: "My lord king, of all the garments you have, you give instructions concerning none but this one?" The king answered: "That is because I wear this close to my body." So Moses said to God: "Master of the Universe, out of all the seventy original nations that You have in Your world, do You command me concerning none but Israel, saying, Command the children of Israel (e.g., Num. 28:2), Speak to the children of Israel, Say to the children of Israel (Exod. 33:5)?" God answered: "That is because they cleave to Me." Thus it says, "For as the girdle cleaves [is worn close] to the loins of a man, so have I caused the whole house of Israel to cleave unto Me" (Jer. 13:11).[63]

The parable tells a story of literal, physical intimacy—direct contact between the king and his underclothes. In spite of their lowly status as adornment, the king is intimately concerned about them. The analogy with the children of Israel, whom God describes as *cleaving—devukin—*to Him, creates an ironic effect. The Hebrew term conveys both a passive sense of "worn next to the skin" and an active *adherence.* This latter sense evokes the term—*devekut—*for both erotic intimacy and mystic union.

The prosaic intimacy of the parable is developed in the proof text from Jeremiah. A linen girdle is hidden in a cleft in the rock. By the time it is restored, it has rotted, it is good for nothing. So the Israelites have been singled out: "As the girdle cleaves to the loins of a man, so have I caused the whole house of Israel to cleave unto me."

The bizarre parable castigates the people for failing to honor their own position of intimacy with God. The thrust of the midrash emphasizes the confounding physicality of the underwear image. This is *chavivut*—familiarity, intimacy—in an uncanny, even a sexual register. Israel are neither the largest nor the greatest[64] of the nations: they are simply the bearers of an almost impersonal intimacy with God. Rather than experiencing epiphanies, they simply live a way of life that adheres in its most prosaic details to the nature of the godly in the world.

The physical intimacy of the couple is transposed to a theological key. The Creation story culminates in, "Therefore a man shall leave his father and his mother and *cleave* (*davak*) to his wife" (Gen. 2:24). "You who *cleave* to God are all of you alive today!" (Deut. 4:4). The aspiration of such a way of being is a state of closeness to God. In the end, this becomes a matter of survival.

The Rabbis ask a practical question: How is it possible to cleave to the consuming fire that is God? And answer by displacing that intimacy onto the quotidian realities of the social-religious order: by marrying a Torah scholar, or by helping him with his business interests.[65] Such a translation of a mystical ideal expresses the rabbinic understanding of the *intimacy* of the material imagination. Human marriage and sexuality and economic survival are the "underclothing" of the king—areas in which unconscious fantasy is powerful. Here, in the midst of life, proximity to God is experienced.

Of course, there is a certain conscious irony in this kind of intimacy. In the first person, accepting responsibility for the gap between social practice and aspiration, irony may arrive to disrupt routine. The words *clinging to God* strike one anew and complicate practical identity. Perhaps what God loves in Moses's language is the playful and the disruptive. Like the inadvertent sin and the good deed that fortuitously "comes to one's hand," it breaks rigidity wide open, whether for good or ill. An opportunity is created; possibilities for new possibilities become visible.

In the world to come, the midrashic chapter on *chibah* concludes, this mode of familiarity with God, once concentrated in Moses's singular way of speaking, will be disclosed to all humanity: "And God's glory will be revealed, and all flesh shall see together, for the mouth of God has spoken" (Isa. 40:5).[66] In the meantime, we are left with the midrashic style of intimacy, a modest way of translating sublime understandings into the religious language of the world of the material imagination. Here, parables tell of process and activity.

In the biblical narrative, a home, a Tabernacle, becomes available for the expression of intimate values. At the heart of the sacrificial rituals is the uncanny presence of the inadvertent sinner. And behind him, the ghost of the Golden Calf. A process is under way. We may call it a process of *working through* compulsions and anxieties. The sacrifices are offered in the midst of life; as Rosenzweig puts it, "Only from the center does there arise a bounded home in the unbounded world, a patch of ground between four tent pegs, which can be posted further and further out."[67] The process recognizes fantasies, dark drives, defenses, that pretend to hold the world together. Israel is invited into that "patch of ground." Here, practices and rituals may open a way to accept responsibility for the out-of-joint reality of creaturely being. And from the awkward passion of those who atone and pray, larger areas of love and compassion may become visible. Perhaps even the possibility of loving one's neighbor as oneself.

2

Tzav

Golden Calf, Clouds of Glory

INSTALLATIONS

For seven days, the priests who will officiate over the sacrificial rituals of the Tabernacle undergo a period of initiation. During this time, they are trained in the practices of priesthood: all the detailed procedures of the sacrifices are rehearsed, as well as the ceremonies of inauguration—blood-sprinkling, anointment, bathing, vestments.

These are called days of *miluim*—of installation, investiture into their new roles. It is God who, the Torah declares, will *fill* (*yimale*) their hands (Lev. 8:33). But it is Moses who will, during these seven days, act as High Priest and instructor. Everything that Aaron and his sons will perform from the eighth day onward is first performed by Moses. Again, most obviously, his role is to demonstrate and rehearse the rituals. But when we turn to the midrashic literature, this transitional period releases unexpected meanings.

Here, for instance, hidden tensions between Moses and Aaron are uncovered:

All seven days that Moses was at the Burning Bush, God told him, Go on My mission! and Moses answered, Send whatever messenger You choose [excluding me]! This happened the first day, the second day. . . . God said: I am telling you, Go! And you tell me, Send someone else! As you live, tomorrow I will pay you back! When the Tabernacle will be completed, you will expect to serve as High Priest, and I will tell you, Call Aaron to serve in that role. . . . There is a calling that is to greatness, as in "Moses called Aaron" (Lev. 9:1). Moses told Aaron, So God

told me to appoint you as High Priest. Aaron replied, You have
labored over the Tabernacle and I am made High Priest! Moses
answered, As you live, even though you have been made High
Priest, it is as though I had been made High Priest! Just as you
rejoiced for me when I rose to greatness so do I rejoice in your
rise to greatness [1]

The midrash proposes that Moses is punished for his original resistance to God's call: since he has "disappointed" God, he will experience his own disappointment by having his expectations thwarted; he
will play the priestly role for seven days, only to yield it thereafter to
Aaron. The price of "disappointing" God at the Burning Bush will be
Moses's disappointment about filling the priestly role himself.[2] Both
narratives are introduced by the verb "to call."

However, the midrashic narrative focuses on the mutual nobility
with which Moses and Aaron deal with this situation. Aaron empa-
thizes with Moses's loss and Moses remembers how generously Aaron
had responded, after the Burning Bush, to Moses's rise to power;
he now finds it in himself to be equally magnanimous in his own
moment of disappointment.

What is portrayed here is the complex reality of an experience of
investiture and *divestment*. Dressing Aaron in his priestly robes means
that Moses strips himself of a symbolic function with which he has
deeply identified. Wearing the white robes of priesthood for seven
days has gratified a long-standing sense of himself. Losing this role to
his elder brother means not simply surrendering his claim, with all its
history of desire. It means accepting responsibility for that desire and
converting its energy to a deepened identification with his brother.

The moment of investiture is a fraught moment in which a person assumes dignities and functions within a shared symbolic universe. There is pleasure in this "rise to greatness." Through a kind
of performative magic, power and authority clothe one. But, as Eric
Santner suggests, there may occur an "investiture crisis," in which
one finds oneself unable to recognize oneself in the call. The result
is a dysfunctional excitement, a sense of being invaded or seduced.
Moses's unease with being invoked by God at the Burning Bush and
the midrashic narratives about the mutual generosity displayed by the

brothers imply an intimate struggle with a kind of idolatry. If Moses is later called "the most humble of all men," perhaps this humility is a function of the hidden ethical work that the midrash gestures at here.

The theme of symbolic investiture is given a strange turn at the end of the long training descriptions (Lev., chapters 6–8). During this period, we learn, Moses and the priests are placed under a kind of house arrest, under pain of death:

> And you shall not go out from the entrance to the *Tent of Assembly* for *seven days* until the day that your installation [*miluaichem*—lit., your filling] is completed; for your installation will require [lit., God will fill your hands] *seven days*. Just as has been done today, God has commanded to be done [for seven days], to make expiation for you. You shall remain at the entrance of the *Tent of Meeting* day and night for *seven days*, keeping God's charge, so that you do not die, for so I have been commanded.
>
> And Aaron and his sons did all the things that God commanded through Moses. (Lev. 8:33–36)

Moses's last words to Aaron and his sons strike a very different note from the technical tone of the duties and preparations that had occupied him until now. Now, in summation, Moses invokes symbolic frameworks: three times he refers to the seven-day period, and twice to the entrance to the Tent of Assembly. These are the liminal time and space of the action during this transition.

What fills these frameworks? A process that is repeatedly called *milium*—lit., filling. This means installation, the fitting of a jewel into its setting; or the investiture where one's hand is filled with a symbolic authority.[3] Either actively or passively, a filling process takes place at the entrance to the Tabernacle during these seven transitional days—"until the filling days are filled" (Lev. 8:33).

Between interior and exterior space, a drama takes place. The priests are not to go forth from that threshold; they are to stay there day and night. The word *teshvu*—you shall stay—echoes the seven-day festival of Sukkot: "You shall stay—*teshvu*—in booths for seven days, in order that your generations may know that you stayed in booths when I brought them out of the land of Egypt" (Lev. 23:43). Strikingly, Moses uses the same key terms in both texts—going forth, staying, seven days. To stay is both to rest, to dwell, and to be, in a sense, suspended, held back. The booths are a reminder of the Exodus experience, of a departure, a going forth, into the wilderness world. The apprentice priests reenact the first part of the Exodus, the Passover night, when God had instructed the people, "You shall not go forth from the entrance to your homes (till morning)" (Exod. 12:22). During the Passover night, too, the people were under house arrest, girded and booted for the journey, eating the Paschal offering. Suspended between past and future, this was a moment of focused attention, *staying* in the rich older English sense of the word (holding back, delaying).

Franz Rosenzweig beautifully observes: "In Judaism, man is always somehow a remnant. He is always somehow a survivor, an inner something, whose exterior was seized by the current of the world and carried off while he himself, what is left of him, remains standing on the shore. *Something within him is waiting*" (my italics).[4] The posture that Rosenzweig describes here is implicit in the expression *leil shimurim*—the Night of Watching.[5] The epic event of Exodus—going forth, expression, liberation—is predicated upon the previous night of *shimurim*, of expectation, vigilance, watching, waiting.

KEEPING WATCH

The same expression marks the seven-day period of inauguration: *U-shmartem et mishmeret Ha-Shem* ("You shall keep God's charge" [Lev. 8:35]). At root, *shamar* means to conserve, preserve, observe. In relation to the Tabernacle, the idiom refers to guard duty. In relation to God, it means observing His prohibitions; resisting, in this case, the urge to depart, to leave. It is used often in the book of Numbers. And in the account in Exodus 12 of the preparations for the Night of Watching, it appears several times, notably in the commandment *U-shmartem et ha-matzot* ("And you shall observe, watch over, the matzot—unleavened bread" [12:17]).[6]

However, *shamar* holds a rich ambiguity. When Jacob hears Joseph's dream, we read, "His father held (*shamar*) the story in mind" (Gen. 37:11). Rashi comments: "He waited in expectation for when it would come true—as in Isaiah 26:2: 'A nation that *keeps faith,*' and in Job 14:16: 'Keep watch over my sin.'"

Rashi spells out the dynamic implications of the root *shamar.* He notices the *future* movement of the word, the attention that is also an intention. In the midrash, indeed, Jacob is imagined as taking pen in hand and recording the date of the dream and its content: "I have seen things *me-mashmeshim u-ba'im*—gradually, slowly, gropingly moving toward realization."[7] The fulfillment of the dream is at the moment unimaginable, but it is *feeling its way* toward him. He is vigilant, expectant, turned to past and future at once. In the precise formulation, in a different context, of the French philosopher Maurice Blanchot, he keeps watch over absent meaning.[8]

Observing God's mandate, then, may imply being vigilant, sustaining a sense of trust, keeping faith with a future yet to evolve. In a word, waiting. It also evokes a kind of freedom from what Eric Santner calls "the repetition compulsions—the Egyptomaniacal labors—that sustain idolatrous attachments."[9]

Santner argues that the Exodus from Egypt is also—and perhaps most significantly—a liberation from the "Egyptian mania" that underpins the Golden Calf. Some rigidity, some fixation, keeps the people enslaved, addicted. In Hasidic thought, this mania is called, simply, idolatry. Exodus is liberation from this slavery.

THE MANIA OF IDOLATRY

How is the Golden Calf positioned in relation to this project? According to Rashi, the Golden Calf originates in the people's inability, precisely, to *wait* for Moses to return from Mount Sinai:

> And the people saw that Moses was delayed in coming down the mountain. And they gathered against Aharon and said to him, Rise up and make us gods who will walk before us, for this Moses, the man who brought us up from the land of Egypt, we don't know what has become of him. (Exod. 32:1)

Rashi reads the word *boshesh*—delayed—as a pun on *ba shesh*—"the sixth hour has come." Moses promised to be back by midday on the fortieth day. The people miscalculated the day and fell into panic:

now, since Moses has failed them, they need another object to "walk before them"—for them to fix their eyes upon.

Without Moses, in Rashi's words, the world is "darkness and gloom and chaos." This is the vision that Satan creates for them. Without Moses, their world has lost its light; it appears uncentered, incoherent. But this panic experience is imagined as a *satanic* fantasy. Perception is distorted; madness has them in its grip.

This midrashic scenario implies a hidden connection between Moses and the idol that comes to replace him. This implication is spelled out by the modern commentary, Meshech Chochmah: the people see Moses as "the man who brought us up from the land of Egypt."[10] In a word, their basic delusion is to view Moses *idolatrously.* They may pay lip service to God's power, but it is Moses whom they experience as their savior. Because of this basic distortion, God quotes their words to Moses when he reveals their sin: as though to say, *This is what your people think of you!* When Moses fails to appear, the Golden Calf fills the gap created by idolatrous desire.

This reading is quite startling. In the midrashic scenario, the time elapsing between faith and betrayal is not even forty days: *instantly,* by failing to appear on time, Moses precipitates a regression to more generic forms of idolatry. (Calves and oxen are classic idols in Near Eastern culture.) Like the fetish that has failed the child, Moses is "destroyed" and replaced. What is at issue is not *what* god is worshipped but the *way* it is worshipped. As Meshech Chochmah remarks, many things can become idols—Shabbat, the Sanctuary, perhaps God Himself.

Essentially, the people have returned to Egypt, to the ancient idolatry; they have undone the Exodus, which offered liberation from the "Egyptian mania." In a sense, they have never really emerged from that mania.

A scandalous midrash tells of the bride who commits adultery during the wedding (*tachat chupata*). While the marriage celebrations are still under way ("While the king was still feasting, my myrrh exuded its fragrance"[11]), the bride is palpably interested in another lover.[12] By analogy, in the midst of the Revelation at Sinai, the people desire another god. No time gap at all intervenes between Revelation and betrayal. The marriage is "forgotten" by the bride even as she commits herself to it. If the bride is still moved by an old desire, an unimaginable state of affairs becomes conceivable. Her way of entering into marriage does not preclude such ambivalence.

The mania of total subservience has been transferred to other objects—to Moses, perhaps, who fails to function according to the fantasy of idolatry. It takes no time at all for that fantasy to target a different object. Even as the people commit themselves to God, they are already mulling over another desire:

> [How many days were they with God?] . . . Not even one day! Even as the people stood at Sinai and declared with their mouths, We shall do and we shall listen, their hearts were attuned (*mechuvanim*) to idolatry, as it says, "They seduced God with their mouths but their hearts were not attuned to Him." (Ps. 78:36)[13]

Their attachment to God and the new world He offers them proves to be superficial. It has left little mark on their being. The delinquent bride is haunted by a passion that diminishes her freedom. If, as Levinas puts it, God is offering a "difficult freedom" at Sinai—if Judaism is indeed a religion for adults[14]—the Golden Calf represents the psychic constraint of primal attachments.

God describes the Calf worshippers as a "stiff-necked people" and on that basis decides to destroy them: "And now, let Me be and My anger will burn against them and totally destroy them, and make you into a great nation!" (Exod. 32:9–10). A people who are rigid in their passions hold out no hope for change. It is striking that God does not charge them with infidelity—they are not, for instance, a *fickle* people—but, on the contrary, with excessive *piety.* They have in effect never moved away from their old idolatry. Not even for one day were they, in the words of the midrash, *with God.*

In this radical reading, the people have never truly awakened to the call of Sinai. Their acceptance of the covenant is judged to be lip service only; the heart remains unattuned to its music. Being *with God* represents an alternative to the psychic rigidity embodied in Calf worship. It means being together *with* the Other, responsive to the Other, responsible for one's own otherness. A conversation becomes possible with that which is not oneself.

Encountering the Other means, in part, being able to wait, to remain vigilant, expectant, turned toward the future. This posture, as we have seen, is articulated in the word *shamar*—to keep watch. This is what God asks of the priests who remain for seven days within the precincts of the Tabernacle. Such *waiting* is part of their initiation rites. It represents faith and the ability to live with the unrealized possibility; it runs counter to the idolatrous posture that can tolerate no delay. Paradoxically, the waiting posture is informed by a kind of *alacrity,* a controlled vitality.

FAITHFUL AFTER ALL?

In midrashic and Hasidic traditions, building the Tabernacle becomes a therapeutic response to the Golden Calf. This work enacts a return, in a new iteration, to the "difficult liberty"[15] of Sinai.

Citing Freud and Rosenzweig, Santner declares: "God is above all the name for the pressure to be alive to the world."[16] This God opens us to the singular pressure of being *with* our neighbor, with his "touch of madness."[17]

From this perspective, the Tabernacle project has at its heart the movement of a people to construct a symbolic world in which this difficult God may dwell. His demand—framed, according to midrashic chronology, on the Day of Atonement, the very day of His forgiveness for the sin of the Golden Calf—is, "Let them make for Me a sacred place so that I may dwell among them" (Exod. 25:8). Concretely, this refers to the structure that will stand in the center of the Israelite camp. Less concretely, it refers to the intimate world of the human being, in the core of the self.

Throughout the process of constructing and assembling the parts of the Tabernacle, the people live through their recovered desire to remain faithful, *after all,* to the call of Sinai. By "after all," I mean, "after Sinai and the Golden Calf." Perhaps, after all, the radical reading we have been considering can be tempered? Perhaps, in spite of everything, the Egyptian mania was indeed interrupted by the freedom offered at Sinai? Perhaps the bride comes to acknowledge the vitality of her love for her husband? A life force breaks through the deathly repetition compulsions of Egypt. In this sense, Sinai represents a radical interruption, an exodus, from the mania of Egypt, while the Golden Calf signifies an equally radical regression to that mania. In building the Tabernacle, the Israelites attune themselves once more to the possibility of God's presence in their midst.

CLOUDS OF GLORY

Many a midrashic narrative engages with the question of this aspiration and with the ways it relates to the Golden Calf. Here is an evocative passage from the commentary of the Gaon on the Song of Songs 1:4:

> When they made the Golden Calf, the Clouds [of Glory that had accompanied them from the time of the Exodus] departed and did not return until they began to make the Tabernacle.

The Gaon presents a chronology of the departure and return of the Clouds of Glory. These Clouds play a significant role in midrashic accounts of the wilderness time. In this midrashic tradition, they depart when the people make the Golden Calf and are restored on 15 Tishrei, which now marks the festival of Sukkot, at the very *beginning* of the Tabernacle work. We have here the hidden story behind this festival, a story of joy at this restoration.[18]

According to the tradition that the Gaon describes, there exists, between the lines of the biblical account, a repressed narrative of loss and return. The sin of the Golden Calf transforms the structure of Israelite experience. What had preceded it had been a state of *hakafah:* of being enveloped, protected, contained by luminous clouds. This state abandons them as they turn to the Golden Calf. When they begin work on the Tabernacle, this *encompassed* state returns.

Functionally, these clouds are said to safeguard the people *on all sides;* to protect them from heat, snakes, uneven ground, perhaps even to give them wings. But beyond their pragmatic uses, the clouds come to represent a condition of enveloping love. In our celebration of the festival of Sukkot (Booths), we remember the recovery of that condition of being *held.*[19]

The primal experience of the infant is represented in this imagery of encompassment. D. W. Winnicott writes of an essential human aloneness, which "can only take place under maximum conditions of dependence." Michael Eigen develops his understanding of this core of aloneness: the ability to be alone is only possible if one is thus supported by

> an unknown boundless other. . . . Our lives tap into a sense of holiness connected with a background aura of infinite unknown support. . . . When the support basic aloneness needs cracks, vanishes, or is threatened, emergent self-feeling veers toward cataclysm."[20]

What Eigen describes here in the world of child development is an early experience of madness. In the imagery of the midrash and of the Gaon, the cataclysm has always already happened. The Golden Calf—completed, blatant, brutal—signifies the loss of the unknown infinite other. Eigen emphasizes the *unknown* otherness of the experience. The baby is *not aware* of being held in this way. Only when the support is lost does the madness tell of what has been lost.

At first, Winnicott writes, "we are concerned with an infant in a highly dependent state and *totally unaware* of this dependence."[21] The Golden Calf—a moment of breakdown—banishes this state; creating the Tabernacle restores it, with a difference. But the vanishing of the Clouds of Glory is neither recorded nor remembered. In a strange sense, it "has not happened yet because the patient was not there for it to happen to."[22] "Nothing happened" may be an authentic account of a kind of emptiness that belongs to the past but that demands to be expressed in the present, when a certain degree of maturity may make the experience accessible.

Perhaps the disappearance of the Clouds of Glory—unrecorded in the Torah text—is that unexperienced emptiness: "nothing happening when it might have happened."[23] Only when the people give themselves over to the everyday creativity of work with the materials of the Tabernacle do the Clouds of Glory return. Does this mean simply that the work on the Tabernacle and the return of the Clouds *attest* to the people's recovery from breakdown? Or perhaps the work on the Tabernacle is *in itself* the movement of recovery, the opening of space for the Clouds of Glory?

What does this theme of the Clouds of Glory add to the explicit narrative in the Torah about the Tablets of the Law, which, in similar pattern, are given to Moses, smashed by him, and then replaced by a second set of Tablets, in token of forgiveness? In the tradition about the Clouds, I suggest, loss and recovery become intimate indications of inner states—precisely because they are impalpable, volatile, they signify indescribable depths of experience.

When the Clouds return, they coincide with the *Mishkan* work and bring knowledge of a particular kind: an original unawareness has been transformed into a new sensitivity.

The moment when the work begins is thus in itself a sacred moment. An experience of emptiness is confronted for the first time. For the first time, the Clouds of Glory are humanly experienced, in and through the working hands of the artists. Simply beginning the work opens the wings of hope:

> *Hope is the thing with feathers—*
> *That perches in the soul—*
> *And sings the tune without the words—*
> *And never stops—at all.*[24]

INORDINATE JOY

The notion of the return of what has been lost introduces a melancholy note into the joy of the Sukkot festival. But the melancholy is subsumed in the "inordinate joy" that Rambam describes in a vivid passage in *The Laws of Lulav:*

12. Although it is a mitzvah to rejoice on all festivals, on the Sukkot festival there was a time of inordinate joy (*simchah yeterah*), for it is written, "You shall rejoice before God your God for seven days." And how was this done? On the eve of the first holiday they would arrange in the Temple a place for the women above and for the men below so that they might not mix with one another. And they began to rejoice from the night after the first holiday, and continued on every day of the intermediate days of the holiday. They began after the Tamid offering was made in the evening to rejoice the rest of the day and through the night.

13. And how was this joy performed? The flute was struck and the violin, harps, and cymbals were played, and everyone

played any instrument he knew how to play. And those who knew how to sing, sang. They danced, and clapped their hands and thighs, and spun, and whirled, each according to his ability, and spoke words of praise and song. But this merriment does not supersede the Sabbath or the Holy Day.

14. It is an obligation to enter fully into this merriment. This was not done by the folk of the land or whoever so wished, but the greatest Sages of Israel and the heads of the Yeshivot and the Sanhedrin and the pious ones and elders and the men of virtuous deeds, they were the ones who danced and clapped and played instruments and rejoiced during the days of Sukkot. But the entire people, the men and the women, all would come to look and to listen.

15. The joy that a person should express in performing the commandments and in the love of God who commanded them, is a great worship of God. Whoever avoids expressing this joy is worthy of punishment, as it is said: ". . . in return for your not worshipping God your God with joy and with gladness of heart." And whoever carries himself haughtily and takes pride in himself and considers himself too dignified in such places is a sinner and a fool. Concerning this, Solomon admonished and said: "Do not dignify yourself in front of a king." But whoever lowers himself and makes light of himself in such places is the truly great and dignified person who worships God out of love. So did David, King of Israel, say: "and I would be even less worthy than this and would be lowly in my own eyes." There is no greatness and honor but rejoicing before God, as it is said: "And King David was spinning and whirling before God."[25]

Inordinate joy belongs to this festival alone. Other festivals are characterized by joy, pure and simple. Only Sukkot entails this *excess* of joy, which, of course, has its dangers. This is taken into account in the separating of men and women in the Temple and in the warning that Shabbat may not be overridden by the celebrations.

The ritual performance of this inordinate joy is detailed in cascading lists of words: the array of musical instruments, the various forms of dancing—wheeling, clapping, cavorting—physical and vocal expressions of intense emotion. The Hebrew language is mobilized to find arcane verbal equivalents for extravagant expressions of ecstasy.

The mitzvah of merriment is to be unstinted, without the usual restraint that characterizes public life. It is, paradoxically, the saintly, pious, and scholarly of the people who are to engage in it, as a kind of spectacle, a performative art form. The elites model for the people authentic worship of God, "with joy and gladness of heart." All self-consciousness set aside, the elites forget their egos and give free—even undignified—reign to passionate movement.

This last remark of Rambam shifts our perspective on the meaning of excessive joy. Love of God and its expression demand a kind of abandonment of dignity; *kavod,* the inhibiting sense of social status, becomes a sin, even a folly, "in such places." The religious ecstasy represented in somersaults or juggling[26] exposes one to mockery. They make one look "light" rather than "heavy"—without gravitas, shameless.

In the last sentence, Rambam refers to the paradigm case of David, who cavorted joyfully in the presence of God when he brought back the Holy Ark to Jerusalem. His wife Michal sneers at him when she sees him "leaping and dancing": "How dignified was the king of Israel today when he was exposed before the eyes of the handmaids of his servants, as one of the empty fellows shamelessly exposes himself!" (2 Sam. 6:20). David answers her: "In the presence of God will I make merry! And I will be yet more shameless than this, and will be lowly in my own eyes! . . . And Michal daughter of Saul had no child until the day of her death" (6:23).

In Michal's eyes, David exposes his "emptiness" in his dancing. But her sense of the "weight" of her dignity makes her barren; she cannot achieve the "lightness" that would open her womb.

Perhaps the central expression in Rambam's text is "in these places." What is out of place in other places is appropriate in the Temple, in the space of God's presence. In Rambam's presentation, David's case is the paradigm. David's genius lay in casting off the symbolic gravity of his royal role and being *me-fazez u-mekarker*—spinning and wheeling in praise of God. Such uninhibited behavior arouses his wife's contempt; it is, however, perfectly attuned to the "inordinate joy" of the Sukkot festival "in these places."[27]

It is interesting to notice that *mekarker* (spinning around in circles) occurs in a midrashic comment on the ways God interacts with human beings—with Sarah, for example: "How many *kirkurim* (circuits) did God perform in order to hear the intimate talk of righteous women!"[28]

In announcing to Abraham the news of Sarah's imminent pregnancy, God wheels from two indirect dialogues to a direct dialogue: first addressing Abraham so that Sarah overhears and laughs (Gen. 18:9–10), then addressing Abraham, who conveys His words to Sarah (18:13–14), and finally affirming directly to Sarah, "No, but you did laugh!" These indirections succeed in eliciting from Sarah her genuine response to the prospect of childbirth.

The classic notion is that God desires to hear the prayers of righteous women. In this midrash, God is willing to go through undignified "hoops" in order to access Sarah's prayer life in all its pain and disappointment. The rhetorical flourish of *kirkurim* removes God, as it were, from His social position so that He can be privy to the elemental passion of this "righteous woman."

If we turn back now to the whirling dance motions of the dignitaries in the Temple, we can appreciate the paradox in Rambam's description. Like David, those who cast aside self-conscious dignity in the moment of love and joy know true dignity. Those who stiffen into their public roles are sinners and fools: incapable of the demands of that inordinate joy that is the modality of Sukkot. So the idea of *kavod* (dignity) is not, in effect, abandoned; rather, it is reinterpreted, stood on its head. By applying the somersaults of the dance to God, the midrash conveys the ultimate seriousness of such swerves. The laws of celebration perform a transformation of understanding.

But still, we might ask, why these excesses of merriment, these spinnings, loopings, reversing, weavings? What inordinate experience has generated such intense feeling? Rabbi Yitzhak Hutner associates this dance with the reappearance of the Clouds of Glory.[29] Those who have lived the catastrophic emptiness, the loss of the "unknown boundless Other," will respond to a return of the Clouds with new awareness.

To be held in an embrace of which one is unconscious, like an infant in its mother's ambience, is one thing. Living an interruption and then a recovery of that state is another. The vanishing Clouds are more than an indication of a spiritual crisis: they are the crisis itself. The theological moment is the experience of *loss-recovery*. The movement of the Clouds—departing/returning—is the moment of encounter with God. Recovery is more than a return to the *status quo ante*: it represents the excess in "excessive joy."

Wordsworth, too, tells a story about clouds: "Trailing clouds of glory do we come / From God, who is our home"; but now, "there hath passed a glory from the earth."[30] Mourning for an inevitable loss, Wordsworth looks for consolation in natural beauty and in human brotherhood. But the loss is irrecoverable, like childhood. The light has gone; clouds now lack the essential glory. In the rabbinic tradition, on the other hand, the clouds return in a newly intensified version of their original glory.

THE TRIPTYCH OF EXPERIENCE

In these midrashic traditions, there is a recurrent attempt to catch the singular quality of the sequence: joy–grief–excessive joy:

> "For the Cloud of God was over the Tabernacle by day, and fire would appear in it by night" (Exod. 40:38). When the Israelites saw the pillar of God resting on the Tabernacle, they rejoiced, saying: Now God has been reconciled with us! But when night came, the pillar of fire descended and surrounded the Tabernacle. Everyone saw it as one flame of fire and began to sorrow and weep, saying, "Woe to us! For nothing (lit., emptiness) we have labored! All our great work has been burnt up in a moment!" They rose early next morning and saw the pillar of cloud encompassing the Tabernacle. Immediately, they rejoiced with an inordinate joy, saying, "This is testimony to the world that if they wanted to make such a thing they could not. Why? Because of God's abundant love for Israel." That is why it says: "His shade I desired and sat in it, and his fruit was sweet to my palate" (Songs 2:3).[31]

Again, joy is followed by grief and then by excessive joy. The pillar of cloud *rests* (*shachen*) on the Tabernacle, a sign of reconciliation with God; at night a pillar of fire *surrounds* (*sivev*) the Tabernacle, transforming it in an instant into flame; the next morning, the Cloud returns—*mekif* (*enveloping*) the Tabernacle. The people then speak of *edut,* of testimony to the quality of transcendent (excessive) love in their experience of God. This triptych yields a quality of transformation through time—day, night, day. The changing positions of the Clouds—resting, surrounding as flame, enveloping—in themselves express the changing relations between the human and the divine. An unconscious state of being becomes one of total engulfment and then of conscious encompassment.

At night, the destructive fire makes *nothing* of all human creation: "Woe to us! For *emptiness* we have labored." The next morning, the people sense the significance of their own experience. It swells into a register of unaccountable grace. The midrash catches a moment of fraught encounter—with emptiness and fullness, with meaninglessness and meaningfulness.

THE TESTIMONY OF SPICES

A classic theme in the midrashic literature on the Golden Calf is that of the wife who is abandoned by her husband, who then returns to her:

> This [the *Mishkan*] is a testimony to the whole world that Moses was appointed by God to erect the Tabernacle. R. Issak said: It can be compared to a king who took a wife whom he loved very dearly (lit., too much). In the course of time he became angry with her and deserted her, and her neighbors taunted her, saying, "He is never coming back to you!" Subsequently, the king sent her a message: "Prepare my palace and make the beds, for I am coming back on such-and-such a day"; and when that day arrived the king returned to her and became reconciled to her, entering her chamber and eating and drinking with her. Her neighbors at first would not believe all this; but when they scented the fragrant spices, they at once knew that the king had become reconciled with her.
>
> So did God love Israel, bringing them before Mount Sinai, giving them the Torah, and calling them a kingdom of priests, as it says: And you shall be to Me a kingdom of priests (Exod. 19:6). However, after only forty days they sinned. The idolatrous na-

tions then said: "God will no longer be reconciled with them," as it is said, Men said among the nations: "They shall no more sojourn here" (Lam. 4:15). But as soon as Moses pleaded for mercy on their behalf, God forgave them for it says: And God said: "I have pardoned them according to your word" (Num. 14:20). Moses then said: "Master of the world! I personally am quite satisfied that You have forgiven them. But make it known before the eyes of all the nations that You have no resentment in Your heart against them!" God answered him: "As you live, I will bring My Shechinah to dwell in their midst," for it says: "Let them make Me a sanctuary, so that I may dwell among them (Exod. 25:8). By this shall all nations know that I have forgiven them [the Israelites]." This is why it says, "the Tabernacle of the testimony," because the Tabernacle was a testimony to the Israelites that God had pardoned their sin.[32]

Here, the perspective of the neighbors gives meaning to the private relations of the King and his wife. Chorus-like, they knowingly comment on the vicissitudes of the marriage: "He is never coming back to you! . . . They could not believe it (that the marriage had recovered)." They are finally convinced only when they scent the fragrant spices wafting from the palace. Now, they are silent, as though this fragrance leaves them speechless.

The parable of the neighbors represents both the force and the weakness of social interpretations. Metaphorically, the neighbors represent the idolatrous nations, who are set to skepticism about the possibility of redemption. The history of God's "excessive" love for His people can never be fully known by the other nations. Ironically, however, its history is powerfully told precisely through the oblique filter of their experience. This intimated history becomes the larger setting for hope.

Moses becomes the catalyst of full return of the relationship with God. His prayer presses the issue of forgiveness beyond minimal meanings: "Make known before the eyes of all nations that You have no more resentment *in Your heart* against Israel!" God responds with the words, "I will bring My Presence to rest among them." This mysterious phenomenon—the indwelling Shechinah—becomes the people's own deep awareness of reconciliation. In the end, the echo of the outside world brings home to the people the resonance of their intimacy with the divine.

In all this, an original divine desire is worked out. "Let them make for Me a sanctuary, so that I may dwell in their midst" (Exod. 25:8). A narrative of sin, anger, abandonment may be judged according to the knowing criteria of the world. But the truth lies elsewhere. Moses knows it, and wants his people to know it. The best understanding that the idolatrous nations can have is through the imagery of smell—at once the most physical and the most "spiritual" of the senses. What the neighbors nonverbally apprehend is an intimacy beyond imagining. What the Israelites know is that, in all their emptiness, they are now full. The way they know is partly through the words, the testimony, of the neighbors.

STRANGE SWEETNESS

Excessive joy is, then, a response to catastrophic anxiety. Even after the clouds have returned and the Tabernacle has been set up, it remains empty of God's presence—uninspired—until an internal event, the resting of the Shechinah, has occurred. Loss and recovery remains a recursive motif, played out in different layers of midrashic narrative.

In the end, as *Midrash Ha-Gadol* implies in its conclusion, the quest of the Israelites can only be understood through sensual experience and its limits: "His shade I desired and sat in it, and His fruit was sweet to my taste" (Songs 2:3). The people develop their own idiom of love, a personal taste for the shade of a tree that offers no shade:

> This apple tree—everyone flees from it in the hamsin [the hot, dry season], because it has no shade. So all the nations fled from God when He gave them the Torah. But "I desired His shade and sat in it."[33]

The satisfactions offered at Sinai may be objectively austere. But strangely, His people find a sweetness and a protectiveness in this austerity. On occasion, they become aware of their own unconventional sensibility.

SHAME, KNOWLEDGE, INORDINATE LOVE

The moment of return is such an occasion for self-awareness. The past is restored with a difference. Perhaps this is one implication of the Shechinah coming to rest within them. The original experience returns, with its rupture within it. There is a fragrance that was never there before.[34]

This recovery is publicly celebrated in the giving of the rewritten Tablets. This second edition is described by the Gaon as "more *mechubadim,* more dignified than the first set."[35] This new set is heavier to hold, since it contains an excess.

A classic statement about inordinate love is found in *Pirkei Avot* (3:4):

> Beloved is man, since he is created in the image of God. But inordinate love—that it is revealed to him that he is created in the image, as it says (Gen. 9:6): "In God's image He made man." Beloved are Israel they are called children of God. But inordinate love—that it is revealed to them that they are called children of God.[36]

Here, the motif of excess—*chibah yeterah*—is explicitly contrasted with simple *chibah* (love). In both the examples quoted here, a state of grace—being created in the image of God, or being called children of God—acquires an intensive edge once the human being becomes aware of that state. Such knowledge arises where there has been loss. The intensity—the surplus quality—is the fruit of *knowledge* in its most intimate form. Once one has become aware of being in the divine image, that knowledge acts on one's imagination: a project begins to form, a way of envisioning the future. A claim has been made upon us.

Knowledge becomes hope. But the excessive dimension of awareness is often dearly bought. Building the Tabernacle will, at every stage, be haunted by the possibility of failure. The ghost of the Golden Calf persists to the very end of the seven days of inauguration. Even on the eighth day, tremendous anxiety attends the completion of the priestly training period. Will the Shechinah really come to rest upon the work of their hands?

"And they came out and blessed the people" (Lev. 9:23)—they said the words that conclude the Prayer of Moses (Ps. 90:17): "May the beauty of God our God be upon us"—that is, May it be God's will that the Shechinah may rest upon the work of your hands! They invoked just this blessing and not another formula, because during the whole seven days of the installation, when Moses was setting up the Tabernacle and officiating in it and dismantling it daily, the Shechinah had not rested upon it and the Israelites felt ashamed, saying to Moses: "Our teacher Moses! All the trouble that we have taken was only in order that the Shechinah might dwell among us, so that we may know that the sin of the Golden Calf has been atoned for us!"

That is why he had said to them: "This is the thing which God commanded that you should do, so that the glory of God may appear to you" (Lev. 9:6)—[that is, only after these offerings have been brought by Aaron (9:7) will God's glory appear to you]. "My brother Aaron is more worthy and excellent than I am, so that through his sacrifices and worship the Shechinah will rest upon you, and you will know that God has chosen him to bring His Shechinah upon you."[37]

Rashi comments here on the blessing of Moses and Aaron on the eighth day, after the inauguration process has come to an end. The content of the blessing tells us why it was necessary. There had been an expectation that God's presence, the Shechinah, would come to rest in the completed structure. Instead, nothing happened. The people's overwhelming reaction is *shame*. They have failed to achieve full forgiveness for the Golden Calf. This is the meaning of the emptiness they experience.

Moses reassures them that once Aaron has taken over the role of High Priest, all will be well. He thus demonstrates to the people that God has indeed chosen Aaron—and stoically accepts his own demotion. Together the two brothers then bless the people that their work may now be crowned with success.

It is striking that, as with the disappearance of the clouds, we have a story of failure after seeming success—the essential event fails to happen. Once again, the significance of this failure is that full forgiveness has been withheld. This time, the frustration is associated with *shame*. After all this work—nothing. . . . As in the *Midrash Ha-Gadol* narrative, there is a natural lament at the emptiness, the pointlessness of all the effort.

The shame is connected with the failure to *know* that the Golden Calf has been fully atoned. The aim of all the work was *knowledge,* an awareness of God's presence. This is a subjective failure; they have not been worthy of such knowledge. They have failed, in a sense, to love enough. The scene is resolved when Aaron offers sacrifices. Then, the people *know* that he is God's choice, and at that moment the Shechinah descends.

The choice of Aaron is, of course, relevant to the Golden Calf narrative. Since Aaron experiences shame and guilt about his role in the making of the idol,[38] the knowledge that he is essential to the process of reconciliation shapes the sense of self-worth of the entire people. In their subjective experience, Aaron becomes a catalyst of their own movement from shame to healing.

Such a sense of intimate knowledge is embodied in the laws of the sukkah, too. The required height of the sukkah—up to twenty cubits—is explained in terms of spatial awareness:

A sukkah that is more than twenty cubits high is unfit. How do we know? Rabba said, as the verse states: "So that your future generations will know that I caused the children of Israel to reside in *sukkot* (booths)." Up to twenty cubits high, a person is aware that he is residing in a sukkah; more than twenty cubits high, a person is not aware that he is residing in a sukkah, because his eye does not perceive the roof.[39]

The reason for the maximum height is that one should be aware of the internal space in which one resides. A visible roof gives one a sense of being housed, of being *inside.* But this consciousness is complicated by the fragility of the structure: Will it stand or fall? The sukkah must allow one to see the stars through the overhead branches; one must know the uncertainty of a "temporary dwelling." One is situated in a home that may fall apart.[40]

This consciousness haunts the Israelites who have survived the disappearance of the protective clouds—which we remember when we build the sukkah—and have lived to see them return. Being inside, being enveloped, is the existential meaning of the sukkah. If we take into account the Gaon's narrative, this intimacy is one that has been lost and then restored. So a tragic edge now frames awareness. One now knows something about the fragility inherent to being held.

CREATING TORAH

We can return now to our original text, the biblical description of the seven days of inauguration. Beyond the rituals of investiture and sacrifice, these days represent transitional time and space. During these days of *miluim* (lit., filling), the priests are fitted into their new setting, like a jewel into its setting. At the same time, empty hands are filled: "He will fill your hands" (Lev. 8:33). Bodies are invested with significant roles, so that they may play their part in a larger drama. During this transitional period, no one is to leave the courtyard area at the entrance to the Tabernacle; they are to dwell there day and night, in order to "observe God's mandate" (*u-shmartem et mishmeret Ha-Shem*).

This last expression, as we have seen, can be understood as a project of scrupulous attention to the details of the rituals. The apprentice priests are in full training mode, anxious not to neglect any essential information. This is a matter of practice as well as theory. They are preserving a body of practices that Moses has been demonstrating for them. In this sense, there is little room for improvisation. Anxiety—scrupulous attention[41]—is inherent to their protective role. The sense of God's presence in their midst depends on it.

On this level, the seven days of inauguration look largely to the past. But as with the night of *shimurim*—the Passover night, which is called the Night of Watching—there is also an implicit vigilance about the future. This is a stage of expectation, of unconsummated hope. What is the inner work of such a period? Like pregnancy, the Passover night and the seven days' inauguration open up a time between being and nonbeing. During the Passover night, too, no one leaves the house entrance till morning. However, during that night, Ramban observes, they are called *yotz'im*—in the process of leaving—even though the physical exodus will take place only on the following day.

In some essential way, redemption happens during this night, even though it is enacted only the following day.[42] During the night of *shimurim,* long-expected, filled with observances, a process of liberation is under way, hidden from the naked eye—an intimate movement toward the future. Keeping faith with God involves this forward, creative movement.

In a different but related idiom, the observances of this night and of the seven days of inauguration are interpreted as the intellectual process by which the future becomes real. Ha'amek Davar has a striking and consistent reading of the words, "And he did—*Va-ya'as*—all the things that God had commanded" (Lev. 8:36). He rejects the obvious reading—"He obeyed God's instructions"—perhaps because there are no positive instructions in this passage. Instead, he reads, "They *created (made) the Torah* by their careful attention, structuring God's words to convey precise meaning." He understands this as a creative process by which God's words are interpreted anew. Beyond their role as apprentices learning various skills, they closely and thoughtfully study the divine words.

With conscious anachronism, Ha'amek Davar reads in these biblical texts an intimation of the creative mode of Talmud study called *pilpul.* This is a form of ingenious play with the boundaries of meaning. On one occasion,[43] he writes: This is a process of *silsul*—swinging high, raising up, holding in high esteem by elaborating, turning in all directions, twirling—of God's words. Nuances are elicited, at the level even of the letters of the text. In his reading, the main objective of the Giving of the Torah is that the people will themselves come to engage in this virtuoso act of interpretation. The repeated root in *silsul, pilpul* reminds us of the intricate dancing of *kirkur*—repeated activity that has, apparently, no purpose beyond itself. All this in praise and love of God.

Ha'amek Davar often returns to this understanding of the words *lishmor la'asot*—calling this the work of the Oral Law. For him, this work has preserved both the Torah and the Jewish people through the ages. *Making* the Torah is fundamental to learning it.

Here is a striking example of this reading:

And God said: Take to heart all the words with which I have warned you this day, so that you may instruct your children to observe and to do all the words of this Torah. For it is not an

empty thing for you: it is your very life; through it you shall
have long life on the land that you shall possess upon crossing
the Jordan. (Deut. 32:46–47)

According to Rashi, this passage refers to the scrupulous attention to
be paid to the complexities of the law. This is not fruitless labor, since
there is much reward for such obedience.

As against this, Ha'amek Davar notes that the passage does not refer
to observing the commandments: How would the notion of *emptiness*
("it is not an empty thing for you") be relevant? Instead, he cites the
reading of the Jerusalem Talmud: "It is not an empty thing for you—if
it is empty, the emptiness is *from* you (lit., *mikem*); because you have
not worked hard on study of Torah, it is empty."[44] He understands this
to refer to the intellectual work of interpreting the text. This "labor"
of *making* the Torah involves more than research; it requires a keen
receptivity to the hints and nuances of the text. This is no empty
work, for "it is your very life." Here, he speaks of the spiritual and
physical vitality generated by "making the Torah."

The notion of *emptiness,* however, resounds strangely in this context. In this reading, the specter of emptiness is banished in the *making* of Torah ("It is *not* an empty thing"). Nevertheless, the very notion
of possible emptiness is troubling. How could studying the Torah be
an empty thing?

As Freud famously points out, inserting the negative is sometimes
a way of sponsoring unacceptable meanings. At the least, the text
alludes to a possible experience, in order to repudiate it. It is the fear
of emptiness that impels one to creativity.

Perhaps the Torah is pointing to a stark, existential choice: either
emptiness or *making*—that is, the vigorous play of interpretation. "If
your Torah had not been my play/delight" says the Psalmist, "I should
have perished in my affliction" (Ps. 119:92). David may be thinking of
particular hardships in his life, but his words resonate widely and
deeply with those who speak them as though they had birthed them.
The Torah is for him *sha'ashua*—a medium of play, of fertile inven-
tion. Practiced in the mind and in the heart, it saves David's life.

EPISODES OF EMPTINESS

Both these texts evoke the tension of *eros* and *thanatos,* with eros embodied in the activity and process of Torah. Remarkably, the sense of emptiness makes frequent appearances in the midrashic literature around the completion of the Tabernacle.

We have already seen one example. In the passage from *Midrash Ha-gadol,* the people rejoice when they see the Cloud of divine glory resting on the Tabernacle; but when the pillar of fire descends and surrounds the Tabernacle, consuming it, they sorrow and weep: "Woe to us, we have labored for naught (lit., for emptiness)." The polarities are stark: there is the indwelling Cloud of Glory and there is the engulfing destructive fire that reduces all human effort to a void. That void is where they live during that night. The following day when the Cloud returns, and *envelopes* the Tabernacle, their joy has a painful edge to it: it is *excessive;* and they sense in this recovery the excessive/inordinate love of God.

The void disrupts states of joy. The Golden Calf that originally emerged from fire has the power to evacuate the Clouds of Glory. A process of atonement follows, culminating in the work of the Tabernacle and the recovery of the Clouds. The Clouds evoke a "background aura of infinite unknown support." When they are lost, joy is banished and replaced by shame. But when they are recovered, joy is intensified by the knowledge of shame. And even after they have been restored, the void returns in further midrashic episodes of failure.

All the seven days of inauguration, for instance, the priests erect the completed Tabernacle and then dismantle it—twice a day, or, in another view, three times a day:

> All seven days of inauguration Moses was erecting and dismantling the Tabernacle, and on the eighth day he erected it but did not dismantle it—as it says, "And it was on the day that Moses finished erecting the Tabernacle" (Num. 7:10)—that is, on the day that his constructions came to an end.[45]

The Talmud points to a process of doing and undoing—that comes to an end on the eighth day. Erecting the Tabernacle requires skill and practice; this is rehearsed many times during the seven-day period.

On another level, there is an existential rhythm that the priests live through during these days: destructive and reconstructive, *thanatos* and *eros,* emptiness and fulfillment. Even as the rituals of the future structure are being rehearsed, the days are punctuated by fallings, vanishings.[46]

Seforno offers an interesting note on Moses's first erection of the Tabernacle: "Moses erected the Tabernacle" refers to the ten inner woven curtains, which constitute the essential Tabernacle (the Tent). Before erecting the boards and sockets and other supports, the curtains are held in the air, whether by human effort or by miracle.

An essential instability haunts the process of raising up the Tabernacle. On the other hand, as Seforno points out, the ten woven curtains are not dismantled during these seven days; they somehow remain in place, even as the supports are taken apart. The Tabernacle as Tent is sustained, its fabric billowing, without boards. Like a shadow Tabernacle, an intimation of worlds not realized.[47]

On the eighth day, the routine of raising up and taking apart comes to an end. The priests enter into their role. But again, midrashic narrative comes to punctuate what reads in the Torah like harmonious consummation. A past history of effort and failure resurfaces—undertones of despair and skepticism are heard.

Rashi summarizes the midrashic material:

"And they brought the Tabernacle to Moses" (Exod. 39:33): because they could not raise it up. Moses had not done any of the craft work in the Tabernacle, so God left him its raising up, which no human being had been able to do because of the weight of the boards which was beyond human strength; but Moses raised them up. Moses said to God: How is it possible for a human being to raise it up? God answered: Busy yourself with your hands and you will look as if you are erecting it, while it rises up of its own accord. That is why it is written, "the Tabernacle was erected"—it was erected spontaneously.

The Tabernacle is constituted by its supportive structure, the boards; Rashi emphasizes the human impossibility of raising it up. Where all others have failed, Moses succeeds, single-handedly, in erecting the heavy boards. In some of Rashi's midrashic sources, the weight of the boards is said to be the difficulty; in others, the nature of the difficulty is less clear. Moses simply speaks of a human limitation, implying an almost metaphysical challenge. "How is it possible for a human being to raise it up?" God's answer to Moses acknowledges the problem: Moses is to go through the motions of construction, and it will rise up of its own accord.

In the Torah narrative, all the parts are simply gathered, and Moses blesses the people; Moses then point by point fulfills God's instructions in assembling the structure (Exod. 39:41–40:17). The work process is presented in orderly and focused fashion. In sharp contrast, the midrashic traditions drive wedges of failure between the stages of the process. When the craftsmen, even Bezalel and the master craftsmen, cannot achieve this construction, voices of rebellion and despair are heard. The people suspect Moses of unnecessarily complicating the work; of delaying completion for (in one view) three months (the parts were ready three months from the tenth of Tishrei but the construction date was set at six months, on the first of Nisan):

> Why did the *Mishkan* not rise up immediately? God's intention was to mix the joy of the Tabernacle with the joy of the day when Isaac was born. That was the first of Nisan, so God declared, "I shall mingle your joy with another joy." Then the mockers of the generation said: "Why is the structure not immediately erected, even though the work has been completed?"
>
> About this King David said, You have rejoiced me, O God, with Your work—I shall exult in the work of Your hands (Ps. 92:5): "You have rejoiced me, O God, with Your work"—this refers to the Tent of Assembly; "I shall exult in the work of Your hands"—this refers to the future construction of the Temple; "How great are Your works, O God, how profound Your thoughts!"—this refers to God's thoughts of mingling one joy with another, the day that Isaac was born with the day that Moses took ten crowns; "A boorish man shall not know this"—this refers to the mockers and fools of the generation who did not know God's thought.[48]

The hope of the people—to have God's presence animating this structure—vanishes as the structure fails even to come together. Their bitter recriminations are recounted in the midrash, extending even to suspicion of Moses's integrity. The project of constructing the *Mishkan* becomes a target for resentment and fear. At every stage, the people are dogged by the anxiety of *emptiness*. In one passage, they point out each detail of the work that they have labored over so conscientiously; they speak of their total obedience—they have done everything God has asked for: Why then does the structure not rise up, come alive? Why does the divine Presence not come to dwell in the work of their hands?

Moses recognizes this problem as a *human* problem. How is it possible for a human being to find total reassurance in the face of guilt, fear, and shame? The expression "the mockers of Israel" becomes a motif in these midrashic sources, a quasi-sociological reference to a recognizable group of Israelites. These mockers speak with disappointed idealism, a kind of defensive righteousness.

TWO LAUGHTERS

But what are we to make of God's thoughts about delaying the date of completion? His intent is given as "thoughts of mingling one joy with another"—the date of completion with the date of Isaac's birth. This divine thought is left cryptic, its depth unfathomable to boors and scoffers. But these scoffers represent the link between the two moments of joy.

The "mockers of the generation" make their first midrashic appearance in the earlier generation when Sarah, barren, in her nineties, receives the prophecy of pregnancy and birth. Then, too, there were scoffers galore.[49] The embarrassingly hopeful notion of a pregnant Sarah was only too easy to mock—Sarah herself laughed at the very idea—and experienced an embarrassing dialogue with the angel who had announced the miracle (Gen. 18:12).

The notion of the withered female body returned to sexual vitality engages a universal female fantasy. Strikingly, the Rabbis underline and even elaborate on this theme, restoring to Sarah the markers of youth—lustrous flesh and hair. In a sense, what is there to do but laugh at the notion of resurrection from the dead? Nothing is more ludicrous than such a transformation of the adamant physical reality. Here, time is embodied: How can time be reversed? Perhaps what makes resurrection truly unthinkable is the strength of the fantasy of just such a reversal.

Abraham, too, laughs when God, in an earlier scene, announces that he will become a father (Gen. 17:17). Strangely, Rashi understands this as a different quality of laughter: "Abraham believed and rejoiced, while Sarah did not believe and mocked." In support of this distinction, Rashi cites the commentary of Onkelos (the ancient, authoritative translator of the Torah into Aramaic), who uses different expressions to translate the two laughters. Such a reading is supported by the fact that God is critical of Sarah's laughter but not of Abraham's.

Two laughters: of faith and of skepticism, of wonder and of scorn. The difference between the position of wife and husband—of potential mother and father—is sufficient to explain such different responses. For Sarah, the body, which is her own self, has lived and aged and yields intimate testimony to the organic reality: "And Sarah laughed *within herself*,[50] saying, After I have withered, shall I have pleasure?" (Gen. 18:12). Abraham's laughter is accompanied by the unembodied words of a third-person observer: "And Abraham fell on his face and laughed. And he said in his heart, Shall a hundred-year-old man have a child, shall Sarah at ninety give birth?" (17:17). Sarah speaks with the subjective knowledge of the one who is to be resurrected; Abraham remarks on the objective improbability of such a miracle.

After the birth, too, Abraham celebrates his son's circumcision, while Sarah says, "God made me laughter! Everyone who hears will rejoice (*yitzachak*) for me!" (Gen. 21:6). Or should we read, "Everyone who hears will *laugh at* me!"? Even when the miracle has happened, it remains implausible, and therefore, literally, *incredible*—vulnerable to the aggressive remarks of others.[51]

In the story of the Tabernacle, the scoffers mock the notion of a similar resurrection. This is symbolically represented in the impossible project of erecting the Temple. There is so much at stake in this project, so much hope of renewed life after the catastrophe of the Golden Calf, that a world-weariness, a knowing despair haunts the words of the mockers. They slander Moses *behind his back* (*melitzim achar Moshe*). How can the collapsing object ever be made to rise up and come to life? The sexual and existential imagery evokes an existential shame.

In the midrashic literature, Moses, too, speaks of the human impossibility of the project. For him, as for Sarah, this is a personal experience of inadequacy. The heroes of these narratives share the sense of the *incredible* nature of such an event.

A midrashic story is told of R. Abbahu, who, as he is departing this world, is given a vision of the bliss that awaits him in the world to come. His reaction is to rejoice and say, "All this for Abbahu! And I said, For emptiness I have labored and for naught and vanity I have exhausted my strength! [Indeed,] my right is with God" (Isa. 49:4).[52]

R. Abbahu represents the righteous person, whose life has known the hopelessness, the emptiness of those who witness the Tabernacle burning up in a pillar of fire. It is not only boors and scoffers who make use of the quotation from Isaiah.

"She laughs at the last day":[53] R. Abbahu laughs in wonder at what he glimpses on his last day. But his wonder is deepened by his memory of his own skepticism. His laughter is an expression of the tension between an embodied sense of *emptiness,* and the revelation just before death. Such a revelation would not be possible in the midst of life; only the righteous are granted such a clarifying vision before they leave the world.

In another reading in the same passage, the proof text refers to a different kind of laughter:

> It is written: "Strength and dignity are her clothing; and she laughs at the last day" (Prov. 31:25). What is the meaning of "at the last day"? All the reward of the righteous awaits them in the world to come. . . . This refers to Moses, of whom it says, "And Moses did not know that the skin of his face sent forth beams" (Exod. 34:29). "And she laughs at the last day" refers to those Israelites who scoffed at him and said to one another: "Is it possible that the Shechinah should find a home at the hands of Amram's son?" Moses did not delay but as soon as God commanded him to raise up the Tabernacle, *he began to laugh at them,* as it says, "And she laughs at the last day." Moses said to them: "Come let us raise up the Tabernacle," whereupon each one began to carry his portion of the work to Moses, as it says, "And they brought the Tabernacle to Moses" (Exod. 39:33).[54]

As soon as God told him to erect the Tabernacle, Moses "began to laugh (*sochek*) at them!" In the face of their mockery at the very notion of the project, the Holy Spirit comes to rest on Moses, who triumphantly consummates the work. The war of laughters touches on the complex field of reference of the word *sechok* or *tzechok:* sport, sexual license, murder, idolatry, triumph in battle—these are all among its associations in biblical and rabbinic sources. There is an aggressiveness, a malice in laughter, as Freud knew. There is also, more obviously, joy. The Rabbis even suggest that one should not "fill one's mouth with laughter in this world."[55]

"He who laughs last laughs best." Moses's "last day," here, is the day when God's presence rests on him. This is a moment of grace, a sense of almost dying. We sometimes call this "inspiration," the experience of being filled with spirit. Those who have not experienced inspiration mock its very possibility. In this sense, inspiration is a form of resurrection: life breath filling the emptiness. "*Then* shall our mouth be filled with laughter!" says the Psalmist.[56] Then, and only then, says the Talmud. "It is forbidden to fill one's mouth with laughter in this world; as it is said, '*Then* shall our mouth be filled with laughter.' When is that? At a time when it is said among the nations, 'God has done greatly with these ones!'"[57]

Living in a world of suffering and death, and of hostility and scorn from "the nations"—from the Other, internal and external—how can one indulge in full-mouthed laughter? The sense of emptiness is, in this sense, unsurprising. To proclaim fullness in this world is perhaps to whistle in the dark. In the view of the midrash, the end of days is the natural time for laughter; only when the fullness of meaning is revealed to all will there be full laughter.

Until then, what do we have? The processes of *miluim,* on the one hand, and the seven days of Sukkot on the other. *Miluim,* the "filling" time, the transitional seven days of investing and divesting, erection and dismantling, meaning accomplished and shelved. The hope for inspiration, for the moment when God's spirit comes to dwell; but also anger, shame, mockery, as the people wait for that moment.

Milan Kundera offers a highly ironic observation:

(On Two Kinds of Laughter)
World domination, as everyone knows, is divided between

demons and angels. But the good of the world does not require
the latter to gain precedence over the former (as I thought when
I was young): all it needs is a certain equilibrium of power. If
there is too much uncontested meaning on earth (the reign of
the angels), man collapses under the burden; if the world loses
all its meaning (the reign of the demons), life is every bit as
impossible.

Things deprived suddenly of their putative meaning, the
place assigned them in the ostensible order of things . . . make us
laugh. Initially, therefore, laughter is the province of the Devil.
It has a certain malice to it (things have turned out differently
from the way they tried to seem), but a certain beneficent relief
as well (things are looser than they seemed, we have greater
latitude in living with them, their gravity does not oppress us).

The first time an angel heard the Devil's laughter, he was
horrified. It was in the middle of a feast with a lot of people
around, and one after the other they joined in the Devil's laughter. It was terribly contagious. The angel was all too aware
the laughter was aimed against God and the wonder of His
works. . . . He opened his mouth and let out a wobbly, breathy
sound . . . and endowed it with the opposite meaning. Whereas
the Devil's laughter pointed up the meaninglessness of things,
the angel's shout rejoiced in how rationally organized, well
conceived, beautiful, good, and sensible everything on earth
was. . . . People nowadays do not even realize that one and the
same external phenomenon embraces two completely contra-
dictory internal attitudes. There are two kinds of laughter, and
we lack the words to distinguish them.[58]

For Kundera, the joke is that there is one laughter turned to two
opposite purposes. Even if we had words to distinguish them—words
like "mockery" on the one hand, and "joy" on the other—in terms
of this world we would still be talking about a disruptive, disorderly
phenomenon, invented by the Devil.

But, on contemplating Kundera's parable, one wonders whether
the angels do not, after all, manage to find their own authentic music.
The achievement of the angels is to modulate their laughter to a different key. Between the destructive extremes of the meaningless and

the overly meaningful, there is the brave, uncertain, still laughable "imitation laughter" that is alone possible in this world. As the Talmudic Sages say, "*Then* shall our mouths be filled with laughter." In the midst of life, fullness and emptiness live together. Or perhaps inhere in one another.

LOVE AND SHAME

The transitional seven-day period of inauguration evokes both anxiety and hope—fear of emptiness and hope for a real fulfillment. Here is the symbolic process of *investiture*—in which acts of instituting, raising up, making real, clothing in dignity—will achieve their performative magic.[59] Hope is bound up with anxiety, for the stakes are high. The trauma of the Golden Calf hangs heavy; residues of the past affect the present and the future. Will the Tabernacle repeat the idolatry that it is supposed to heal? Will the pattern of sin and guilt remain undisturbed? Will the people remain subject to the compulsions that sustain idolatrous attachments?[60]

The sense of psychic inertia gives rise to the essentially human experience of shame. In midrashic narratives, as we have seen, the theme of shame recurs. Perhaps the experience of shame characterizes one who is now, in Franz Rosenzweig's words, in the "grip of love." This shame, rather than guilt, arises from the new awareness that one has been, in the past, "loveless." Rosenzweig addresses the particular shame of "lovelessness." The "soul is ashamed of its former self, and that it did not, under its own power, break this spell in which it was confined."[61]

What makes us ashamed, as Santner points out, is precisely our total investment in the paralyzing "dignities" of personhood, in the public roles that engulf us. For these very dignities tend to assume "the quality of defense mechanisms. Against what? Against the kernel of 'indignity' . . . produced *by* every symbolic investiture."[62] Only what Rosenzweig calls the "shock of love" can elicit the shame that is the awareness of a past absence of love. This love/shame can free one of the "spell" of the defense mechanisms that are embodied in "dignity."

The seven days of investiture, of inauguration of a new period of "dignity," bring with them just that awareness of the past self that, precisely, seeks out those vestments, these rituals. Installation into the symbolic forms of dignity offers a defense against the "kernel of indignity" that is evoked by those forms.

The problem that Rosenzweig is raising is that the symbolic roles of authority, even those commanded by God, cast a kind of spell that may confine the self. Forms of dignity may easily become empty vestments, evoking the same shame that the people feel when the Tabernacle refuses to come together or when the presence of God remains absent. This shame is a valid protest against the spell cast by defensive dignities.

Love and shame, for Rosenzweig, inhere in each other. In this sense, the Golden Calf will not be exorcised from their midst. There is forgiveness, there is a new awareness of love—which evokes the old shame of "lovelessness."

For Levinas, too, shame may be a salutary phenomenon. This is the "shame of the I for its naïve spontaneity." In Santner's words, this "marks a break with the posture of the knowing, conscious subject."[63] Shame breaks the spell of self-satisfaction; it jars one awake from the repose of narcissism. Facing the other creates a traumatic upheaval—what Levinas calls the "worry," the rupture of uncontainable otherness. "Are there not grounds for imagining a relation with an Other that would be 'better' than self-possession?" This is an awakening, perhaps a form of revelation.

"Worry, questioning, seeking, Desire," Levinas claims, have as their "original mode" that "inspiration" which "lies in obedience to the Most High by way of the ethical relationship with the Other."[64]

A NEW ETHICS

We turn back now to the themes of anxiety and joy, dignity and shame in the Tabernacle and, later, in the Temple.

The seven-day inauguration period of the Tabernacle, with its erection and dismantling of the structure, its two kinds of laughter, its fragile hope for inspiration, provides one model for life before the "last day."

The other model is the seven days of the festival of Sukkot. We remember Rambam's discussion. The celebrants in the Temple are described as clapping, spinning, whirling—all acts of exceeding, even excessive joy. Rambam declares this joy a mitzvah—the celebration of love of God and His commandments—a "great form of worship." Here, "in these places," self-conscious dignity becomes not only irrelevant but wrongheaded. In opposition to the idea of dignity (*kavod*, related to *kaved*—weighty), Rambam speaks of lightness and lowliness, citing King David when he responds to his wife Michal's mockery: "I would be even less dignified than this and I would be lowly in my own eyes." This posture goes beyond humility: it affirms a real identification with those outside the circle of social dignity. Only saints and Sages of this kind are truly dignified. ("Only he is truly great and dignified who worships out of love.")

Indignity becomes a value-bearer when it expresses love of God. "In certain places or institutions, dignity is out of place," writes Giorgio Agamben. "The lover, for example, can be anything except 'dignified,' just as it is impossible to make love while keeping one's dignity." Remarkably, he tells us, the ancients classified erotic matters under the genre of comedy.

In love, there is no space for dignified compromise between external image and internal truth. Life itself is the only norm. Auschwitz—another extreme situation—marks the end of dignity as an ethical value. On the contrary, Agamben suggests, survivors testify to the fact that "it is possible to lose dignity and decency beyond imagination, that there is still life in the most extreme degradation." Here begins "a new ethics, an ethics of a form of life that begins where dignity ends."[65]

In Rambam's account, "these places" refers to the Temple courtyard, but perhaps also to the radically human moment when one becomes conscious of that which is not oneself. This dazzling/desolate human moment is embodied precisely by the nation's spiritual and intellectual elite. Publicly abandoning ego, they manifest both this transcendent consciousness and the limits of its human expression.

The whirling movements of their dance on Sukkot express excessive joy, to the point where time falters and something is laid bare.[66] In Rosenzweig's words, the "moved, gripped, seared soul" comes alive.[67]

In this dance, the movement is circular. Sometimes, at the center, someone is dancing, alone or with others, holding a Sefer Torah (Torah scroll), embracing, gripping. Or, as in the famous midrash about the world to come, the dancing circle of the righteous point toward God at the center, as they wheel ecstatically beyond time and death.[68]

But whether or not the circle is empty at the center, the whirling proclaims something about a universe beyond hierarchies. Here, there is no high and low, no dignity and loss of dignity. Indignity becomes dignity; embracing and being embraced are undifferentiated; one is part of an intricate infinite otherness.

Like the Clouds of Glory, whose restoration the festival celebrates, the power of the dance contains, envelops, may even engulf. But there is something else. The dancer's place in the circle is not like the place of a soldier in the army, or a clerk in the bureaucracy. Being a part of the dance invokes the excessive joy of containing the whole dance in oneself.

The moment of the dance, whirling, endless, merely human, has the immediate function of bringing the Shechinah to rest: "Whoever is humble will ultimately cause the Shechinah to dwell with the human on earth, as it is said, "So says the One who is exalted and lofty dwelling in eternity, holy is His name" (Isa. 57:15).[69]

Stripped of the masks of dignity, the dancers come to represent the very site of God in the world. Admired public figures all, they are spun to a humanness that obscures hierarchies. This is where God lives in the world, far from the divisive structures of society. Bringing God to rest in this way evokes a paradoxical power. The humble, in this sense, create a new reality, a natural lodging for the "one who is exalted and lofty."[70]

Embodied in the dance is the whirling, ever-changing human condition. It is striking that in the work of R. Nahman and other Hasidic thinkers, the arbitrary spinning of the top becomes an expressive image for the contingency and the inscrutable possibility of human life.

The fact that the Golden Calf worship included *mecholot*—circle dancing of just this kind—further deepens the paradox. The orgiastic, undifferentiated spinning around the Golden Calf becomes part of the unconscious memory of the people. When the Clouds of Glory are restored, what is restored with them is a possibility of shame, a way of "working through" the intensity and rigidity of their own fantasies, a way of turning these to face what is in their very midst.

BECOMING A MOTHER

One more turn of the top:

> "And I shall dwell in their midst": It does not say "in its midst,"
> suggesting that the place they are to sanctify for His dwelling is
> in the midst of the Israelites, who are to encompass (*yakifu*) the
> Tabernacle with their banners on all sides. Perhaps these words
> were God's response to the desire of the people when they saw
> at Mount Sinai that God was encompassed by the angels' ban-
> ners, while He was a sign in their midst. They lovingly desired
> that so He should be in their midst. So the response of the One
> who penetrates the human heart was, "Let them make Me a
> sanctuary and I will dwell, as they wish, within them."[71]

"In their midst" means that the camp of Israel will actively hold,
embrace, encompass—*yakifu*—the Tabernacle at its core. But perhaps, says the Or Ha-Chaim (tentatively, speculatively), these words
were originally God's response to an unexpressed desire of the
people. As a classic midrash has it: the Israelites saw God at Sinai,
encompassed—mukaf—by the angels' flags; to encompass God like the
angels became the people's deepest desire.[72]

In this transformative reading, Or Ha-Chaim centers the drama in
the human heart. A desire—to hold the Other at one's very center—is
evoked by a vision at Sinai. Otherworldly images: ranks of angelic
banners encompassing God who acts as a "sign"[73] or a banner of transcendent meaning. The visual image generates a human fantasy: col-
lectively and individually to hold the Other in the very midst of life.

What first reads like a simple command from God becomes, in this
reading, a profound human wish. The desire to encompass reverses
the desire for the Clouds of Glory, which embrace and protect the
people. Here, we have a dynamic, feminine desire to hold, to contain.
This is an erotic and perhaps a maternal image. The wish to be protected by encompassing clouds is converted here into a more mature
desire: to nurture, to protect the Other. This might be called an ethical
desire. It has something of Levinas's "worry," even of "inspiration."
Reaching beyond self-possession, it allows itself to be awakened: "The

'less' is forever bursting open, unable to contain the 'more' that it contains, in the form of 'the one for the other.'"[74]

God's response arrives at the same moment as His forgiveness and the return of the Clouds. Along with the building of the Tabernacle, there awakens a hope that the vision at Sinai may be embodied *in their midst,* at the heart of human desire. Holding and being held: perhaps the wish is to go beyond the differentiation of lover and beloved, of mother and daughter:

> "Go forth and look, O daughters of Zion, at King Solomon, in his crown with which his mother crowned him on his wedding day and on the day of his heart's joy" (Songs 3:11): Rabbi Shimeon ben Yochai asked Rabbi Elazar: Did you perhaps hear from your father what is the meaning of "the crown with which your mother crowned him"? He answered him: This is like a king who had an only daughter whom he loved exceedingly. He did not stir from his love of her until he called her, My daughter, as it says, "Listen, daughter, and see" (Ps. 45:11). He did not stir from his love of her until he called her, My sister, as it says, "Open for me, my sister, my darling" (Song 5:2). He did not stir from his love of her till he called her, My mother, as it says, "Listen to Me, my people and hearken to Me, My mother (*le'umi*)" (Isa. 51:4). Rabbi Shimeon ben Yochai rose up and kissed him on the head.[75]

Israel plays various roles successively in relation to God. Daughter, sister, mother: through all these transformations, God remains constant in His love for her. The intense love, *exceeding* love, of the King in the parable remains unchanged, even as its object moves from the position of daughter to that of mother. This divine love might have yielded to some other force—perhaps to the hostile voices that emphasize her less lovable aspects. But the King *did not stir from loving her (me-chabva)* through all their relational shifts, which clearly only raise her in his esteem.

These transformations hold a truth of human experience—in both psychoanalytic and mystical terms. Reading the mother position from the texts of the Song of Songs, Psalms, and Isaiah is no simple matter. Here, Israel in the position of mother is, as it were, God's fantasy. As such, it strikes a chord with Rabbi Shimeon ben Yochai, who kisses his younger colleague on the head in congratulation—a fatherly kiss, corresponding to the mother who crowns Solomon, her son. The midrash began with the older scholar asking the younger if he remembers hearing from his father an explanation of the verse about Solomon's mother; continues with the presumed report of the father's interpretation, and ends with the kiss of another "father." A text about motherhood engenders a discussion between men—a movement of Oral Torah from father to son—which frames another movement: God's relation to Israel as daughter, then sister, then mother. The feminine subject moves from the position of inferior to that of equal to that of "motherhood."

God as the object of His people's feminine desire breaks through all the conventions of religious language. A difficult text is read strongly, issuing in the radical imagery of motherhood. On his wedding day, on the day of his heart's joy, the king's mother crowns her son. What day is this latter day? asks Rashi. "This is the eighth day of the inauguration of the Tabernacle in the wilderness."[76] This second wedding day—after much has been lost and recovered—holds a singular joy for God: the day when Israel becomes "mother," nurturer of the divine in their midst.

Desire remains, at each stage of the people's history, like a "sign" in their midst, infinitely eloquent in its yearning. "But the soul—the *nefesh*—cannot have its fill" (Eccles. 6:7). The *nefesh*—the ensouled life force—cannot fill its emptiness. Its yearnings arch beyond what is possible. A dance enacts what cannot otherwise be known.

3

Shmini

The Desire for Desire

"And it was on the eighth day" (Lev. 9:1): that day was joy for God, like the day when heaven and earth were created—"And it was morning and it was evening . . ."[1]

The Talmud invests the commonplace narrative formula *vayehi* (*"And it was"*) with all the wonder of creation. This is the historic moment when, after seven days of inauguration, the Tabernacle is graced by the appearance of God's glory. This moment is compared in the Talmud to the appearance, day by day, over seven days, of the divine creation of the world. Those original seven days included the Sabbath day of divine rest. In mystical thought, this was followed by an unrealized eighth day transcending the boundaries of this world. This eighth day is in a sense enacted at this Tabernacle moment of divine joy. Some deep desire of the divine has been realized. This day, the first day of Nisan, says Midrash Seder Olam, took ten crowns of distinction:[2] the day itself is somehow dazzlingly bright.

The day climaxes with the revelation of God's glory.

And Moses and Aaron came into the Tent of Assembly, and they came out and blessed the people. And God's glory appeared to the whole people. And there came forth a fire from God's presence and consumed on the altar the burnt offering and the fats. And whole people saw and they exulted and fell upon their faces. (Lev. 9:23–24)

It seems clear that the fire is identified with the revelation of glory. In consuming the sacrifices, the fire emerging from the Holy of Holies testifies to God's acceptance and favor—the grace of His presence. The people's reaction is *vayaronu*—"and they sang in exultation." Never before or after this moment do we read of this quality of song in a narrative context.[3] So powerful is their experience that it apparently prostrates them (they collapse on the ground). This moment mirrors the divine joy of which the Talmud speaks. In human experience, however, it has a cataclysmic quality; the people are overwhelmed.

What is the nature of this song? In kabbalistic and midrashic traditions, it seems to represent a complex rather than a simple moment of joy. The Zohar remarks that from the time of the Song at the Red Sea, there was no joy like this joy of the eighth day. Sefat Emet[4] notes that the difference between the two songs is that in the miracle of the sea the song is fully communicated in words, while on this eighth day there is just the cryptic description, "They sang/exulted." The first song, at the sea, he writes, was created for all generations: this is the *Ur*-song, the foundational expression of wonder in the miraculous event. However, with the sin of the Golden Calf, song fell silent. Once the rupture had been healed, the people were capable again of singing the eternal song, but with the words obscured.

In other words, the Song of the eighth day is both less and more than the original Song at the sea. The eternal song has been interrupted, and is now restored with a difference. Now it comes without words. Now it includes, as Sefat Emet puts it, the knowledge of having been forgiven. The ecstasy at the appearance of the divine fire is overwhelming; it throws them on their faces, at a loss for words, "blocked"—blocked, dumbstruck. For they are now *ba'alei teshuvah*, "penitents in the world of hiddenness." They no longer belong in the expressive ranks of the righteous who have never been "interrupted" by sin. Theirs is an explosive song, uncontainable, mysterious even to themselves.

ONE FIRE

Uncannily, at that very moment, Aaron's two sons, Nadav and Avihu, are struck down by fire:

Aaron's sons, Nadav and Avihu, took each his own censer and placed in it fire and set incense on top; and offered up before God strange fire that was not commanded them. And fire came out from the presence of God and consumed them; and they died in the presence of God. (Lev. 10:1–2)

Fire is everywhere and everywhere it is mysterious. The revelation of God's presence—was that expressed in the fire that consumed the sacrifices? Or, as some read, are these two distinct phenomena? Then there is the "strange fire" offered by Nadav and Avihu. In what lies its strangeness? Is this a technical problem with inappropriate fire? How does this become the crime that merits such dire punishment? And, finally, there is the fire that consumes *them*—is this the same fire that consumed the sacrifices? Does this fire now find a macabre second object of consumption?

Rashbam offers a dramatic reading of this complicated narrative. The divine fire that consumes the sacrifices is indeed identical with that fiery "appearance of God's glory" that evokes such overwhelming joy in the people. Moreover, this fire is identical with the one that consumes Aaron's sons.

"Fire came forth from before God": from the Holy of Holies first to the golden altar, in order to burn the incense offering there . . . The fire found Aaron's two sons there, near the golden altar, and it burned them to death. Then the fire went out of the Tabernacle to the copper altar where it "consumed the burnt offering and the fats on the altar."[5]

In a single economical gesture, one fire signifies acceptance and forgiveness on the one hand and destruction on the other. The horrifying double object of the fire—animal sacrifices and human beings—is indicated in the syntax of the verse.

As for the "strange fire," Rashbam offers a further unusual reading. This fire would have been appropriate on any other day—it was "private fire" (*esh min ha-hediot*), which means domestic or *regular fire* from their own ovens. On this specific day, however, Moses had not commanded the routine procedure, since he was praying, precisely, for *divine* fire. On this day, they should have waited for the miracle, "so that God's name would be sanctified, when everyone realized that fire had come down from heaven."[6]

The narrative of sin and punishment should, then, be read in the pluperfect: "Aaron's sons had taken . . . And they had died in God's presence" (Lev. 10:1–2).

They could not wait for the miracle and instead brought private fire to the altar. Rashbam's reading places the catastrophe *before* the appearance of divine glory, whereas most midrashic sources place it *afterward*, as an effect of overenthusiasm. However, as Meir Yitzhak Lokshin points out, the Sifra does seem to support Rashbam:

> When Aaron's sons saw that all the sacrifices had been offered and all the deeds had been done and the Shechinah had not yet come down, Nadav said to Avihu, Does anyone cook a meal without fire? Immediately, they took strange fire.[7]

Pragmatically rushing in with domestic fire, they are interrupted in their priestly duties by the divine fire, which "finds" them in the wrong place at the wrong time.

NORMOTIC PRIESTHOOD

The tragedy arises from a compulsive drive to normalcy. The two priests cannot tolerate the tension of waiting; they thus lose the opportunity for sanctifying God's name. Going about their priestly business, they are caught in the trajectory of divine fire, moving between altars.

It is striking, in fact, that the language used is the normative language of cultic law. The verbs reverberate from the world of ritual sacrifice: *place, set, approach, incense.* The religious language is immaculate. All the sacrifices to this point have been scrupulously performed; and this in itself inspires the young priests to what we might call a *normotic* madness.

Here is the psychoanalyst Christopher Bollas, who coined the expression:

> Normotic illness is distinctive as a turning outward into concrete objects and toward conventional behavior. The normotic

flees from dream life, subjective states of mind, imaginative living and aggressive differentiated play with the other. . . . We could say that if the psychotic has "gone off at the deep end," the normotic has "gone off at the shallow end."[8]

In our context, Aaron's sons become, in a sense, intoxicated by the power of ritual, of predictable routines scrupulously followed. Faced with the gap in which, after all the procedures have been immaculately performed, *nothing happens*—when everyone is waiting, praying, blessing—the two young priests resort to the local vocabulary of the system. Concrete objects and the human movements that operate them must make the epiphany happen.

In this, Aaron's sons are, in effect, fully inhabiting their role. They are acting *as priests,* keeping the priestly procedures going. More specifically, they are acting as the sons of Aaron, who has a personal history that makes the gap, the waiting, particularly intolerable:

> When Aaron saw that all the sacrifices had been offered and all the rites performed, and yet the Shechinah had not come down for Israel, since the heavenly fire had not come down to consume the sacrifices, he was distressed and said, I know that God is angry with me and that it is because of me that the Shechinah has not come down for Israel. He therefore said to Moses, My brother Moses! Do you act thus with me? You know that I went into the Sanctuary at your bidding and I have been put to shame! Moses at once went into the Tent with him and they begged for compassion and the Shechinah did come down for Israel.[9]

In the moment of failure when God's glory pointedly *does not appear,* Aaron recognizes his own shame. His role in the Golden Calf debacle is the sin that blocks the divine Presence. *B'shvili,* he cries—it is because of me! All the procedures were correctly performed—which exacerbates Aaron's shame. The problem is not in the world but in me.

Aaron is haunted by his role in creating the Calf. Even after the specific sacrifice has been offered—the Sin Offering, involving a calf to atone for the Golden Calf—*nothing happens.* God had commanded, "Take for yourself a calf" (Lev. 9:2). On this, Rashi comments: "To make it known that God brings atonement through this calf for [Aaron's] role in making the Calf." This and other sacrifices were to clear the slate, so that "on this day God will appear to you" (9:4). The connection between sacrifices (expiation) and divine Presence is repeated in verse 6.

THE SHAME OF "NOTHING HAPPENS"

Here, however, the midrash drives a wedge between the two halves of the promise. The biblical text reads straightforwardly as describing the fulfillment of the promise. After Aaron has carried out the priestly rituals, "the glory of God did appear to the whole people" (Lev. 9:23). But the midrash reads the narrative for a sense of God's *absence:* "And Moses and Aaron *came into* the Tent and they *came out* and they *blessed* the people—and the glory of God appeared to the whole people."

Why this mysterious entry-and-exit by Moses and Aaron? And why the apparently redundant blessing (see v. 22)? The midrash detects a gap, when shame overwhelms Aaron. The Calf returns to incriminate him as, still, *nothing happens*—the divine Presence fails to appear. Only after Aaron, in his own mind, has been singled out in this way for disgrace, and only after Moses has joined him in prayer and blessing, does the divine Presence appear.

The midrashic saga of repeated pulses of divine absence and human shame is focused in this instance on Aaron, whose role in the Golden Calf story is ambiguous. (Is he merely accessory to the people's sin? When, immediately after the sin, he tries to justify himself to Moses, does that palliate his sin or exacerbate it?) Here, he draws all responsibility into himself.

This drama of guilt and shame is, however, visible only in the midrashic reading. And it is only in the midrashic reading that a more general, internal anguish is experienced by the whole people. Rashi continues his midrashic story by remarking on the next clause:

> "And they came out and blessed the people": They said the words that conclude the prayer of Moses (Lev. 9:23). They invoked just this blessing because during the whole seven days of the installation when Moses was setting up the Tabernacle and officiating in it and dismantling it daily the Shechinah had not rested

upon it. And the Israelites felt ashamed, saying to Moses, "Our teacher Moses! All the trouble which we have taken was only that the Shechinah may dwell among us, so that we may know that the sin of the Golden Calf has been atoned for us!"

Once again, Rashi reads the text for failed Presence: the second blessing is given by both Moses and Aaron. Rashi spells it out: "May it be God's will that His Presence may come to dwell in the work of your hands!" In Rashi's reading, this blessing is haunted by the failure implicit in the seven days of inauguration. During all those days, Moses had acted as High Priest, performing all the sacrifices. And during all that time, the people had experienced *nothing happening*—their attempts to expiate their sin have failed.

Here, the element of Aaron's priesthood complicates the situation. The national experience of shame is related to the memory of the Golden Calf. On the one hand, the event is in the past; the Golden Calf was ground to dust; it is, by this time, dead and gone. But on the other, it haunts the people, in the way that something neither dead nor alive haunts the present moment. Their shame, then, is hard to define, both familiar and strange. In order to resolve this shame, Aaron is assigned the role of High Priest, who, by his sacrifices of atonement, is to expiate both the national and his individual shame. It is he who feels most acutely responsible for what happened—and for what is not happening now.[10]

But it is his sons, Nadav and Avihu, bearing the scorch of their father's shame, who will die in their compulsive need to make things happen. Tragically, this leads them deeper into the fire. Unable to bear the tension of waiting for divine fire, they rush in with regular fire from their own oven. *Rushing in* sometimes represents retreat; performing impeccably, they fail to sustain the tension of the day.

This kind of fervor relates father to sons in a more radical way. The Golden Calf is also born of a kind of impatience: "And the people saw that Moses was delayed in coming down the mountain . . . and they said, Rise up and make for us gods that will walk in front of us! For this Moses, the man who brought us up from the land of Egypt, we don't know what has become of him!" (Exod. 32:1). The people turn their impatience, their sense of uncertainty, of living in limbo, upon

Aaron. It is Aaron who organizes their fear of chaos, who fires their gold jewelry into the cold fixity of the Calf.

The idol answers to a need for order. It seems to put an end to ambiguity; stable, predictable, it emerges from the fire as though demonically possessed.[11] All the turbulence of inner life can be resolved in one gleaming image. Delay and uncertainty bred the Golden Calf. Now, Aaron's sons respond in a priestly, pragmatic way to the limbo of *nothing happens*. The need for certainty *now* is associated with the compulsive need for the stable, completed image.

Shakespeare knew of this kind of despair when he wrote of "th'expense of spirit in a waste of shame."[12] So much energy expended to no avail, the *waste* of it is hard to bear! So Aaron's sons abandon the waiting posture and waste themselves totally in the divine fire that consumes both sacrifices and sacrificer.

THE SHY BRIDE

In Rashbam's reading, shame does not play an active role. But in midrashic tradition, it is central. The Sifra offers an unexpected analogy for Aaron's shame:

> "Come close to the altar" (Lev. 9:7): To what can this be compared? To a human king who married a wife. She was shy of him. Her sister came to her and said, Why did you get into this matter if not to serve the king? Steel yourself and come and serve the king! So Moses said to Aaron, Aaron my brother, why were you chosen to be High Priest if not to serve God? Steel yourself and come and fulfill your service![13]

Using the cultic language of *krav, sharet, avodah,* the midrash evokes the bride who is embarrassed about entering into intimate relations with her new husband, the king. Moses encourages his brother, *Krav*—Come close: overcome your inhibitions about the spiritual intimacy of your priestly function. The analogy of the shy bride inflects Moses's words. On the one hand, there is the pragmatic imperative of sexual intimacy: Why else did she get married? *Hagisi da'atech,* her sister urges her: steel yourself—or more literally, mobilize yourself,

toughen up, be practical, make yourself *coarser.* The image is mascu-
line, crude, military. Aaron, too, is similarly urged by his brother. Why
were you chosen? In a situation where the sacrificial act of atonement
is required, your shame is a luxury.

But on the other hand, there is the inner world of the shy bride
who is asked to coarsen her sensibilities. A strangely erotic tension
is set up. The word *krav* expresses the movement into intimacy, a
movement fraught with desire and fear. Rashi succinctly summarizes:
"Aaron was embarrassed and afraid to come close." Shame and desire:
the gap between the human and the divine is impossible to bridge.
How can "coming close" be merely pragmatic? The demand is unnerv-
ing, particularly if the Golden Calf history is borne in mind. If there
is an analogy in the bride parable to the element of the Golden Calf,
it may be the dread of "nothing happening," of the perils of intimacy.

Sefat Emet offers a profound reading. "Why are you shy/ashamed?
For this you were chosen!"—"Precisely because of your shame, you
were chosen!" Aaron brings to his priesthood the singular history
of the *ba'al teshuvah,* of the penitent. Unlike his naturally righteous
brother, Aaron comes by his readiness to serve through a painful process of sin and repentance.

Achieving intimacy with God means surrendering one's ego to
His service. But Aaron is inhibited by his history. There is a distance
between himself and God that will need time and process to overcome. Aaron becomes the prototype of the person arrested by self-
consciousness who is yet moved by the divine demand. The Other
who desires, "Come close!" brings out a responsive energy in the self.

In this reading, shyness/shame is the natural and proper response
of a human being who has sinned. However, this shame is to allow
itself to be released into the flow of life.

TRAUMA, SACRIFICE, PRAYER

Returning now to the Sifra, we read further:

> "Some say that Aaron saw the altar in the form of an ox, and he
> was afraid of it. Moses said, My brother, are you afraid of it?
> Steel yourself and come close to it! That is why it says, Come
> close to the altar!"

Here is fantasy alive in the world. The altar itself shifts shape and becomes the Calf. Now shame becomes fear; the inner world and the external world conspire to paralyze Aaron. And again Moses urges him, "Come close—move through and beyond your obsession!"

Shame and fear threaten to make of the Golden Calf an enduring obstacle. In effect, shame and fear block the way to atonement. "My sin is constantly up against me," says the Psalmist, intimating the danger of traumatic obsession.[14]

And one more passage from the Sifra:

> "Take *for yourself* a young calf as a Sin Offering" (Lev. 9:2). This teaches that Moses said to Aaron, Aaron my brother, even though God has been appeased to atone for your sins, you need to put something into the mouth of Satan! Send a gift ahead of you before you enter the Sanctuary, lest he block your path into the Sanctuary.

The calf of atonement is *lecha*—for you, homeopathic healing for your trauma. God may be reconciled with you, but *you need* to placate *Satan,* so that he does not block your way. Satan, your Opponent, who is always on the lookout to petrify impulses of life, has to be, in a sense, paid off. Here, the payoff is a calf to neutralize the malign Calf of fantasy.

The language of the midrash is magical, hallucinatory, to express the need for release from the past. It evokes the practice, on Yom Kippur (the Day of Atonement), of the *Sa'ir la-Azazel*—the goat thrown off the rock in gift to the wilderness goat-god (Lev. 16:8). Ramban describes Azazel as the power that rules in places of destruction. The Israelites were to placate this power *at the command of God.* It is not always clear whether such powers live in the internal or the external world, or both.

Aaron's fear and shame perhaps represent the anxiety that the future will inevitably be like the past; that there will, in fact, be no future. At heart, this is anxiety about loss of love: God's presence will not come to dwell in their midst. "Take *for yourself* a calf": there is a need to accept, to engage the Calf, who will not be exorcised in any other way.

Perhaps this is what Jonathan Lear means when he speaks of

accepting responsibility rather than *holding oneself responsible.* The latter move is the work of the superego; the former makes it possible to acknowledge an inner world and to work with it and through it.

Moses exhorts Aaron: "Mobilize (*hages*) yourself!" Even placating a demon requires a movement of energy. If Aaron is to "come close" to the altar, he must, in a sense, go into battle. The word *krav* itself can be translated as "go into battle."

In his commentary on this text, Ha'amek Davar (known as the Netziv) brings up the association of the *krav* moment with that of prayer. Prayer, he suggests, is an act of war against the "opponents" (*mastinim*), against the forces that petrify one's being. Sacrificial rituals (*korbanot*) enact a struggle against inertia.

After the destruction of the Second Temple, prayer will replace sacrifice. Essentially, they have the same dynamic value. Prayer is not a state of intimacy with God but a process of *coming close,* of overcoming impediments to intimacy.

The Netziv elaborates on the military image for prayer. He refers to the practice of urging the prayer leader: Come and wage battle! (*Bo u-krav!*) He also cites a classic wordplay: "'With my sword and with my bow (*be-kashti*)' (Gen. 48:22): with my prayer and my request (*bakashati*)" (Targum Onkelos). This, he concludes, refers to the force of daily prayer, which faces down the many obstacles between self and God.

The pursuit of Jewish spiritual life, for the Netziv, is full of impediments. Overcoming these impediments demands courage and a kind of tactical intelligence. Daily prayer, in its repetitiousness, even its tedium, arms one with words and stories that penetrate unconscious life. Daily prayer engages with anxiety about survival, about the economics of everyday life and the energies required to sustain that life.

THE INTIMATE ORDER

The writings of Georges Bataille provide a language for thinking about the principle of sacrifice. In his *Theory of Religion,* Bataille sets the sacred against the profane world of things and bodies.[15] This is the "real" world that can provide objects for human use as tools. Killing an animal for food implies that it has been defined as a *thing* to be skinned, cooked, roasted.[16] The human body, on the other hand, is haunted by the spirit that is closely linked to it; it is ambiguously both thing and spirit.

> The principle of sacrifice is destruction, but though it some-
> times goes so far as to destroy completely (as in a holocaust), the
> destruction that sacrifice is intended to bring about is not anni-
> hilation. The thing—only the thing—is what sacrifice means to
> destroy in the victim. . . . [I]t draws the victim out of the world
> of utility and restores it to that of unintelligible caprice. . . . The
> sacrificer declares: "*Intimately,* I belong to the sovereign world
> of the gods and myths, to the world of violent and uncalculated
> generosity. . . . I withdraw you, victim, from the world in which
> you were and could only be reduced to the condition of a thing,
> having a meaning that was foreign to your intimate nature. I
> call you back to the *intimacy* of the divine world, of the pro-
> found immanence of all that is."[17]

The movement from the values of the thing-world discloses the falsehood of those values. No longer is the thing valued for its dura-tion; paradoxically, death affirms the countervalue of intimate life.[18] As against the neutral order in which the individual functions in the society of labor, death reveals the truth of the intimate life that has been lost. Suddenly, there is uncovered a "ground of things that is dazzlingly bright."

Sacrifice, then, "restores a lost value through the relinquishment of that value. But death is not necessarily linked to it, and the most solemn sacrifice may not be bloody. To sacrifice is not to kill but to relinquish and give." Sacrifice focuses attention on the moment. What it consumes is the thing-ness, the usefulness, of the object. Sacrifice is, in this sense, "gift and relinquishment."[19] "This is the meaning of 'sacrificing to the deity,' whose sacred essence is comparable to a fire. To sacrifice is to give as one gives coal to the furnace."

The blaze of the furnace as it accepts and consumes the coal offers a moment of truth, of pure gift. Bataille speaks of this moment as one of inexpressible *intimacy.* The individual who sacrifices identifies with the victim in his "anxiousness to remain personally alive. . . . [He] would have no anguish if he were not the individual (the thing), and it is essentially the fact of being an individual that fuels his anguish. . . . Man is afraid of the intimate order that is not reconcilable with the order of things. . . . Because man is not squarely within that order, but only partakes of it through a thing that is threatened in its nature. . . . Intimacy, in the trembling of the individual, is holy, sacred, and suffused with anguish."[20]

Bataille creates a difficult but suggestive language of intimacy and sacred anguish set against the realm of labor: productivity, utility, and duration. The sacrificial victim seen in this way is withdrawn from playing a purely instrumental role in the world. Now, he exists not for his usefulness but for his absolute intimacy with a world of "violent and uncalculating generosity." To this intimacy individuality must be sacrificed. Since defining this intimacy is impossible, Bataille resorts instead to metaphor: "What is intimate is what has the passion of . . . the *imperceptible sonority of a river.*"[21]

Can this language be brought into conversation with the biblical and rabbinic notions of the sacrificial as intimacy? One association is the image of the consuming fire of the divine Presence. "The vision of God's glory was as a consuming fire at the top of the mountain, before the eyes of the Israelites" (Exod. 24:17). The visual impact of God's glory includes the essential awareness of *consumption.* What fire does is *consume:* its destructiveness is visually understood. Into that unimaginable intimacy with the divine Moses vanishes for forty days and forty nights. When he fails to reappear on the fortieth day, the people assume the worst. He has been taken up into that sacred intimacy.

This is Moses's second encounter with consuming fires; at the Burning Bush, what first draws his attention is the revelation of an angel in the midst of fiery flame: "And he saw, and behold, the bush was burning in fire, but the bush was not consumed" (Exod. 3:2). This "great vision"—of an *un*consumed bush burning in fire—draws him out of his path: "Let me turn aside and see this great vision—Why is the bush not consumed?"

The routine of Moses's life as a shepherd is interrupted by an anomaly—the failure of this fire to do what fires do—to consume the fuel offered by the Bush. This scene is followed by God's call to take off his shoes, for the ground he treads is holy ground. Moses is then called to prophecy, without any further reference to the mysterious Bush.

In some readings, the Bush represents the Israelites suffering in the fire of Egypt, which will ultimately fail to destroy them. However, in Rashi's reading, the Bush speaks directly to Moses's anxiety ("Who am I . . . ?" [Exod. 3:11]). God interprets:

"I will be with you" (Exod. 3:12): You will go to Pharaoh on My business, not yours. And the vision you have seen in the Bush will be a sign of your success in My mission: just as you have seen the Bush fulfilling My mission without being consumed, so you will go on My holy mission without being damaged.

Intimate encounter with God represents both desire and danger. In Bataille's language, an individual suddenly discovers "a ground of things that is dazzlingly bright." Stability and duration are endangered in a realm of consuming fire. But where there is fire there is also "unintelligible caprice." Moses is drawn away from normalcy—in this case, even from the normalcy of fire itself. What he sees is an exceptional fire, which promises him survival and a future of utility,[22] even in the very heart of the fire. He is to be the Bush that remains *un*consumed.

His personal fate will be the sign that God's other promise to save the Israelites from Egypt will be fulfilled. But Moses as burning bush is not, in the usual sense, a sign that proves the truth of God's promise. It is rather an image, something seen, that gives rise to other images. It is Moses's imagination that opens a future that is, precisely, a movement beyond any fixed image. His is a sophisticated imagination, familiar with the clichés of consuming fire and the dangers of intimacy.

Gaston Bachelard writes of the imagination that is "a kind of spiritual mobility" that renews the heart and soul. Images are the spark that fires the poet toward new images. "To imagine," he says, "is to absent oneself, to launch out toward a new life."[23] The *unconsuming* fire leads Moses to God's Own name for Himself, "I shall become what I shall become. *Ehyeh asher Ehyeh*" (Exod. 3:14). God's name is a verb, it is movement. Not only that: Moses is charged with the impossible task of transmitting this name to the Israelites: "*Ehyeh—I-shall-become* has sent me to you!" (3:14).

Bataille's discovered "ground of things that is dazzlingly bright" has become a different kind of instability. In this new country, "*Ehyeh—I-shall-become* will be with you." Damage and destruction become a moment in the imaginative voyage.

AN ALTERNATIVE TO IDOLATRY

What the divine Name and the unconsuming fire most powerfully evoke is an alternative to idolatry. The Golden Calf has of course not yet happened. But the ground for it is being laid in this first dialogue between God and Moses on the subject of exodus from Egypt. The project of *yetziat Mitzraim* (the Exodus) is, at its core, a project of separation from the gods of Egypt, from the culture of the master race that holds the slaves in thrall.

Immediately after the first commandment ("I am the Lord your God who has brought you out of the land of Egypt, from the house of slaves") comes the second commandment—almost as though after a colon: "You shall have no other gods in My presence." The Exodus represents a break for freedom, and the construction of a new identity based on that freedom. An important aspect of freedom is the separation not just from Egypt but from the fascination with Egypt's gods. The Exodus is an iconoclastic project; entering a covenant with the One God is an attempt to break the idolatrous spell.

Eric Santner offers a psychoanalytic understanding of what he calls *Egyptomania.* His concept of Egyptomania can be connected with the rabbinic wordplay on *Mitzraim/meitzarim*—Egypt/straits. In this symbolic world, Egypt becomes a Jewish cultural memory, the site of constraint, of constriction, angst, anguish. This rigidity is associated with the practice of idolatry. Freedom would mean loosening the grip of the fascinations and defense mechanisms of a hindered life. This is exodus—the turn to the worship of the one God, *Who-will-become-what-He-will-become.*

Eric Santner sets himself to explore the metaphor of Egyptomania, the Egyptian madness. (It is striking that God raises the subject of a peculiar "Egyptian sickness" [Exod. 15:26] immediately after the Israelites have crossed the Red Sea.) For Santner, Exodus involves finding a way "to separate from the various forms of Egyptomania that so profoundly constrain our lives."[24] In the biblical narrative, it soon emerges that the "stiff-necked" people regress almost immediately, while the divine fire still burns at Sinai, to the compulsive appeal of the Egyptian bull, Apis.[25] Even when the immediate outbreak of Egyptomania has been suppressed, its residues remain. The Calf still fascinates and appalls. As we have seen, it provokes fear and shame; and the fantasy of eradicating the past informs the hope of God's presence coming to dwell in the midst of the people.

The biblical law is clear: "They shall no longer offer their sacrifices to the goat demons after whom they stray. This shall be to them a law, for all time, throughout the ages" (Lev. 17:7). But the very force of this taboo indicates the counterpressure of reality. For, in fact, the fascination and the struggle with the goats and bulls of the past will linger. Idolatry will return periodically, in repressed form, to create perpetual unease.

One of its appearances is on the terrible night of national weeping after the Spies bring back their anxious report from the land of Israel. This night is later, in his last months, remembered by Moses: "You sulked in your tents saying, It is because God hates us that He brought us out of the land of Egypt, only to give us over into the hands of the Amorites to destroy us" (Deut. 1:27). Thirty-nine years after the fact, Moses gives new words to the paroxysms of that night. The people bewailed the destructive *hatred* of the God who had delivered them only in order to annihilate them at the last moment.

In Moses's account, the people have transformed the Exodus into a story of divine hatred. In the commentaries of Seforno and, centuries later, of Ha'amek Davar, it is the Israelite history of idolatry that produces such a guilty narrative of divine resentment.[26]

The most interesting aspect of this is what it indicates about the state of the people. Rashi points out that their complaint is an instance of projective identification. The people are possessed by guilt, shame, and resentment about their idolatrous past; they project their hatred onto God. They put into God unbearable elements of their inner world. In doing so, they constrict their world of possibilities and, in effect, prophesy their own fate.

According to the midrashic Sages, the Golden Calf never dies. It remains to haunt the generations. After the sin, God tells Moses: "When I make an accounting, I will bring them to account for their sins" (Exod. 32:34). The Jerusalem Talmud comments: "You never have a single generation that does not have a small measure of the generation of the Golden Calf."[27] The generation of the Calf—its desires and anxieties—leaves a stain on all generations. These are remainders of Egyptomania. However minute the remainder—*onki* is a minuscule measure—some Calf substance ferments in all generations.

Against the constraining force of idolatry, God announces Himself at the Burning Bush as *I-shall-become-who-I-shall-become.* He is the mystery of Becoming, of that which opens the realm of possibility. Even the image of the *un*consuming fire enacts this, as it destabilizes the classic image of the consuming fire. In arousing Moses's "spiritual mobility," God invites Moses to free himself from fixed images of all kinds.

FETISHIZED PRACTICES

Returning now to the fire that consumes Nadav and Avihu, we remember that the same fire consumed the sacrifices. Animal sacrifice was supposed to replace and symbolize human sacrifice. Instead, the divine fire burns both human and animal, one after the other, as though some essential symbolic process has failed.

Their priestly training had habituated them to ritualized behavior. This habit becomes pathological when they reach compulsively for home fire. But exceptionally, on this day, routine has been suspended. Home fire is today *strange* fire, inappropriate to this time and place.

This day (Lev. 9:4) makes its own singular demands of them. A gap punctuates the reassuring normalcy of the rituals, a gap of expectation, anxiety, waiting. Compulsively, they fill the gap with routine action. A passion for procedures, for *things,* possesses them. They are caught in the order of things, incapable of living in the gap.

The passion for ritual—and the way it mimics idolatry—is addressed by Ha'amek Davar. He cites the Song of Songs:

> "Draw me—*moshcheni*—and we will run after you!" (Songs. 1:4) The beloved responds fervently to the merest hint from her lover. But the Rabbis inflect this to *meshachani*—"*He withdrew His presence from our midst, therefore we run after You!*"
>
> Know that it is so, that they did not mourn for all the troubles that the Golden Calf brought upon them. But when Moses told them, "I will not go up in your midst," immediately,

they mourned . . . Israel were impassioned for God's presence, as it is said, "Let my beloved come into his garden" (*le-gano/le-ginuni*—his wedding canopy).

The passion for God's presence is most ardently experienced in His absence. Rereading the word *moshcheni,* the midrash dwells on the state of loss and the passion it generates. Paradoxically, the Golden Calf brought this loss and this passion upon the people.

Ha'amek Davar discusses the pathological potential of this kind of fervor. The word in the midrash is *lehutim*—fiery, frenzied, intoxicated, infatuated. This (literally) overheated state of mind can result in sectarianism, each group creating its own rituals, fragmenting the unity of Jewish practice. He cites the Sifra:

> "Moses said, This thing is what God has commanded that you do" (Lev. 9:6). Moses said to Israel: Remove *that evil inclination* from your heart and be all of you of one fear and one counsel to serve God. Just as He is one in the world, so you be one in your singular worship of Him. As it says, "You shall circumcise the foreskin of your heart." Why? "Because the Lord your God is supreme God and supreme Lord" (Deut. 10:17). If you do so, "God's glory will appear to you."

Worship of the one God demands discipline. "*That* evil impulse" refers to the excessive fervor that tends to create new religious rituals to express the urgent passion of the moment; fragmentation results. At the same time, the Netziv clearly appreciates the spiritual passion behind such movements. This is a passion "to achieve love of God in its holiness." If it ends in death, "[t]he death of His pious ones is precious in God's eyes."

In a fine rhetorical move, he interprets the later phrase, "who shows no favor and takes no bribe" (Deut. 10:17). What could conceivably act as a bribe to God? Spiritual dedication and exalted passion, he answers. There can be nothing more "seductive" than such spontaneous sacrificial movements of love. But the divisiveness that results is not "the way of God"; ultimately, it does not please Him.

Ha'amek Davar here speaks from his own historical moment and ideology. Witnessing the rise of the Reform movement in the nineteenth century, he deplores its divisive effect on the Jewish people. At the same time, he seems to acknowledge the genuine religious passion that drives it. For him, Nadav and Avihu personify the potentially tragic encounter between human religious passion and inscrutable divine desire.

The singular quality of this collision is indicated in the midrashic term *lehutim*. From the root *lahat*—a flame—it implies, as we have suggested, immature ardors, intoxications, infatuations. There is an edge of adolescent melancholy to such passions. What it wants is the thing itself. Experience teaches that the thing is what cannot be had; like the ice cube on a hot day, it melts in the hand. Or, in Bataille's language, what can be had is the empty objectivity of things. The true desire is for intimacy, which is not to be *had*.

Nadav and Avihu are on fire to bring God's presence into their midst. Only in this way will the shadow of the Golden Calf be removed. This passion is pragmatic in its thrust: to resolve the suspense of waiting for the sacrifices to be consumed. It is, starkly, a passion to consummate the sacrificial rituals. The Netziv imagines the situation—the crowds of Israelites waiting for the revelation of the consuming fire: an element of social pressure plays its part. Moses forewarns him: "This thing, and this thing alone, you shall *do*—[that is, you shall make authentically meaningful]—so that God's glory will appear to you." The Netziv reads the word *la'asot*—to do or make—as he often does, referring not to practical action but to the close study and precise interpretation of God's words.

The real danger of the sacrificial rituals is that they will become replacements for the Golden Calf—fetishized practices to satisfy a similar hunger. Nadav and Avihu act on their passion for the rituals. The sense of God's absence inflames them to a kind of willful frenzy. They will make the world conform to a predictable, intelligible order. Tragically, their pragmatic desire for order reduces them to thing-hood.

As we have seen, obsession with the normative typifies "normotic" illness. Christopher Bollas remarks on the personality type that repudiates the subjective element in everyday life.[28] An unimaginative passion constricts life into Egyptomaniac forms.

FETISHIZING GOD

The theological problem, of course, is that God is not necessarily a normative, predictable God. One of the hazards of religious systems is the attempt to house God in any system. On the one hand, the purpose of cultic rituals is to please God and affect His behavior; on the other, a certain delicate balance can easily be lost, when God is casually incorporated into the system. God then becomes part of a fetishized reality. At such times, His autonomy and unpredictability reassert themselves, momentarily disrupting theological certainties.[29]

A similar analysis of the inexplicable deaths of the young priests is offered by R. Meir Simcha Hacohen (known as Meshech Chochmah). Writing in the nineteenth century, he is familiar with the various explanations given in the midrash: because they officiated in a state of intoxication; because they acted without proper authority; because they were not married; because they had no children. And many more explanations are offered by commentaries throughout the ages. But the number and variety of these explanations only highlights the fact that none is fully satisfying.

R. Meir Simcha Hacohen focuses on the inscrutable nature of the narrative. Tracing these deaths back to the sin of the Golden Calf, he surveys the narrative of sin, punishment, and restoration. He notes how quickly the catastrophe is resolved. In short order, in less than a year, God's presence comes to dwell among the people.

Here, however, in this restoration of order, lies the problem. Israel will say, God is easy to pacify. The world is governed by systems of sin and forgiveness in which God plays His orderly role. In order to reaffirm His autonomy, God strikes down those who enable the rationality of the system.

God's violent gesture is intended to regenerate the religious sense of the incalculable gravity of His presence. The only words of explanation He offers are the enigmatic, "Through those that are close to Me I shall be sanctified; in the presence of the whole people I shall make my gravity felt (*ikaved*)" (Lev. 10:3). The death of the young priests is a reminder of the dangers of everyday life with God. It is the work of a moment, an abrupt flash of fire, the truth that reveals "the *invisible* brilliance of life that is not a *thing*."[30]

SWEET FIRES

Once as Ben Azzai sat and expounded Torah (*doresh*), the fire flamed (*me-lahetet*) around him. They went and told R. Akiva, saying, Rabbi, Ben Azzai is sitting and expounding Torah and fire is flaming around him. He went to Ben Azzai and said, I hear that while you were expounding Torah fire flamed around you? He answered, That is so. He said to him, Were you perhaps engaging in the secrets of the Divine Chariot? No, he replied. I was only combining the words of Torah with one another and then with the words of the prophets, and the prophets with the Writings; and the words rejoiced as when they were delivered from Sinai, and they were sweet as at their original utterance. And was it not in fire that they were originally delivered from Sinai, as it says, "And the mountain burned with fire"?[31]

Here, again, is fire, flaming around Ben Azzai. The sight arouses wonder in his students. Perhaps like Moses at the Burning Bush, they are mystified by the fact that the teacher is not consumed. Three times the phrase repeats, becoming an incantation in the mouths of the narrator, the students, and R. Akiva. Ben Azzai himself only responds to R. Akiva's troubled questions. His concern is only for the *d'rashah*, for the creative movement of his teaching—making links, threading beads between texts of Torah.

The flaming fire produced by Ben Azzai's words is described as *melahetet*, with the familiar *l-h-t* root that described the frenzy, the anxious greed of the Israelites after the Golden Calf. But here the fire represents not sacrifices but the threading of beads, the electric contact of words with words. The image from the Song of Songs ("Your neck is beautiful with beads" [Songs. 1:10]) presents an almost domestic idyll, far from the dangerous mystical suspicions of R. Akiva. But this "threading" action symbolically retrieves the consuming fire of Sinai. In Ben Azzai's words, the original fire, with all its terror, is transformed into sweetness and joy. Somehow, the erotic passion has lost its sting of anxiety. He is not constructing a system of perfect order. Rather, he is uncannily demonstrating the effect of God's presence within him.

Shall we say that the passion has been tamed, has lost its frenzied quality? But the *lahat* is still there and Ben Azzai, unawares, is generating it. It flames around him but does not consume him; it characterizes the fire and not the man; it is a verb and not an adjective. It evokes the intimacy that is not a thing. It animates one of the most poetic descriptions of learning/teaching Torah in its midrashic mode—as if to say, "Really, this is how it was, then as now."

MOURNING AND MELANCHOLY

The narrative of Nadav and Avihu represents the ultimately mysterious nature of events. Perhaps no reading of the story can be completely satisfactory. Nevertheless, I would like to explore one specific midrashic reading, just because it is so specific. According to *Vayikra Rabbah* 20:6, Nadav and Avihu officiated while in a state of drunkenness. This is deduced from the placing of the taboo on priestly intoxication immediately after the narrative of Nadav and Avihu.

Addressed specifically to Aaron and his surviving sons, this taboo is read by the Netziv as addressing the problem of melancholy and mourning in the life of the priest. In the first stage of mourning (*onen*), the priest is barred from participating in the very rituals that create a sense of intimacy with God. Since he is then considered to be in a depressive state, he may be tempted to use intoxicants to overcome his sadness. He cites a verse from Proverbs: "Give alcohol to one who is lost, and wine to the bitter of spirit. Let him drink and forget his destitution" (Prov. 31:6). This tactic—intoxication as an antidepressant—is forbidden in the Sanctuary.

Nevertheless, the Netziv recommends a metaphorical antidote—the wine of Torah! He interprets the following verse, ". . . to distinguish between the sacred and the profane, and between the impure and the pure," as referring to the study and teaching of Torah, with its work of clarifying differences, even in the gray areas of doubt between polarities. This nuanced work, he remarks, is the best antidepressant, with no negative side effects!

As he evokes the "intoxicating" effect of Torah study, the Netziv is clearly most interested in those areas of doubt that require sober intellectual and ethical work. The ground for this creativity is the encounter with loss, mourning, apparent meaninglessness. In her *Black Sun,* Julia Kristeva describes the *despondent intoxication* with which the depressive engages with the losses inherent in living.

In Kristeva's Freudian view, melancholy states emerge from a failure to acknowledge primal loss—the loss of the mother. "If I did not agree to lose mother, I could neither imagine nor name her."[32] Mourning for this loss is an essential element of development; the inner world of a human being is made of the work of mourning. To refuse to acknowledge loss results in depression: "My depression points to my not knowing how to lose—I have perhaps been unable to find a valid compensation for the loss? . . . The depressed person is a radical, sullen atheist."[33]

For Kristeva, psychoanalysis offers the opportunity to rediscover desire in the process of mourning. Learning how to lose is a sobering but liberating process. Dialogue between two speaking subjects offers a way out of the silence that shrouds unacknowledged loss.

For the Netziv, the practice of learning and teaching Torah in the mode of midrash has a similar effect. The priest in mourning, temporarily deprived of the practices of his priesthood, exemplifies the dilemma of one who desperately seeks to fill the emptiness of melancholy. The work with the words of Torah involves generating those new strings of language that reenact the "sweetness and joy" of the original words of Sinai.

In the rabbinic imagination, Nadav and Avihu seek comfort in intoxicants. But this form of ecstasy is surrounded by the penumbra of melancholy that blocks them from entering into the midst of life. Other midrashic diagnoses of their sin suggest that they are childless and that they are unmarried—"What woman is fit for us?" These diagnoses also hint at a depressive, narcissistic state: marriage and parenthood involve exchange with the imperfect Other. Holding themselves apart, the young priests are caught up in an impossible mourning for the ideal *thing.*

In the end, the whole people are to "weep the burning that God has brought about" (Lev. 10:6). Perhaps this refers to the work of mourning that offers a therapeutic response to loss. The melancholy subject refuses to mourn, refuses even to acknowledge loss. Moses urges on the whole people that they enter a period of mourning for very real loss—in part, for the loss of their own idolatrous fantasies.

EUPHORIA AND PRAYER

An association: Adam driven out of the Garden of Eden is forever barred from return. "God stationed (*va-yashken*) east of the Garden of Eden the angels and the flame/blade (*lahat*) of a turning sword, to guard the way to the Tree of Life" (Gen 3:24). So ends the primal narrative of loss: Paradise lies behind Adam and Eve, the fiery angels block return. Under these circumstances, will Adam and Eve rivet themselves to the gates of Paradise?

The word *lahat* here refers to the blade of the sword, sharp, pointed, polished. It represents terror and also the fascination of flashing fire as it "turns."

Also remarkable is the word *va-yashken,* here translated "stationed." But this word will come to denote the Shechinah, God's presence in the *Mishkan* (Tabernacle): "I will dwell (*ve-shachanti*) in their midst." These angels are doing God's work with their dazzling swords.

Here is the *Midrash Ha-Gadol:*

When a human soul longs for the Garden of Eden, it moves eagerly to enter. But when it approaches it finds angels standing with flaming swords, and it recoils. . . .

Another reading: What is the turning flaming sword? This refers to the angels who turn into many forms—sometimes angels, sometimes men, sometimes women: as the moment requires.

"To guard the way to the Tree of Life": God hid that Tree that would render anyone who ate of it immortal, and gave us in its place His Torah which is the tree of life, as it says, "It is a tree of life to those who hold on to it" (Prov. 3:18). A person looks at it and sees divine wisdom and the structure of creation and the structure of the world with its comings and goings and customs; he sees God's righteousness and the commandments and statutes and judgments. Instantly, *he returns to his mind* and engages with them and acquires life in this world and the world to come.

These angelic guards are there to frustrate human desire, the desire to reenter Paradise. It is they who "turn," transform themselves like fire, according to the needs of the moment. From the perspective of loss, the human being sees divine wisdom, the metaphorical Torah of life, which now *replaces* the literal taste of eternity. Thus he "returns to his mind," to his *da'at,* which releases him to the symbolic world of Torah.

This turning sword has a bewitching effect, like the illusory work of the Egyptian magicians.[34] It changes shape in accordance with human desire. But even as it arouses desire, it bars access. An alternative way opens up—the way of the symbolic, of words, and texts, and wisdom. The mouth that craves the fruit will instead speak words of Torah.

This shift of desire represents a *return to one's mind,* in the striking phrase of the midrash. As though mourning, the acceptance of loss, moves one back from the realm of fantasy to that of consciousness. Loss of the object threatens one's mind. What Freud calls "the work of mourning" constitutes a process of ethical engagement that restores life.

Elsewhere, the Rabbis warn against intoxication—the potentially suicidal dream of return to the Garden. "One who is drunk is forbidden to pray."[35] Why is it specifically the religious act of prayer that forbids intoxication?

R. Yaacov Leiner, the late-nineteenth-century Hasidic commentator, engages with the metaphysics of intoxication. The human being is constituted by the sense of *chissaron,* of an incompleteness that turns one to God in prayer. The impulse that connects the human being with God is this awareness of deficiency. This consciousness, he affirms, lies at the heart of human religious experience. The prayer impulse arises from awareness of a gap in the self, which leads one to the Source of goodness.

There can be no true prayer, R. Leiner teaches, without this awareness. This is why the Talmud forbids the intoxicated to pray. Transforming the rabbinic injunction to a metaphorical register, he articulates his theology of prayer. The intoxicated, in this larger sense, can no longer perceive their own human limitation.

To pray while in a state of euphoria, then, is to "speak falsehood before God." This would be a moment of "double talk," belying the existential posture of one who prays. Ecstasy unhinges the basic sobriety of the mind. Euphorias are fantasy states, with anxiety built into them. Self-awareness vanishes, and with it the realistic recognition of *chissaron* that can generate authentic prayer.

For R. Leiner, yearning is vital to spiritual life. The illusion of *wholeness*—of needing nothing—is like drowning, sinking in momentary pleasure so that one *forgets oneself.* Since this pleasure is spiritual, the problem is not the sensuality of pleasure but its deranging effect. To remember oneself and one's yearning, a sober mind is needed. He calls this state *yishuv ha-da'at,* the "settled" mind that opens one to the presence of the Other.

This is a psychological account of the tension within prayer. We remember Bataille's description of the religious desire to transcend oneself, to achieve intimacy with God, to the point of abandoning the order of reality, and even to the point of self-sacrifice. Inherent in the religious sensibility is a desire for individuality to be consumed. This is the passion for life-in-the-moment—which means some form of death—ignoring the future and the utility of the world of things.

R. Leiner points to the dangers of this ecstatic posture. His emphasis on *chissaron*[36] reframes prayer as a disenchanted awareness of the true relations between the human and the divine. Difference, rather than ecstatic merging, creates the dynamic of relationship. In this and other teachings, he engages with the pathology of the religious mind. The individual is drawn back by prayer into the world of words.

Prayer and sacrifice are, of course, connected. The impulse to offer sacrifices to the divine is rooted in the same consciousness of imperfection and need. An active energy reaches out to God. For the dynamic to be effective, it must arise from self-awareness.

Nadav and Avihu represent one mode of religious pathology. They are absorbed in the need to escape their helplessness. Focusing on the normative practices of the Sanctuary, they become intoxicated with a quasi-technical power. This is a kind of madness: the normotic response that, for Christopher Bollas, marks a blank inner life. Conventional behavior becomes a form of idolatry. Common sense obviates any other kind of sense. One "goes off at the shallow end."[37]

In both Hasidic and psychoanalytic thought, normalcy becomes a fraught notion. For R. Leiner, to be a normal human being is to acknowledge inner trouble and to pray. For analytic thinkers like Bollas and Jonathan Lear, the normal mind can be easily distracted by fantasies of wholeness. This obscures the sense of responsibility for one's inner world. Returning to oneself, to one's mind, one rediscovers one's erotic attachment to the world.

In accepting responsibility for one's inner world, Lear remarks, one must "take up and be infused by the instinctual life for which one is assuming responsibility."[38] The mind becomes active in the body; living words are erotically charged. They take on an instinctual intensity, become vital, even playful.[39]

HOPE AND THE IMPOSSIBILITY OF HOPE

Adam Phillips describes psychoanalytic theory as "a set of stories about how we can nourish ourselves to keep faith with our belief in nourishment, our desire for desire. . . . What we now call desire is both hope and impossibility of hope; that the life in us is not always on our side."[40]

Phillips takes as his subject the loss of basic interest in life. He asks how hope may work with such despair. This is a question, I have been suggesting, that hovers over the narrative of Nadav and Avihu, whose willed pragmatism places them in the direct line of divine fire. How can one keep faith with the belief in nourishment when life seems to sabotage it?

Here is one more midrash about the impossibility of hope:

R. Acha and R. Ze'ira opened their discourse with the text: "At this too my heart trembles, *va-yatter* out of its place" (Job 37:1). What is the meaning of *va-yatter*? "It leaped." As you read, "to leap upon the earth" (Lev. 11:21).

Elihu said, Shall the sons of Aaron not even be like his rod, which entered dry and came out full of sap? The wicked Titus entered the interior of the Holy of Holies with his sword drawn in his hand. He cut into the curtain and his sword came out full of blood. He entered in peace and departed in peace. But Aaron's sons came in to offer incense and came out burned, as is borne out by the text, "After the death of the two sons of Aaron, when they drew near before God, and died."[41]

The midrash moves between two proof texts, beginning with Job describing his shocked response to a lightning storm and ending with the postscript to the story of Nadav and Avihu. Both texts describe the traumatized mind.

First, there is Job, perhaps the classic sufferer of trauma. "My heart/mind jolts from its place," he says. The midrash picks this up and applies it to the confounding mystery of evil in the world. What sense can be made of the comparison between Aaron's sons and Aaron's staff? In what seems like a purely formal comparison, both enter the Sanctuary: one flourishes, and the others are burned to death. Or, in another strange pairing, Titus and Aaron's sons both enter the Holy of Holies; the one who desecrates emerges unscathed, the others who sacrifice emerge burned to death. The mind is jolted by the impossibility of finding justice—or, simply, meaning—in the motives and fates of the individual.

The final proof text is quoted from the later reference (Lev. 16:1) to the Nadav and Avihu narrative. "After the death of the two sons of Aaron . . ." Rashi quotes *Torat Kohanim:*

R. Elazar ben Azaria said, Here is a parable: A sick man was visited by his doctor who told him, Don't eat cold foods, don't sleep in damp places. Then another doctor came and told him, Don't eat cold foods and don't sleep in damp places, *so you don't die as X died*. The latter doctor has a greater effect on the patient! That is why it says, "After the death of the two sons of Aaron."

Unexpectedly, the death of Aaron's sons becomes a textbook example of sin and punishment. The real-life story makes the teaching more forceful. Strangely, this mysterious narrative now sponsors a lucid story of sin and punishment. What, then, makes Job's heart jolt at the impressionistic analogies that so painfully fail to make sense?

SONG WITHOUT WORDS

The thrust of those analogies goes further than the acknowledgment in Ecclesiastes 9:2: "The same fate befalls the righteous and the wicked, the good and the pure and the impure, the one who offers sacrifice and the one who does not." On that verse, too, there is also a wealth of doleful midrashic material. These teachings simply note, with some outrage, the ineluctable fact of death that makes no distinction between good and evil. Our midrash, however, exacerbates the outrage by focusing on the aesthetic details of the analogies (the flowering stick and Aaron's sons; the bloody sword and the burned bodies). The point is not the undiscriminating nature of death but the impossibility of any kind of moral aesthetic.

The unusual word *va-yatter*—to leap—is translated by reference to another proof text, about winged swarming things (Lev. 11:21). Since locusts and crickets have a capacity to "leap on the ground," they may, in principle, be eaten. Rashi, however, rules out any way of identifying the permissible species—their features are so complex that they are impossible to categorize: "We do not know how to distinguish between them."

The very word *va-yatter* thus carries with it the recognition that the task of taxonomy—of creating meaningful categories—is sometimes impossible. In our midrash, Job's heart—and the heart of the reader—jolts at a reality that defies orderly categories.

Our midrash engages with the various acts of mind by which we seek meaning. The comparison of Aaron's staff with his sons, for instance—a whimsical parallel, to be sure—is the product of a lively mind that seeks analogies of a poetic order. But these, too, only succeed in negating meaning.

The Nadav and Avihu narrative becomes the very type of that which eludes a stable context of meaning. It is particularly striking that the midrashic sections that follow are all concerned to ascribe guilt of one kind or another to Aaron's sons; in other words, to rationalize their fate. Some of these claims we have noticed. But our midrash nevertheless brings us into the mind of trauma, of the unfathomable moment that disrupts structures of meaning. The stories that connect events into a coherent whole suddenly fall apart. Discordant images of triumphant bloody swords and flowering staffs jostle one another.

Job's mind jolts out of place. All the accusing stories of his "comforters" only irritate him further with their falsehood. The mind of the reader is also jolted, to the point where the final quotation, "After the death of the two sons of Aaron," resonates ironically. An event that is construed by some interpreters as a textbook example of the power of particular stories to reveal meaning has now become the paradigm of the unfathomable.

We, too, are traumatized by this midrash, by its idiosyncratic hopelessness and, ultimately, I suggest, by the biblical narrative itself. This is a story that has generated many stories of meaning. But Aaron's response is silence: "And Aaron was silent." Perhaps this is the appropriate response. In itself, it bears many possibilities. Does Aaron's silence signify assent to God's enigmatic summation: "Through those who are close to Me I shall be sanctified"? Or resignation? Or tight-lipped self-control?

Silence holds many possibilities; as of course does language, which is fraught with ambiguity. The narrative of Nadav and Avihu gives us perhaps too many possibilities with an unresolved gap in their midst of each. What is not explained or reduced to narrative order is the divine itself. What cannot be fully known ("I shall become what I shall become" [Exod. 3:14]) makes us both hopeful and hopeless. To recall Adam Phillips: important stories are "about how we can nourish ourselves to keep faith with our belief in nourishment, our desire for desire . . . What we now call desire is both hope and the impossibility of hope; that the life in us is not always on our side."[42]

Hope and the impossibility of hope: vivid inner life is made of such material. The artist Pierre Bonnard wrote in his notebook: "The practice of cropping of the visual field almost always gives something which doesn't seem true. Composition at the second degree consists of *bringing back certain elements which lie outside the rectangle*."[43] The artist recognizes both the terror and the opportunity of breaking the frame of an elegantly composed picture. Bringing back what has been excluded "makes it a frame for something that seems true." What seems true can also seem baffling and unstable: a story about desire.

We remember the song of joy that began the day of God's joy. "It was on the eighth day . . ." *"Vayehi b'yom ha-shemini . . ."* The same word—*Vayehi*—may signal either joy or distress, or both. A new kind of song includes both. Since the Song at the Red Sea, says the Zohar, this people have not sung. Time has passed; losses have been incurred. Now a new song, without words, with knowledge of contraries.

4

Tazria/Metzora

Isolation and Compassion

SKIN SYMPTOMS

The subject of impurity plays a central role in the book of Leviticus. A glance through a concordance yields many listings for the word *tamei* (impure): multiple references, for instance, to animals that are impure and that cause impurity in those who consume them (or even have contact with them). Other biblical sections list impurities that "issue from the human body" (*ha-yotzot mi-gufo*). These begin with the woman who has given birth (chapter 12). A process of purification is described. Then follow the sections that deal with the skin pathology called *tzora'at*. Traditionally, this was understood to be leprosy, but, as we shall see, there is good reason to read the term *tzora'at* as an idiopathic disorder, a form of psoriasis.

A long section deals with the many eventualities in the progress of the disease. Diagnosis is a complex matter, sometimes requiring two weeks to complete. Treatment is total isolation outside the camp. Other forms of *tzora'at* follow, affecting clothing and housing—perhaps a form of mildew. However, classifying the human body together with clothing and housing creates a bizarre category of symptoms. It is difficult to find an analogy in modern clinical understanding.[1] And, indeed, the traditional rabbinic understanding of the origin of this disorder is, as we shall see, not medical.

Tzora'at, as a category of "issues from the human body," is set apart from impurity originating in the world outside. Here, impurity originates not in consumption or contact with the world; rather, it emerges from the unknown interior of the body onto the body surface. Its progress through time is a significant factor in diagnosis; the lesion is periodically examined by the priest for its changing appearance—extent, color, and other physical changes.

Symptoms appear on the skin, that sensitive envelope that separates the body contents from the outside world. The skin is a liminal area, a space between, in which are registered both inner malaises, physical and emotional, and reactions to the outside world. It is a responsive organ, reacting to food, touch, climate, to attractions and repulsions, fears and pleasures. The Hebrew word for skin is *or;* in these Torah passages, it is often called *or bessoro* (the skin of his flesh). It functions as a porous barrier between inside and outside. The Hebrew *or* evokes alertness, responsiveness, vitality. The pathology of *tsora'at,* in which the skin is bleached of color, is associated with death.

The word *bassar,* as Samson Raphael Hirsch points out elsewhere,[2] has the double meaning of *flesh* and the act of *announcing:* the skin of the flesh carries impressions and communicates them in both directions, between inner and outer worlds. It is a borderland between the private and the public, telling more than one knows. It can also provoke self-awareness.

Ramban offers a psychosomatic reading—or, better, a *psycho-theological* reading. Addressing the blight on clothes and houses, he writes:

"When the plague of leprosy is in a garment": This is not in the natural order of things, nor does it ever happen in the world outside Israel. Similarly, leprosy of houses is not a natural phenomenon. But when Israel is wholly devoted to God, then His spirit is upon them always, to maintain their bodies, clothes, and houses in a good-looking state. Thus as soon as one of them commits a sin, a deformity appears in his flesh, or on his garment, or in his house, revealing that God has turned aside from him. It is for this reason that the Torah states, "I shall put the plague of leprosy in a house of the Land of your possession" (Lev. 14:34), meaning that it is God's punishment upon that house. Thus this law applies only in the Land, which is "the inheritance of God," as He said, "When you have come into the Land of Canaan, which I give you for a possession." Now the reason why this law does not apply outside the Land of Israel is not because it is a requirement that attaches to the ground, but because this matter of divine indication of sins occurs only in the Chosen Land, where the glorious Name dwells.

The house can be polluted only after the conquest and distribution of the Land has been achieved, so that each recognizes *what is his.* The reason is that then they are settled to know God so that His Presence can dwell among them.[3]

Ramban's opening statement is arresting: this physical phenomenon is not a *natural* physical phenomenon. It occurs only in the Land of Israel, and only in the context of a society that is highly attuned to the godly. In such a sensitized environment, any sin manifests as an *aesthetic* blemish. This blotch on skin or clothing or housing indicates a disorder in the spiritual world. Such a situation in which physical symptoms directly indicate spiritual disorder is a unique dispensation, paradoxically a kind of *gift* ("When you come into the Land . . . I shall *give* the plague of *tzora'at*" [Lev. 14:34]).

Ramban emphasizes the connection with the Holy Land, not because of any particular agricultural commandment but because the Chosen Land is the site of God's presence. In this heightened atmosphere, human misdeeds register directly.

Furthermore, he cites *Torat Kohanim* to the effect that *tzora'at* on houses appears only after the Land has been fully conquered and apportioned. Only when "each recognizes what is his," only in a state of *yishuv ha-da'at,* of general social and cultural order, is the individual capable of "knowing God." And only in such a condition can *tzora'at* manifest itself.

In a nation finely tuned to holiness, individual disruptions will register in the aesthetics of skin and clothes and walls. When the baseline of spiritual life is set high, the *tzora'at* phenomenon becomes a privilege; it constitutes a miracle.

ALTERNATIVE SYSTEM OF RATIONALITY?

Ramban here addresses the physical conditions in which a human being lives—the "envelope" of clothing and housing. Since the skin condition of *tzora'at* has the same name, we can assume that his comment here applies to that situation as well. Some underlying spiritual configuration connects all three phenomena. That the problem is not, in the modern sense, purely medical is indicated by many anomalies: the diagnosis is made by a priest; the priest does not measure the blotch or examine private parts of the body; examinations are not done on Shabbat, festivals, or during a bridegroom's seven days of celebration (when he will be most exposed to others, with the heightened danger of infection). Diagnosis is required only in walled towns; the furniture in the house is not cleared out. And, in diagnostic terms most strikingly, if, after a quarantine period, the whole body is affected, the patient is declared *pure:* while if some healthy skin returns, the patient is *impure.* The patient who plucks out signs of *tzora'at* is declared *pure;* and if a healthy spot appears within the blotch, he is *impure!*

Clearly, the fear of infection is not the significant factor in this pathology. Nor does common sense seem to shape the rules of diagnosis. We are faced with a system of classification unlike any other. This is reminiscent of a passage in Jorge Luis Borges's "John Wilkins' Analytical Language," where he refers to a certain Chinese encyclopedia called the *Heavenly Emporium of Benevolent Knowledge:*

> In its distant pages it is written that animals are divided into (a) those that belong to the emperor; (b) embalmed ones; (c) those that are trained; (d) suckling pigs; (e) mermaids; (f) fabulous ones; (g) stray dogs; (h) those that are included in this classification; (i) those that tremble as if they were mad; (j) innumerable ones; (k) those drawn with a very fine camel's-hair brush; (l) etcetera; (m) those that have just broken the flower vase; (n) those that at a distance resemble flies.[4]

Reading Borges, Michel Foucault writes of "the wonder of this taxonomy." We can apprehend not only "the exotic charm of another system of thought" but also "the limitation of our own, the stark impossibility of thinking *that.*"[5] He opens his *The Order of Things* by crediting this passage in Borges with the "laughter that shattered . . . all the familiar landmarks of my thought—*our* thought that bears the stamp of our age and our geography—breaking up all the ordered surfaces and all the planes with which we are accustomed to tame the wild profusion of existing things, and continuing long afterward to disturb and threaten with collapse our age-old distinction between the Same and the Other."

Does such an encyclopedia exist? Did Foucault take it seriously as an alternative system of rationality? Did Borges? The diagnosis and treatment of *tzora'at* evokes such a sense of wonder. Cutting across the body/mind division, as well as the human and inanimate worlds, the *tzora'at* taxonomy, too, threatens with collapse our sense of the Same and the Other.

SLANDER CULTURE

As we have seen, one legal condition of this pathology is that it can occur only after the land of Canaan has been conquered and divided up among individual families, so that "each recognizes what is his own." This sense of being personally stabilized in the geography of the Holy Land is the condition for the individual homeowner to bring his *tzora'at* to the priest. The intimacy of possession is the ground on which blotches become meaningful.

An interesting modern reading is provided by Ha'amek Davar. He goes on the basis of the traditional explanation that *tzora'at* is caused by the sin of slander, *evil speech*. Citing a midrash, he understands the word "Canaan" to refer to the collective of *traders*.[6] He proceeds to develop a psycho-geographical theory: since the Canaanites lived close to the seaboard and carried out extensive trade throughout the Mediterranean lands, a culture of gossip and slander developed; they traveled between countries, competing with one another, talking up their own wares and bad-mouthing their rivals. An aggressive verbal culture is linked to the trafficking mind—unlike the culture of those who work the earth and who have fewer opportunities for exchange and comparison.

In this theory, trading sharpens one's eye and ear for difference, competition, and jealousy. Here, *talk* is the stuff of life, for good or ill. The Holy Land, by virtue of its long seaboard, becomes the scene, for good or ill, of a lively verbal culture.

Geography, economics, and culture interweave. This theory of slander culture creates a different scheme for understanding *tzora'at* from that of the midrash. There, a psychology of being well settled, of *knowing what is one's own,* is the necessary condition for the *tzora'at* on houses. Here, a restless movement between countries and cultures breeds the psychology of slander.

Perhaps the biblical text is describing the moment of tension between two values: stability on the one hand and the agitation of competitive economies on the other. This moment—the seriously ethical moment—cannot happen to either a vagabond, whose life is cut off from all roots, or a taciturn tiller of the ground. This powerful moment arises in the space between a strong sense of identity and an avid involvement with others. In rabbinic language, these are the modalities of the *sea* and the *yishuv,* the settled land.[7] We experience this interface as that between the mercantile and the agricultural. What characterizes the mercantile sea world is *discourse* and its shadow, destructive talk.

THE PEDDLER AND THE SCHOLAR

Here is a classic midrash about a trader and his surprising relation to a Talmudic scholar:

> "This shall be the law of the leper." "Who is the man who desires life?" (Ps. 34:13). This may be compared to the case of a peddler who used to go around the towns in the vicinity of Sepphoris, calling out: "Who wishes to buy the elixir of life?" and drawing great crowds round him.
>
> R. Yannai was sitting and expounding in his room and heard him calling out: "Who desires the elixir of life?" He said, "Come here, and sell it to me!" The peddler answered: "Neither you nor people like you require that which I have to sell!" The Rabbi pressed him, and the peddler came up to him and brought out the book of Psalms and showed him the passage: "Who is the man who desires life?" What is written immediately afterward?—"Keep your tongue from evil, depart from evil and do good." R. Yannai said: "Solomon, too, proclaims, 'Whoever guards his mouth and tongue guards his soul from troubles'" (Prov. 21:23). R. Yannai said: "All my life I have been reading this passage, but did not know how it was to be explained, until this

hawker came and made it clear—"Who is the man who desires life? Keep your tongue from evil."

For the same reason, Moses addressed a warning to Israel, saying to them, "This shall be the law of the *metzora* (leper)"— the law relating to one who gives currency to an evil report (*motzi [shem] ra*).[8]

The peddler who circulates in the towns and proclaims— advertises—his wares finds an unexpected customer. What does R. Yannai need from this peddler when it comes to issues of life and death? The peddler himself is embarrassed. The peddler shows the scholar the text in Psalms that offers the remedy in his advertisement. There, the elixir of life is clearly inscribed for all to read: "Keep your tongue from evil." The Rabbi contributes to this strange conversation another proof text from the book of Proverbs and congratulates the peddler for clarifying a text that had baffled the Rabbi all his life.

What has the peddler hawking his wares—often quack cures, home remedies for every ill ("Who desires life, come and buy!")— contributed to R. Yannai's understanding? One reading suggests that R. Yannai in his humility thinks that the worldly peddler may know of some occupational hazard that threatens scholars like R. Yannai. After first protesting that his remedies are not for the elite, the peddler offers a trenchant diagnosis: those who sit and learn Torah work with language, giving rebuke to those under their care. Constantly judging and criticizing, they may fall into the systemic sin of slander. He advises: "*Keep* your tongue from evil!"—Use of the tongue cannot be banned, since there are good behaviors, even commandments, that involve language. So constant care is needed, in order to speak judiciously, to avoid evil, and to do good in the use of language.[9]

The text in Psalms moves from a general advertisement—"Who is the man who desires life?" to a direct, second-person exhortation to the reader: "Keep your tongue from evil!" The reader—in this case, R. Yannai—is addressed in his particular situation and sensibility. This is no all-purpose home remedy; it demands of the scholar a scrupulous self-awareness. The power of the tongue is to be well deployed, for good and not for evil.[10]

R. Mordecai Yosef Leiner (known as the Mei Ha-Shilo'ach) offers a radical reading of the midrash. He links the word *rochel* (peddler) with *rachil,* the term for one who bears slander: the peddler is essentially peddling gossip. When he realizes that the toxic nature of his speech is barring him from society, he repents, changes his ways, and transforms his experience into a vivid object lesson for others. The full existential meaning of the text from Psalms is revealed to him, so that he is well-placed to teach others.

In R. Mordecai Yosef's reading, the motive of slander is *anger.* A dynamic process is required to transform this anger into *tovat ayin*—generosity of vision.

Under R. Mordecai Yosef's influence, R. Zadok Hacohen, a Lithuanian Talmudic prodigy, was converted to Hasidism. He cites his teacher's reading, subtly inflecting it. In his account, the peddler is "rotten with gossip," totally defined by his occupation of *rechilut,* gossip-bearing. When he repents, he feels the *ta'am,* the *taste/meaning* of the verse from Psalms. On his lips, thereafter, the verse holds that "taste" which R. Yannai now registers for the first time. R. Yannai, in his righteousness, had never "tasted" that flavor of slander. Now, at second hand, he understands the radical meaning of the verse, such that only a penitent could comprehend it.[11]

Taste is a private, largely incommunicable experience. The text from Psalms evokes a gamut of associations in the peddler. The "taste" in his mouth infuses the words of Psalms with these conscious and unconscious associations. His spoken words communicate something of value to R. Yannai.

PUNGENT TASTE

R. Zadok often quotes the Talmudic maxim "One cannot master (lit., stand upon) words of Torah unless one has stumbled over them."[12] The implications of this maxim are more or less subversive, depending on how one paraphrases it: that knowledge cannot be fully appreciated unless one has tried and failed; that darkness must precede light, in order that light may become revelation. Or, more powerfully, that it is the very experience of stumbling that jolts one to new insight. In R. Zadok's thought, a shock, a shattering is necessary to transcend the system of things totally understood.

Under this rubric, paradoxes proliferate. In the divine world order, opposites are dynamically connected. Idolatry and prophecy, for instance, go together. When the stumbling block (idolatry) is removed, prophecy, too, comes to an end.[13] R. Zadok quotes: *zeh l'umat zeh assah ha-elokim.* A sublime order exists, with contraries balancing each other out. But, in the same breath, he introduces a principle of disorder: in all things, including all things human, there exists a confusion of good and evil.

Since good and evil are so thoroughly intermingled, it is precisely in the experience of the *slippage*—of getting it wrong, of being embroiled in the inevitable mixture of good and evil, falsehood and truth—that the theological moment is experienced. The moment of the most vulnerable humanity, when one stumbles over the complexity of things, brings one into greatest intimacy with God.

This is a radical reading of error and understanding. One might call it a psychoanalytic reading: the insight that ego, id, and superego are twined together in the inner life. They produce the particular *ta'am*, the flavor of irreducible personal experience of a complex reality. R. Yannai realizes that the peddler, the penitent slanderer, is full of that pungent taste. Once R. Yannai has heard the peddler reading the text in Psalms, he will read that text with new authenticity. In this way, the scholar comes to understand obliquely what he could never understand directly.

This is the work of the Oral Torah, teaches R. Zadok: when direct revelation is lost, the vital process of interpretation begins. In this new world, "the sage is preferable to the prophet."[14] Human creativity is triggered by the *stumble,* or, in kabbalistic language, by the fragmentary sparks after the Breaking of the Vessels.[15]

It is striking that R. Zadok discusses the fable of the peddler within the context of the narrative of the Golden Calf and the breaking of the Tablets. He also cites a famous midrash about Moses and R. Akiva. Moses has a vision of R. Akiva teaching Torah to his students; Moses finds to his dismay that he cannot understand the Torah R. Akiva teaches. Moses is reassured when R. Akiva later explains his reading to his student by saying: "It is the law as taught to Moses at Sinai!"[16]

Here is played out the paradox of continuity and discontinuity in relation to the Written and the Oral Law. The Oral Law is both Same and Other in relation to Moses's Torah. R. Zadok develops one of his grand themes: Moses, at whose birth the house fills with light, represents the integrity of spiritual being and thus becomes the channel for the direct revelation at Sinai—the Written Torah; while R. Akiva, whose personality is more complex and undergoes transformation, represents both the loss of that lucid revelation and the gift of interpretation of the text—the Oral Torah. The loss and the gift, the good and the evil, endow R. Akiva with the complex "taste" of radical experience. He and those like him continue Moses's Torah after Moses's death.[17]

The issue in both narratives—that of Moses and R. Akiva and that of the peddler and R. Yannai—concerns death and life. "Who is the man who desires life?" Life and death are in the balance for all who hear the question. R. Yannai responds because he needs to find a new reading of the question, one saturated with the *taste,* the flavor of the radical issues implicit in the question. It is a matter of life and death. Similarly, Moses, after the crisis of the Golden Calf, faces the rupture of all he has taught his people. He smashes the Tablets, the mystical wholeness of the stone inscribed with the finger of God. A terrible taboo: what could have inspired him to such an act? In a powerful talmudic midrash, God assures him: *Yishar kochacha she-shibarta!*— "More power to you that you smashed them!"[18] The violent moment of disruption, of radical disorder, should signify the death of the entire project of Exodus. But, as the midrash declares, "sometimes the Torah is confirmed by its undoing."

There is something properly absurd about this claim. The paradox jolts us awake. Like the mastery of Torah depending on failure, on the very experience of the stumble and the recovery. Something new and therefore not yet comprehensible transpires in these jolts. The Golden Calf, for R. Zadok, is a typological event of this kind. And the story of the peddler, idiosyncratic as it is, traces the same trajectory. Steeped in unconscious violence, the peddler speaks evil of others. He reaches bottom and begins a depth process that qualifies him to speak of life.

AN ELITE VALUE

R. Yannai deepens himself as he hears the peddler read the words of Torah. He hears a warning about the professional hazard that threat-

ens scholars and teachers like himself. Without the peddler, he would
have had no access to this insight. Only as inflected by the peddler,
the Psalmist's words reveal R. Yannai to himself.

For the role of scholars is, essentially, *lehavdil u-lehorot*,[19] to make
distinctions, to declare difference. Discriminating between similars
is the very stuff of halachic (Jewish legal) thought. The categories of
pure and impure are informed by a well-honed sense for difference:

> "To distinguish and to instruct": It should say, "[to distinguish]
> between a donkey and a cow." But that difference is already
> quite clear. So it says, "between what is pure *to you* and impure
> *to you*—between an animal that has been slaughtered halfway
> through the gullet and most of the way."[20]

Gross differences require no discrimination. The skill of the
scholar lies precisely in the gray areas where differences are not obvious.[21] For this reason, in the previous verse (Lev. 10:9), drunkenness is
forbidden to the priests, who are to exercise this kind of differentiation. Intoxication blurs the ability to distinguish between sacred and
profane, permitted and forbidden.

This function of *havdalah* (differentiation) comes up in unexpected places:

> Whoever separates from his wife close to the time of her men-
> strual period will have children fit to instruct in the laws of
> differentiation, as it says, "to distinguish and to instruct."[22]

Those who are scrupulous in observing the laws of marital purity
will have children who are capable of differentiating in legal matters.
The reward, that is, for religious fastidiousness is offspring who are
scholars. The reward expresses a continuum of critical sensibility—one
reaps what one sows.

Similarly, one who makes *havdalah* (the ritual of differentiation)
over wine to mark the end of Shabbat and the beginning of the new
week will have children who are capable of sharp intellectual distinctions. The link between the act of *havdalah* and the blessing of
talented children depends solely on the adjacency of texts (11:16/12:1).

In contrast with the idea that sexual scrupulousness is rewarded with scholarly offspring, here the link is more obscure. Uttering words of differentiation is a creative act in itself: speech reorganizes the world. The capacity for *havdalah* becomes an aspiration and a privilege. It represents a high value that constitutes a social and intellectual elite.

KNOWING THE NO

The ability to differentiate, to limit and define parts of the "blooming, buzzing confusion" of experience is what allows all human beings access to what we call reality. Symbolic systems select particular aspects of immediate experience. Kenneth Burke offers a definition of the human being, which begins: "Man is the symbol-using animal, *inventor of the negative* (or perhaps invented by language and the negative), separated from his natural condition by instruments of his own making."[23]

He proceeds to celebrate "that peculiarly human marvel, the negative." He points out that there are no negatives in nature: a table is simply a table, but there are endless things one could say about what it is *not.*

In Burke's thinking, the primary use of the negative is in the form of "Thou shalt not"—as a command. He researches the documents on the training of blind and deaf Helen Keller, for instance: the records show that she was taught the "Don't" form before other forms of language. Laws are essentially negative; "mine" equals "not thine." The ethical personality is infused by negativity. Polar terms like yes-no, true-false, order-disorder, life-death, pure-impure come to be distinguished from purely positive terms. They limit each other. "There is an implied sense of negativity in the ability to use words at all. For to use them properly, we must know that they are *not* the things they stand for." Linguistic subtleties like metaphor and irony, too, are infused with negativity: we must know that the metaphor is *not* literal.[24]

In Freud's terminology, too, "the 'unconscious' process of 'repression' involves the fact that the thou-shalt-not's of the 'superego' would negate the desires of the 'id,' that portion of the 'unconscious' which knows no Negation (or, more resonantly, 'knows no No')."[25] The rules are negative; and so are those movements in art, music, and dance that challenge the rules, in the quest to reinvigorate forms of aesthetic expression. Burke remembers a modern-dance instructor: "How to say good-bye in gestures, if you're not allowed simply to wave good-bye, if you can in fact do anything but that!"[26] Burke's mission is to make "the presence of the No" apparent in a world of hackneyed positives.

Returning to our exploration of the value of *havdalah* in the intellectual and spiritual world of the Rabbis, we note the significance of "knowing the No" in the structures of meaning derived from the biblical text. Models of legal and ethical reality are created by the "wonder of the negative"—from the Garden of Eden to the specific genius, in their own eyes, of the Rabbis themselves: the ability to distinguish between pure and impure, on the one hand, and the ability to cut across boundaries that seem all too obvious, on the other—like those separating the disordered human body from housing and clothing. This double-edged genius—continuity and discontinuity—requires the ability, in all cases, to make a "new cut" in the natural world. It is this ability that constitutes the elite group of the Sages.[27]

THE ANGER OF THE RIGHTEOUS

What, then, does R. Yannai learn from the peddler, this hawker of negative language who has come to negate his negativity? The commentaries we have cited (Anaf Yosef, Mei Ha-Shilo'ach, and Pri Zaddik) imagine an uncanny *similarity* between the great scholar and the hawker of dubious remedies. R. Yannai is brought to realize that each in his own way faces the same dilemma. The scholar represents the use of human language to make significant pure/impure distinctions; the peddler redeems his previously toxic speech. Mei Ha-Shilo'ach suggests that toxic speech is motivated by *anger*: the peddler has become an allegorical figure of anger and verbal malice. He is converted by reflection on his resentment as a spiritual disease. The desire for life and goodness transform him not only behaviorally but in a way that invokes his *nefesh,* his soul. ("Whoever guards his mouth and his tongue guards his *soul* from trouble.")

What has R. Yannai gained from the depth of the peddler's experience? R. Zadok carries the question to its radical edge. R. Yannai gains a profound sense of the place where the peddler's inner life meets his own. What is communicated "underground" is the *ta'am*—the taste, the meaning, the flavor—of a checkered inner life.

The *ta'am* of a text, the inflection lent it by one who has been compelled to engage with his own disorders, ironically deepens the understanding of the righteous scholar. "All my life," he says, "I have been reading this text, but I did not know *heichan hu pashut* (lit., where it is stretched out, flattened, plain)." R. Yannai describes the paradox—the class reversal—of the scholar who learns from the peddler, the righteous man who learns from the sinner. What he was looking for all his life was the radical, pungent flavor of the text.

This midrash, then, is a text about basic human impulses—anger, hostility, and their expression in language. Of course, this primal "taste" has found a way of redeeming itself. Transformed, the peddler lives to perform his story. But the happy ending is not in itself the point. R. Zadok is interested in failure, in negativity, in fundamental human lacks. In this narrative, without the sin there can be no redemption. The taste of an *earthy* transformation affects R. Yannai in his own life with language.

What we are not told is *how* the transformation is achieved. But in R. Zadok's thinking, the radical experience of *stumbling-standing*, of "bringing forth the precious from the vile,"[28] becomes a major theme. He cites the prophet Jeremiah on the dynamic of repentance: "If you bring forth the precious out of the vile, *you shall be as My mouth*"; the prophet is urged to refine his inner world, to extract pure from impure, the gold from the dross. No dross, no gold. Then, he will become God's mouthpiece.

As this verse is used in Hasidic teachings (particularly by Mei Ha-Shilo'ach and R. Zadok), it articulates the necessity of confronting the "vile," the repressed layers of human experience. "There is no possibility of standing, of understanding the words of Torah, unless one has stumbled in them, over them."[29]

By this measure, R. Yannai needs the invigoration of the peddler's life taste. For his own professional expertise is suffused by an implicit—or even an explicit—negativity. Critical, analytic, compelled by a quasi-positive vision of purity, repelled by impurity, the righteous Sage may harbor repressed anger.

In a powerful passage on *tzora'at,* the Mei Ha-Shilo'ach speaks of the anger of the righteous.[30] He cites the Zohar, which treats anger as the occupational hazard of *adam*—the superior person, who is largely immune to worldly temptation. Such people, he claims, are prone to anger. In some radical sense, the world irritates them; since physical pleasure means little to them, they can find no gratification in the world. Such people need to cultivate a generosity of vision (*tovat ayin*) that offers healing for anger.

DESOLATE SHALL HE STAY. . . .

Tzora'at is the paradigm case of the way a psychic dis-ease emerges in physical symptoms. What is needed is *birur*. In Hasidic texts, particularly those emerging from the Mei Ha-Shilo'ach and his offspring, this legal term, which means clarification, going to the roots of a problem, analysis, takes on a psychological, spiritual valence. The symptom thus represents an opportunity for essential work.

If we assume that *tzora'at* is a symptom of a psychic disorder, what is the process of diagnosis and treatment? The description in Leviticus 13:1–43 is concerned with the particulars of diagnosis, with the color, size, hairiness, location of the skin disease. In certain cases, the diagnosis is clear and the priest declares the patient either pure or impure. In other cases, the situation is unclear and the patient is isolated—*hesger*—for seven days outside the camp. Reexamined, the patient may be declared pure, impure, or requiring another quarantine period. After another seven days, he is again examined and given the final diagnosis—pure or impure.

We notice that here the binary position of *pure/impure,* which for Burke is suffused with negativity, is complicated by the *perhaps* position, the probationary period in which symptoms are given time to develop either way.

The diagnosed *metzora* is isolated outside all three circles of the camp (priests, Levites, and Israelites). Unlike other cases of impurity, he is isolated even from other sufferers of the same kind:

"And the 'leper' who has the affliction—his clothes shall be tattered and his hair shall be wild and he shall cover over his lip. And *Impure! Impure!* he shall cry. All the days that the affliction is upon him he shall be impure—impure he is. Desolate he shall stay, outside the camp shall be his dwelling." (Lev. 13:45–46)

Already rendered unsightly by his skin disease, his tattered clothes, wild hair, and covered mouth (perhaps a head covering that extends to his mouth) make him an object of revulsion—if there were any observers to be repulsed. He becomes an object of negative sociability: a kind of embodiment of the Other whose appearance, while recognizably human, helplessly proclaims his otherness.

The word that the Torah uses to describe this state is *badad*—alone. This is an unusual term for aloneness,[31] sometimes paired with *yeshev*—"he shall dwell in isolation"; sometimes, it is associated with security, freedom from attack. The singular quality of this aloneness is *separation,* a lone-wolf existence. The covered lip conveys speechlessness, mourning. This impression is reinforced by the singular form of *safam*—as though the two lips are sealed together.

The diagnosed "leper" enacts his own toxic relation to the world:

"Desolate shall he stay": Because no other impure people stay with him. Our Rabbis said: Why is he differentiated from other impure people to stay alone? Since he set husband and wife, and friends apart from each other, so shall he be set apart.[32]

His total isolation evokes the effect of his slander on others. Stigmatizing others, he has exploited the implicitly negative power of language to differentiate, define, isolate. What the "leper" has done is inscribed in his body, on his skin, in the one word that he cries out repeatedly: *Tamei! Tamei!* His slander or gossip (even if true) has divided couples and friends; its effect has been to make intimates feel repulsion for each other; its motive may be a kind of anger at the happy connections of others, and its temptation may be the momentary illusion of identification with those who listen to his slander. A pseudosocial bond is set up by the sheer exclusion of the slandered other. Now, the slanderer has himself become the other, ostracized, his exclusion perhaps feeding a similar instinct of solidarity in the society from which he is expelled.

It is striking that the biblical text enacts the same ostracizing power of language by simply repeating the word *tamei:* three times in the priest's diagnosis in verse 44, twice more in the leper's cry, and twice more in the voice of the narrator—all together seven times in three verses. There is an incantatory, performative power to the word, which conveys the effect of the leper's toxic use of language. In this state, he remains—closed off (*musgar*—in temporary quarantine, or finally diagnosed), until his condition is healed.

There are two moments in the description of his isolation that particularly resonate in their poignancy: the *badad* condition in which he dwells, and the calling out of *tamei! tamei!*

The state of *badad* strikes the keynote of the book of Lamentations: *Eichah yashvah badad*—"How she sits *lonely*, the many-peopled city." Exploring its resonances, we find Rashi's striking translation: "*deprived* (*galmud*) of her inhabitants." *Galmud* has dense associations: menstruous, lonely, weaned/separated from her husband, like a *shapeless, lifeless lump*.[33] An extraordinary midrash on the same text transfers the desolation to God:

> "How she sits lonely." R. Alexander said, "I am wakeful; I am like a lone bird upon a roof" (Ps. 102:8).
>
> God said, "I am wakeful" to rest My presence in the Holy Temple forever. "I am like a lone bird"—just as this bird, when her goslings are taken from her, sits lonely, so I have burned My House and destroyed My city, and exiled My children among the idolaters, so I sit lonely" as it is written, "How she sits lonely."[34]

God becomes the subject of the *badad* description of the stripped city. Like a lonely bird deprived of her goslings, God stays close to the Holy Temple, bewailing the loss of His Temple, His city, and His children. The pathos of the simile is complicated when God reveals that He is the destroyer of His own place in the world. In a surrealistic move, the mourning bird becomes the source of His own undoing. Both victim and aggressor, He gathers into Himself all the resonances of lamentation.

God haunts the scene of loss, even as vital expressions of His being-in-the-world are stripped away. This is a moment of rueful divine reflection. Lonely on the rooftop, the Shechinah-bird is the subject of desolation.

The word *badad*, with its fraught later meanings in Psalms and Lamentations, sheds those meanings back onto its earliest appearance in the laws of the leper. This first use of *badad* enfolds within itself implications that will later unfold. The *Metzora* evokes divine potential come to ruin, the subject of a reflective desolation.

ASKING FOR COMPASSION

What has placed the leper in this desolate *badad* condition? Technically, it is the priest who alone is qualified to diagnose the disease. Even if the priest is no expert (child or imbecile), he alone has the power to examine and to utter the diagnosis. The expert stands beside him and instructs him, "Say *Pure!* "Say *Impure!* Say "Place him in quarantine!" and he obeys.[35] The performative power of language is enacted. The one who knows instructs the one who speaks; and the status of the patient becomes a reality.

In the early stages of diagnosis, the third possibility of *hesger*—quarantine—breaks the binary mode: Yes—No—*Maybe*. Being "closed off" indicates a state of not-yet-knowing—a probationary period while the situation remains undecided. This "closed-off" state, however, is evoked in the very name of the disease. *Tzora'at* is translated in Aramaic by *segiru*. Locked in, the sufferer lives in a state of suspended animation. His pathology represents an interruption of life, a kind of limbo, of not-yet-knowing what to think or what to say, of being engrossed, bewildered.[36] In this limbo condition, a space is made for the Real—that which resists definition. However, even this limbo condition is constructed by the word of the priest.

The patient's situation is passive (as is implicit in the word *patient*). But once he has been isolated and "treated"—tattered clothes, wild hair, lip covered—he comes uncannily alive: "*Tamei! Tamei!* (Impure! Impure!) he shall call out." In his one moment of agency, he declares his own condition—one powerful word. The obvious meaning of this is, as Rashi explains it, to warn others to keep away from him. Here, we remember Kenneth Burke's observation about the primary use of the negative to convey, *Thou shalt not!* The word creates a limitation, a difference.

He is not, for instance, calling *others* impure; he is protecting others from infection by naming himself. This might be an example of what Burke calls a *quasi-positive,* like *This is mine!* Which means *This is not yours!* Where he had so often spoken to isolate others from society, the leper now speaks to isolate himself from society. His divisive power of language is turned, like a leper's bell, to protect others from himself.

Here, it is the patient who isolates himself in the *badad* state. It is the impurity itself that cries out, "Keep away!"

R. Simeon ben Pazzi said: Where is an indication in the Torah that gravesides should be marked? "If one sees a human bone, one should set up a sign by it" (Ezek. 39:15). R. Abbahu suggested that it may be derived from the leper text: *"Tamei! Tamei!* he shall cry." The impurity cries out and warns others to separate from him.[37]

The leper gives voice to his own impurity, in order to protect others. But on the same page in the Talmud, another reading is offered:

> This teaches that he should publicly proclaim his suffering, so that the public ask for mercy for him.

The cry of the leper communicates, not the public health hazard he represents but his sheer pain. In this reading, it is a religious requirement to affect others, so that they will pray for him in his suffering. His desolation creates a connection with others whose compassion is stirred. In terms of modern brain research, we might think of *mirror neurons,* which fire both when one is suffering pain and when one watches someone else suffering. This phenomenon has been credited as the basis for human empathy. It is also associated with the ability to attribute intention to others. In the case of the leper, the Talmud suggests that his crying out (unconsciously) *intends* to provoke others to prayer.

The cry of the sufferer interrupts, appeals, demands. The one who hears him *must* ask for compassion. This is an ethical moment. Whether or not neurons are at work, the moment assumes the reality of com-passion—suffering *with* the other who is apart from him.

The second verse in Lamentations comes to mind: "Bitterly she weeps in the night." Disconsolate, Jerusalem is imagined as a woman crying at night. Why at night?

> Because one who cries at night, his voice is heard. Another interpretation: one who cries in the night, the stars and planets

cry with him. Another interpretation: anyone who hears his cry cries in sympathy.

It happened that the child of a neighbor of R. Gamaliel died, and she was weeping for him at night. R. Gamaliel heard her and wept in sympathy until his eyelashes fell out. The next day, his disciples realized this and removed her from his neighborhood.[38]

A cry in the night pierces the body defenses of the other—eyes flow and eyelashes fall out. On this primal level, R. Gamaliel's students have to rally to defend their teacher who is assailed so mercilessly by the weeping voice. But the range of the sympathetic world widens to include stars and planets, heaven and earth, mountains and hills, ministering angels and God Himself. These forms of otherness—why should they cry for the unseen one whose friends have abandoned him? The human voice in pain, impersonal yet intimate, can arouse to tears the coldest star in the heavens.

These images are examples of what is called the *pathetic fallacy*—the attribution of feeling to objects in nature. Although such attributions are a fallacy, they command great intensity. There is a world in which all barriers fall before the cry of the sufferer. It is striking that the human being who cries in sympathy is said to be crying *kenegdo* (in sympathy, in response) and not, as in the earlier examples, *immo* (with him). This is not simply empathy: the disembodied voice creates a "neurological" connection with the body of the listener. As with the phenomenon of mirror neurons, seeing or hearing the suffering Other causes hormonal changes in the body and emotions of the perceiver.[39] Our attention moves—even the sentence structure rather awkwardly suggests this—between the two subjects, separated by space and time.

The voice of the *badad* condition strikes a common chord with remote others. Moreover, the leper *should* proclaim his pain in public, so that the many (*rabbim*) will hear and ask for compassion. The public sphere is strangely re-created in this uncanny scene. The leper does not ask for compassion, but he knows there is a world of others who will respond by themselves asking for divine compassion.

Where is com-passion primally experienced? The Hebrew word

rachamim (compassion) holds the womb at its core (*rechem*). A world of connectedness is imagined as a *matrixial* condition. As Bracha Ettinger writes, "This compassion is primary; it starts before, and always also beyond, any possibility of empathy that entails understanding, before any economy of exchange, before any cognition or recognition, before any reactive forgiveness or integrative reparation."[40]

THE POSITION OF PRAYER

From a very different context, here is another example of the rabbinic use of this concept of asking for compassion: "No vegetation of the field was yet in the earth and no grasses of the field had yet sprouted, because the Lord God had not sent rain upon the earth and there was no man to till the soil":

> R. Assi pointed out a contradiction between verses. One verse says: And the earth brought forth grass (Gen. 1:12—referring to the third day of Creation), whereas another verse, when speaking of the sixth day, says: No vegetation of the field was yet in the earth (2:5). This teaches us that the plants commenced to grow but stopped just as they were about to break through the soil, until Adam came and *asked for compassion for them;* and when rain fell they sprouted forth. This teaches you that the Holy One longs for the prayers of the righteous.[41]

Rashi presents an edited version of this Talmudic passage. In his text, he traces an elaborate causal chain. On the sixth day, when Creation is complete except for the human being, vegetation has failed to appear. More accurately, as Rashi emphasizes, it has *not yet* appeared (*terem*)—and this despite God's command on the third day, "Let the earth bring forth vegetation"—which was apparently immediately fulfilled: "And the earth brought forth grass." Did the earth obey or did it not? This is a moment of religious significance; something has stalled in the seamless Creation narrative of *"And He said . . . and it was."* It turns out that the earth did obey but stalled the green growth just under the earth-surface. In other words, there is an interruption in the organic fulfillment of God's will.

The reason for this, Rashi continues, is that there is no rain. Why?

Because there is no human being to recognize the need for something that is *not-yet*. Only when Adam is created can he *"till the earth."* In his first religious act, he recognizes the glitch in nature, the crack in the cup—and responds by praying for rain. His human achievement is to recognize the tragic gaps between God's will and reality—and to work. (The word for *tilling—la'avod*—is read in a different register as *serving, praying*).

Human prayer is the response to the moment when the stalled world calls out to the human being in its insufficiency and its possibility. Rashi reads the negatives—the *ayin* ("The human *was not*") and the *terem* (*not-yet*) and the *lo* (*no* rain)—as provocations of desire. The chain of negatives arouses human longing for a different kind of linking. The first human act is a religious act, a prayer, which responds to the insufficiency of the world. For the sake of this act, the biblical text then describes the vapor that rises up from the watery depths, seeds the clouds, and causes the first downpour. All this, says Rashi, for the sake of the *creation of the human*—for the sake of the divine physical creation from the mud of the earth, and also for the sake of the creation of the human act of prayer, which is necessary to repair the world.

The story Rashi tells creates links between the separate moments described in Genesis 2:5–7. Everything tends toward a purpose: the physical creation of Adam and the spiritual moment of his prayer. The teleological thrust of the passage is implicit in Rashi's retelling of the biblical story. But what precisely is the purpose? Is it the growth of vegetation, or is it the prayer that brings it about? The focus in Rashi is probably on the former moment: Adam's creation and prayer bring about the ultimate purpose—growth of vegetation.

However, if we look again at the Talmudic passage, we read simply: the grass grows and waits at the entrance to the earth until Adam comes and *asks for compassion* for it. The rain falls and the grass grows, *to teach you that God desires the prayers of the righteous*. Here, the narrative is unequivocal: the purpose of the whole story is Adam's prayer. The apparent failure of the vegetation to appear is a ruse to arouse Adam to *ask for compassion*. The story ends with a theological comment on God's desire. The rest of the story is instrumental in achieving the divine desire.

One might almost call this an *anti-teleological* narrative. The story ends with the satisfaction of no human protagonist; for that, there will have to be rain. Rather, the divine disturbs the natural thrust of the human story with His unknown desire, and *its* satisfaction. Human purposes are instrumental to another plot ending, of which the human being may or may not be aware. The stability of a teleological narrative with all the arrows pointing to the happy ending is undermined when the story ends with a prayer rather than with the rain.

This is a story about God's desire for the moment of *bakashat rachamim:* when a human being *asks for compassion.* Here, we return to the midrash about the cry of the leper and the response of those who hear it. The expression implies that the human being asks, not for a *thing* (e.g., for rain, or for the healing of the leper) but for a *non-thing—rachamim.* "Com-passion arises in the matrixial embrace experienced in, and symbolized by, the womb. Com-passion is a connectedness that is also a kind of border crossing, and it is the source of responsibility and care."[42]

Before and beyond words, this *rachamim* is generated in a womb-like state of "passive vulnerability." One cries out and the other is passionately responsive. The voice of prayer acts like a touch: in the womb, "borders can be crossed without being removed entirely . . . 'I' and 'non-I' are always linked in the matrixial."[43] To ask for compassion is to be possessed by this connection-in-difference.

This "matrixial" state is experienced as vulnerable, even helpless. Both Adam in a dry world and the leper disconnected from the vital energies that hold the social world together discover this state. *Rachamim* evokes not only the womb but its linkage with the breast that suckles and nurtures life. It is striking that in rabbinic Hebrew the verb *rachem*—to have compassion—becomes the technical expression for suckling in animal and human life. It is used without self-consciousness, as a concrete analogue to its metaphorical usage as compassion. Without this instinctual movement of active interlacing of mother and child, the world could not continue. Perhaps something like this is also true of the human and the divine in the position of prayer. In Aramaic translation, the *rachem* root represents, simply, love.

ANGER AND COMPASSION

For the leper locked into his isolation, others suddenly become available in a new relation. They ask for compassion for him. Where they once were part of his suffering, seeing him, examining him, labeling him, they now become a resource. The pain that he suffers is both physical and social: "[H]e is in pain and, moreover, others see that he is in pain."[44] The gaze of others has a tactile, bruising quality. But now, there is no scrutiny, no exposure to the gaze of others; rather, there is a voice that touches off a new world of com-passion.

An implicit therapeutic process is under way. If it is anger that motivates slander, this is a syndrome to which the great and noble are prone. Moses, Aaron, and Miriam, the three leaders, all experience the skin disease and all are implicated, in midrashic sources, in the sin of slander. As we have noticed, Mei Ha-Shilo'ach discusses Moses's anger with an ungratifying world. Healing for this kind of anger, he says, lies in cultivating *tovat ayin*—a different, generous way of looking at others.[45] We might say that this would be a "matrixial" gaze, which would be more like a tactile than a visual experience. It would be created by *rachamim* and aroused by the cry of the other to recognize a shared world of vulnerability. Prayer would be the spontaneous expression of this state, connecting the matrix to its source. Such a state would become its own gratification: the fulfillment of divine desire.

The movement between anger and compassion is discussed by the Mei Ha-Shilo'ach in other places, too.[46] It becomes a kind of notation for the problem of the individual in a world of otherness. There is a natural anger—for instance, that of the father against his rebellious son—but there is also parental compassion, which God has implanted primordially in the human heart and which is aroused precisely by anger's intensity. A similar dynamic obtains theologically. Divine compassion is primary, but it can only be aroused by its working within the human heart; God is the source, but His compassion can only be imagined and activated from within the matrix of human experience.

That anger sometimes finds psychosomatic expression in skin ailments is now generally recognized. Intolerable conflicts beset the human being, the ensouled body in a world of others. These characterize even—or especially—the *adam*, the evolved spiritual personality, with whom this section of the Torah begins (Lev. 13:2).

The smooth continuity of the skin *breaks up, breaks out*. Something about the phenomenon calls out for recognition. When the vapor rises from the depths in the Creation story (Gen. 2:6), this generates a midrashic meditation on the linkage between heaven and earth. Rain from above responds to the mist rising from below. "Deep calls unto deep" (Ps. 42:8)—above and below; male and female, separate parts of a whole that respond to one another. The vapor—*eid*—that rises up is read as a *shever,* a brokenness in the earth. This *shever* becomes the source of moisture for the whole earth-surface.

Psychologically and spiritually, places of breakdown both endanger and enliven the surfaces of things. In a state of finitude, longing is aroused; depths are stirred; a cry connects with another cry; the one apart senses the whole of which (s)he is a part.

In one midrashic story, the skin, in its impurity, cries, "Keep away!" In another, it cries out to awaken the com-passion in others; a vibration is set up that spreads from center to rim and back.

Paul Ricoeur notes the way in which negation "steal(s) into the heart of the experience of finitude," in the form of lack or need, regret, impatience, anguish. But he then posits the existence of a countermovement, which he calls *de-negation*—the negation of a past negation.

A conversion experience, for instance, is described as a hidden affirmation: "I repudiate a past of myself only because I assume another past . . . I am aware of liberating in myself what remained inhibited, refused, impeded." The turn to the future leads to regarding a decision as a *project*. Value is not merely, as Sartre asserts, a lack, a hole, "which I hollow out before me and which I fill by acts, in the sense in which one fulfills a wish . . ." Value also includes an affirmation of being.

Sartre quotes Camus: "In every act of rebellion, man experiences not only a feeling of revulsion at the infringement of his rights, but also a complete and spontaneous adhesion to a certain part of himself." But Ricoeur adds: "Shall we say that the object of adhesion is precisely what does not exist, since that part of himself which the slave raises before the master has no place in this world?" In other words, it is the act of rebellion that imaginatively, affirmatively, creates that "certain part of himself" that is brought into being by it.

One can, moreover, discern "the nucleus of affirmation shrouded in anger . . . *in fact* one can always find an affirmation implicit to the most virulent negations of consciousness."[47] For Ricoeur, it would *in fact* be true to say that anger holds compassion as a nucleus within it. The sense of nothingness holds at its heart a potential for negating that nothingness. Instead of Burke's *quasi-positives,* we are presented with Ricoeur's conversion experience in which hidden affirmations are couched within the crisis of negation.

In terms of the leper's therapeutic process, this would suggest that within the rupture of anger and slander there lies a possible further rupture: the cry *Impure! Impure!* that creates the "matrixial" world of com-passion with another. This structure would exemplify R. Zadok's paradox: "One does not master words of Torah unless one has stumbled over them." It would shed light on the notion of "bringing forth the precious from the vile" (Jer. 15:19).

STRUGGLE FOR LIFE

Two Hasidic sources elaborate on the dynamic of anger and compassion, separateness and oneness. Here is the Sefat Emet:

> In the midrash, we read, *Metzora* means *motzi ra*—one who utters evil speech. For in every thing there is a mixture of good and evil, and so in the human being. Nevertheless, in as much as one is connected with the root of things, good prevails over evil, since good preponderates. But one should be careful not to extract the evil from the general context. So it is written: "Guard your tongue from evil. . . . Seek peace. . . ." This is to subsume evil to the wholeness of things. So it is written in the purification of the leper: "Two *living* birds . . . *living* water." Every thing is to return and adhere to the root of life. And from this position within the wholeness, evil can be healed.[48]

Two opposing ideas are presented here. In a classic midrashic wordplay, the *metzora* is defined as one who "brings forth evil from his mouth." After this "headline," Sefat Emet then proceeds to cite another classic kabbalistic idea: that in every thing—and in every human being—good and evil are mixed together. On the other hand, the power of the good in the human being can prevail over the evil.

The uneasy mixture of good and evil, however, should not be filtered of its evil elements. Extracting the evil will not allow the evil to be transformed; it must find its place within the mixture, within the *klal,* the wholeness of things. "Seek wholeness (*shalom*) even while turning aside from evil."

The paradox is poetically rendered. The act of *motzi*—the act of bringing forth—is toxic: it constitutes evil speech, and it refers to "extracting the evil from the whole." This act of differentiating, isolating the part from the whole, is dangerous. *Guarding* one's tongue from evil means preserving some sort of inner connection between the evil and the larger context, which is called the *klal*—the dynamic ecology of the inner world. Only in that context, where the aim is to restore vitality to the organism (the live birds and the living water), can the evil elements be healed.

This is a struggle for life. The sense of being held within the embrace of life—or, in the other meaning of *klal,* of social concern—can restore the slanderer to health. (We remember the wicked son on Passover night, who is castigated for "removing himself from the *klal.*") Placing oneself outside the group, one may achieve a certain objectivity: one can analyze positive and negative elements, isolating them from one another; one can see the whole picture. However, the price for such isolation is high: one loses the sense of one's implication in what one observes. Ideally, one would want a judicious balance of the two perspectives, external and internal. The therapeutic process of the leper involves naming his disease, isolating it, proclaiming it, both to warn others off and to create a new place for himself in the embrace of life.

IN PRAISE OF IMPURITY

In *The Periodic Table,* Primo Levi offers his professional/biographical account of his life as a young chemistry student. He writes of the process of preparing zinc sulfate:

> [T]he so tender and delicate zinc, so yielding to acid which gulps it down in a single mouthful, behaves, however, in a very different fashion when it is very pure: then it obstinately resists the attack. One could draw from this two conflicting philo-

sophical conclusions: the praise of purity, which protects from evil like a coat of mail; the praise of impurity, which gives rise to changes, in other words, to life. . . . In order . . . for life to be lived, impurities are needed, and the impurities of impurities in the soil, too, as is known, if it is to be fertile.[49]

With his characteristic gentle irony, Levi chooses to praise impurity. Indeed, as he later admits, he views himself, in his Jewishness, as the impurity "that makes the zinc react . . . I am the grain of salt or mustard." In those years of growing Italian fascism, Levi feels a perverse pride in being impure. The volatile reactions of the impure zinc create drama: the zinc wakes up, there is enchantment.

Levi's point, however playfully expressed, is a serious one. Apparent weakness, the impurity of the zinc, generates a sense of life. He is different, isolated from others. Not even Rita, the woman who attracts him in the lab with her equivalent isolation, turns out to be like him. The attraction between two isolates leaves him feeling as alone as ever. But alive, or at least moderately so. A victory is celebrated over the death that awaits.

There is a profoundly Jewish intuition in Levi's meditation on impurity. The skin disease of *tzora'at* is repulsive, but it contains a potential for deepening life. This can be done only by allowing it to take hold, to be fully experienced in all its ugly implications— the isolation, the failure of language, the abandonment of and by others.

From this personal catastrophe, a different kind of connection with others emerges, "bringing forth the precious from the vile" (Jer. 15:19). As we have seen, R. Zadok likes to quote this verse. This is the art of the metal refiner, extracting the ore from the dross. From the generally mixed state of good and evil, it is possible to isolate and extract the good.

However, R. Zadok is not offering a sterile redemption. Like Sefat Emet, he believes that all things human are mixed. It is the vile, the impure that, in transformation, exhilarates. Or, to return to his other characteristic paradox: It is the one who stumbles who learns to stand. The peddler will never be like R. Yannai, but R. Yannai will learn something idiosyncratic, of impure pedigree, from the peddler.

THE GOOD SPOT

In what he regarded as his most important teaching,[50] R. Nahman takes us through his own process of despair and healing. He begins with the general ethical teaching that one should judge all people, even the truly wicked, favorably. One is obliged to find an iota of goodness, even in such a person. He cites a verse from Psalms, which he reads powerfully: "And yet, in a little while—*od me'at*—the wicked is no more. You will look well at his place, and he is not."[51] Seeking and finding the iota of goodness, the *od me'at*, which R. Nahman calls the *good spot*, brings about a kind of chemical enchantment: the wickedness disappears. A generous vision inspires this quest to transform reality: For how is it possible that there should not be such a good spot, even in the wicked? Then, you look well at him and realize that he is no longer—in the same place.

Only now, R. Nahman turns to his true subject: the duty to seek and find a good spot *in oneself*. This at first seems a hopeless mission: one is full of sin, and still more, sunk in melancholy, which poses the greatest spiritual danger. One searches for and finds a single good act, only to realize that when one looks closely it, too, is infested with ego. One knows oneself too well for illusion. *Nevertheless*—R. Nahman finds many different synonyms for *nevertheless*—in spite of everything, how is it possible that there should not be one iota of real goodness in oneself?

R. Nahman's imagery evokes the skin condition of the *metzora*. Not a healthy spot. But one must look well: the good spot must be found. For it is a religious duty to restore oneself to life and joy. Finding the healthy spot brings one out of the gloom of generalized guilt. Ironically, with the model of the *metzora* in mind, we remember that finding a healthy spot determines the diagnosis of *impurity*! Only in this way can the process of repentance become possible. Working to discover the good spot, one creates oneself anew.

However, R. Nahman, too, believes that good and evil are mixed in every human being. So there can be no purely good spot. *Nevertheless*, he repeats, one can bring it forth from the mixture.

We notice that R. Nahman advocates extracting the good from the mixture, rather than the bad. *How is it possible that there should not be such a good spot?* The question is at the heart of the passage. A double negative, a de-negation, as Paul Ricoeur terms it. Even if it is only a spot, mathematically without dimension, a merely theoretical possibility, it has transformative power. The keyword is *nevertheless:* against negation ("There is nothing unmixed in this world"), it affirms the experience of a "complete and spontaneous adhesion to a certain part" of oneself. But that part of oneself, Ricoeur asks, *does it exist?* It has no place in this world. It is not a matter of factual being, but of a value—the affirmation of an "I am," which means "I have worth."[52]

In the last section of this teaching, R. Nahman moves in on his most striking image. Collecting, gleaning (*leket*) one good spot, and then another—*od me'at*—one creates a *niggun,* a melody. Melodies are composed, graphically, of black dots that unexpectedly sing. Sacred music, as he calls it, is a matter of *gleaning,* separating out the healthy from the depressed strands of the self: in mystical language, it is a process of *birur ha-tov min ha-ra*—identifying the good from within the evil.

The focus on the good spot is a creative process that allows the line of melody to emerge from chaos. But the chaos of good and evil is the place from which the music begins. It leaves a certain taste in the melody.

This is R. Nahman's personal description, his prescription for spiritual despair. At its deepest, he says, this condition isolates the sufferer to the point where prayer becomes impossible ("He cannot even open his mouth"). Sealed apart, like the leper, he must *nevertheless* find that iota that remains alive—his *od me'at.* This is a residual atom of life and joy, especially when it generates a larger melody. "Then, he can pray, and sing, and give thanks to God!"

The story that R. Nahman tells is highly personal. Within his own life as spiritual leader, he gleans the essential narrative. Song and prayer require the isolation of the part from the whole. It is the good part that needs to be imaginatively sought out, though it seems nonexistent. From this dimension of the *od me'at,* the minuscule residue, a new whole, musical dots in time, emerges. The thread of melody makes one into a musician, who can lead others in prayer. As R. Nahman hauntingly puts it, the good iotas long for him! He recognizes "his" notes in others, and their need for him. He can identify these yearnings and offer them a new *klal*—a matrix of life.

"LIFE COMES BACK TO LIFE"

The story begins with anger, and isolation, and sadness, and slander. Of course, before that beginning there must have been some radical loss. The infant-mother matrix remains only as an unremembered but sometimes recognized fantasy. For R. Nahman, working with that fantasy reopens the silenced mouth of the slanderer. This work is a religious duty equivalent to saving a life. It prepares the ground for prayer.

In his introduction to *The Essential Loewald,* Jonathan Lear articulates how, in the psychoanalytic process, the language of the patient can be reinvigorated. He returns to the infant's entry into language, which "will be one of the greatest, if not the greatest, developmental achievement of her lifetime." This emerges out of the "loving matrix" of the infant-mother world. How does this process happen?

Summarizing Hans Loewald's approach, he first rejects the familiar view: that the child experiences objects and is then taught to assign names to those objects. "On this picture, language acquisition is an addition: the child acquires language by learning how names are *added on* to objects. But, then, how does this 'adding on' occur? How can one get two things—an object and a name—to relate to each other?" How do words "stick" to things? A word is just an uttered sound that is heard: Why is it not experienced merely as a thing? And how can one ever bring these two things—object and word—together to create meaning?

Lear reframes the situation:

> The infant is bathed in sounds and smells and sights and feels. "Words here are," as Lowald puts it, "indistinguishable ingredients of global states of affairs." In this situation there can be no question of how words attach to things: there are not yet "things" for words to attach onto. Rather, the question is: how do certain sounds *separate themselves out* so that they become experienced by the child as words? The achievement of linguistic understanding is not the *addition* of language onto an already-given world, it is the *differentiation* of a global field into an experience of language and world. To put it paradoxically, words become "attached" to things by differentiating them-

selves from them. The "connection" of language to world is in fact a kind of separation from it—the kind of separation-in-connectedness we call integration.[53]

In cases where this process of differentiation and integration has failed, "words lose their emotional charge." Psychoanalysis is a response to this manifestation of the death drive: "the *recreation of a loving-field* in which processes of growth and differentiation can resume" (my emphasis). Words again become fraught with possibility. Like the impure zinc that Primo Levi celebrates, interaction with other things can resume. "Words can take on an instinctual intensity." We can play with fantasies and emotions that have now become conscious.

One sentence in this essay is particularly resonant: "Words come back to life and *life comes back to life*."[54] As in R. Nahman's teaching, the struggle is for *life.* The work requires differentiation (the good spot) and integration (the melody). Then, a kind of magic (Lear), or enchantment (Primo Levi) can occur.

THE LOVING-FIELD

"The recreation of a loving-field": for Lear, this is the project of psychoanalysis. The loving-field—what a strange linkage!—has to be *re*-created. For Lear and Loewald, this once existed in the matrixial embrace of mother-and-infant.

In the context of this essay, the expression "loving-field" evokes the "field" of the world before Adam's creation: "No vegetation of the field had yet emerged." This field is in a state of *not-yet,* anticipating the greening that is yet to happen. But the word *siach* (vegetation), too, evokes chains of association:

"All the vegetation (*siach*) of the field": All the trees speak to one another, as it were. All the trees speak to human beings, as it were. All the trees were created for the benefit of human beings. . . . All the discourse—*siach* (prayer)—of human beings is about the earth: O Lord, let the earth produce good harvest! O Lord, let the earth thrive! All Israel's prayers are about the Holy Temple: O Lord, when will the Temple be rebuilt?[55]

Siach refers both to vegetation and to language. What has not yet come into the world is the subject of human discourse about the field, specifically the trees of the field. Human discourse is primally concerned with the economics of daily existence: Have the trees borne fruit? Has the wind destroyed the harvest? Is there sufficient foliage to provide shelter? But first, the trees themselves, as it were, talk to one another: leafy branches sway and rustle in the wind. This is discourse in its mythic animistic form: the life force in nature as an ongoing conversation. Recent forestry studies indicate the existence of nonmetaphorical forms of communication.[56]

Ultimately, there is *siach* as prayer.[57] This, too, is basically about the earth, and its products, and the human need for subsistence. On a different level, prayer is concerned with the Holy Temple, which is also called a field.[58] This is the most spiritually evolved form of human discourse.

This extraordinary midrash focuses the material imagination on the "field" of forces from which language emerges. A field, in the cognitive sense, is a "region in which a body experiences a force as the result of the presence of some other body or bodies. A field is thus a method of representing the way in which bodies are able to influence each other."[59]

We remember Lear's description of psychoanalysis as "the *recreation of a loving-field,* in which processes of growth and differentiation can resume." Against the death drive, there arises the sense of living within a field in which bodies influence each other. Such a field is created by the society of trees, by the society of human beings and trees, and by the society of human beings and God. In all these fields, language is the force through which bodies influence each other. Language as prayer, too, retains the sense of the speaking *body.*

Speaking, or praying, one expresses desire, appeal, demand; and one responds to the equivalent force of others. This, in itself, is an expression of differentiation and integration. Where the field is a *loving-field,* as Lear puts it, it re-creates the original "matrixial embrace." Words are used evocatively so as to reconnect with unconscious experience; now infused with instinctual life, they are liberated to make new connections. What began as words about the trees in the field finds new life in new linkages: "Words come back to life as life comes back to life."

The drama of toxic language is, in part, a drama of dead language.

When one slanders another, the death drive runs amok. Words are used as though they have either lost their instinctual power, or as though an unacknowledged demon of one's own had been let loose. The mouth articulates badly, however glibly the words flow.

There is, one might say, a bad taste in the mouth. The *ta'am,* the flavor, of slander in the mouth of the peddler is the angry experience of an inner world. By its nature, this private experience cannot be directly communicated. And yet, R. Zadok claims, once the peddler has returned to a life of growth within a field of connection, the singular *ta'am* of his history has the power to enrich even R. Yannai's understanding of the text in Psalms: "Who is the man who desires life? Guard your tongue from evil. . . . Seek peace and pursue it." For those who have been gone and back, a new field of connections opens up: the alienation from life and the desire for life; the role of language in isolating and linking; the hard quest for a peace in which two go together in a com-passion that is before and beyond words.

5

Acharei Mot/Kedoshim

Commanded to Aspire

THE ROYAL DECREE

The two Torah portions, Acharei Mot and Kedoshim, are sometimes read separately, sometimes together. Their subjects are indicated in their titles—Death and Holiness. In one, we read the fraught ritual of the scapegoat, which lies at the core of the rituals of the Day of Atonement; in the other, we read a panoply of laws with their great ethical capstone, "Love your neighbor as yourself."

The Day of Atonement and its rituals is introduced with an ominous reference to the story of Nadav and Avihu, the two sons of Aaron who met a violent death in the midst of the celebrations of the inauguration of the Tabernacle:

> And God spoke to Moses after the death of the two sons of Aaron when they came close to God's presence and died. And God said to Moses, Speak to Aaron your brother and let him not come into the sacred area within the Parochet (the curtain dividing areas) at any time . . . so that he does not die. Only in this way shall he come into the sacred area. . . . (Lev. 16:1–2)

The timing of God's message to Aaron is *after* those deaths. Why does God evoke those horrifying moments, just as He embarks on the Yom Kippur laws? The essence of those moments is succinctly conveyed: two priests encroached, came too close to the divine Presence, and they died.

Rashi gives color to that factual *after the death:*

This is like a patient who was visited by his doctor who instructed him not to eat cold foods nor to sleep in damp conditions. Then another doctor arrived and instructed him not to eat cold foods nor to sleep in damp conditions, "so that you do not die as X died!" The second doctor motivates the patient more than the first! So God said, "Let him not encroach, come too close, so that he does not die in the same way that Aaron's sons died."[1]

The second doctor is considerably more effective than the first, simply because he can back up his instructions by pointing to an actual death in similar circumstances. God instructs Aaron about how he is to act on Yom Kippur, the Day of Atonement. Coming *after* the story of Aaron's own sons, God's words have unambiguous authority. There is no mental escape route for the patient. *After* here means "*in the same way* that X died."

Rashi picks this up again in the next verse: "So that he does not die: as his sons died . . . but if he does encroach he will die" (Lev. 16:2).

The consequences of encroaching on the sacred are already a fait accompli; Aaron is being instructed about the specific rituals that will allow him safely to enter the sacred space.

The laws of Yom Kippur are thus given to the High Priest who is also a grieving father. More generally, "In the same way that X died" gestures at the existence of order in the world. The death of the young priests is a warning to all priests. There are dangerous patterns that can be avoided. Common sense is demanded. In addition, perhaps, Aaron must atone for *the way* his sons die. He is identified with them and they with him. He may even be temperamentally inclined to the same emotional pattern that brought them down.

The rituals of atonement are strictly regulated. *Be-zot yavo:* on this one day in the year, in the specific manner of Yom Kippur—enveloped in a cloud of incense—he may enter the sacred space. The service is to be meticulously observed, on pain of death. Aaron's sons infringed these rules of access—although the exact nature of their infringement is not clearly stated.[2]

At the end of this account of the Yom Kippur regulations, we read: "And this shall be for them an eternal statute to atone once a year for

all the sins of the Israelites; and he did as God had commanded Moses"
(Lev. 16:34). The Talmud comments: "All the practices of Yom Kippur
are to be performed in proper order. If he performs one out of order,
he has done nothing!"[3] This order is "an eternal statute"—unalterable,
as though engraved in stone.[4]

Aaron obeys God's commandment. Rashi comments: "When Yom
Kippur came, he did all in accordance with this order. This tells us of
his excellence, that he did not don his vestments for his own grandeur,
but *as one who fulfills the royal decree*." Aaron is praised for not yielding
to the temptations of narcissism. He performs his office purely as an
act of obedience. The motivation and style of his acts is as important
as *what* he does. He adopts a way of being that is *like* fulfilling the royal
decree. This is, apparently, the closest analogy that the midrash can
summon up for Aaron's attitude to his role.

The expression *the royal decree* is intriguing in itself. The royal
decree makes an inexorable demand of the citizen. It attaches to statements like "I am God your God" (Lev. 18:2). Rashi comments: "I am
the One who said at Sinai, 'I am God your God,' and you accepted my
kingship over you. From now on, accept My decrees!"

Accepting God as royal authority implies obeying His edicts. But
were the people at Sinai totally aware of this stringent implication?
What else might they have assumed? Rashi quotes further from the
midrash: "God is well aware that the people will deviate by entering
forbidden marriages in the time of Ezra. For that reason, He comes
down hard on them with the decree, 'I am God your God.' Be aware
Who is decreeing!"

The harsh word *gezerah* (decree) exacerbates the severity of the
legal demand. The root is *gazar*—to cut—implying an incisive force.
The people are told, *Accept!* Absorb the force of God's will, with its
specific demands. The music of this is different from that of a general
acceptance of God as King. All romanticism is cut away: the *gezerah*
enacts rupture, interruption, violence. Its implacable quality is conveyed in the book of Esther, where the king's edict cannot be withdrawn, even by the king himself.[5] Such an edict has a metaphysical
force, related to the notion of divine omnipotence. An impersonal
and irrevocable force attaches to Ahasuerus's written decrees. The
only way they can be countermanded is by a later decree that exhorts
the Jews to defend themselves against the now inevitable pogrom.

Such inflexible modes of law are attended by a kind of absurdity. Another biblical moment has King Solomon literally decree that the baby claimed by two women be *cut in two: G'zor!* he proclaims.[6] In this way, he provokes the true mother to show her colors, actually to perform her motherhood by choosing life. The extremity of such decrees brings truth to light. The unquestionable has something of the irrational—or, at least, of the nonrational. It focuses on the most radical implication of acknowledging God as King. But as we will see, the music of this can modulate in a more romantic direction, after all.

The wording that follows provides a general guideline for the laws of Leviticus:

Speak to the children of Israel and say to them, I am God your God. You shall not imitate the deeds of Egypt where you lived nor the deeds of Canaan where I am bringing you; and you shall not walk in their statutes. You shall act according to My laws and My statutes you shall observe to walk in them; I am God your God. (Lev. 18:2–4)

Rashi comments:

"My laws": These words are stated in the Torah as *laws,* for if they had not been stated, they would have had to be stated. "My statutes" refers to words that are the *royal decree,* to which the evil inclination makes objections: Why do we have to keep them? And the nations of the world also make objections to them—like not eating pig meat and not wearing mixed linen and wool clothing and purification by the water of the Sin Offering. That is why it says, "I am God, I have issued this decree and you are not free of obligation."

Rashi makes the classic distinction between natural law (*mishpat*) and the royal decree (*chukah*). What is the nature of the latter category? Strikingly, this is characterized as provoking rebuttals from the evil inclination and the nations of the world. The royal decree rests upon *nothing but* the arbitrary will of God. Rashi's examples—the ban on eating pig meat, on wearing wool and linen clothing, and the practice of purifying with the water of the Sin Offering—are hard to justify on rational grounds. "I am God" is repeated many times in the *parshah* like a dire incantation.

Strangely, Rashi acknowledges the rational power of the Devil's arguments. The Jew is to obey the divine demand, simply because of his relationship with the One who demands. Walking in His ways is the obverse of walking in the ways of the Egyptians and the Canaanites. In both contexts, *walking* evokes the various forms of compulsion, mythic social conventions that unconsciously shape one's ethical and spiritual world. Choosing between them means adopting a particular set of de rigueur behaviors.

In Rashi's Talmudic source,[7] the examples of natural law are those prohibiting idolatry, incest, and murder, as well as robbery and blasphemy. It is striking, however, that the Talmud lists several examples of nonrational laws that Rashi does not include in his list: the law (*chalitzah*) by which the sister-in-law of a childless widower frees both of the levirate obligation, the law of purification of the leper, and the law of the goat that is cast out into the wilderness. Altogether, the tone of the Talmudic source is more demonic, more radical in every way than in Rashi's version: it is Satan rather than the evil inclination who has objections to these laws; these objections prompt the Jew to say, "These are meaningless laws (lit., the work of the void)." And God's response, "I am God," means that "you may not entertain misgivings (*harher*) about them." In Rashi's version, this becomes, "You are not free of obligation to observe them."

One has the impression that Rashi is toning down the extremity of the Talmudic language. He suggests an internal protest: "Why should we observe this?" The Talmud bans *hirhur:* unruly thoughts, fantasies, wonderings. It even gives a specimen of such ruminations ("These laws are absurd!"). Rashi simply observes that the laws are binding.

The examples that Rashi omits—the ceremony that frees from Levirate obligation, the purification of the leper, and the goat expelled into the wilderness on Yom Kippur—evoke a violent world. Rashi excludes these from his palette. What he retains—forbidden foods and clothing and the paradoxical purification ritual with the ashes of the Red Heifer—these may defy reason but they are not offensive. The Talmud invokes a range of practices that pose moral and aesthetic problems as well as rational ones. *Hirhurim*—unruly thoughts in relation to these practices—are forbidden. Rashi does not mention such subversive "wonderings."[8]

TWO GOATS

We turn now to the most dramatic, even demonic example of the Talmudic *gezerah* (decree) motif: the ritual of the goat expelled into the wilderness on Yom Kippur. This is perhaps *the* constitutive ritual of the day. As we have seen, the laws of the Day of Atonement are summarized as an "eternal statute" (Lev. 16:34). The order of rituals is inflexible; but this specific ritual has the power to disrupt the whole service. Till it has been completed, all is in suspension.[9] It is crucial to the order of the day.

What does it involve? As described at the beginning of the laws of the day (Lev. 16:5–10,20–22), two young goats are taken and "positioned in the presence of God." The High Priest casts lots between them: one goat is "for God"; the other is "for Azazel." The first is sacrificed as a Sin Offering; the other is cast forth into the wilderness as atonement. But first, in the context of other sacrifices, the *vitality* of this goat is twice emphasized: it is "positioned *alive* in God's presence" and the priest lays his hands on the head of the *live* goat while he makes confession of the people's sins, projecting them onto the goat's head. After that, the goat is cast forth into the wilderness, under the escort of an *ish itti,* a man who has been prepared for this role.

This is the original biblical *scapegoat.* It bears on its head the sins of the people when it is loosed into what the Torah calls "the land of *gezerah.*" Of edicts? Of sharp cuts? Of arbitrary determinations between life and death?

The Talmud reads *gezerah* on different levels. Concretely, the tradition is that the goat is pushed over the edge of a sharp cliff. In its descent, it is cut in pieces. This ritual is commanded by God as a decree about which one may not *wonder.*[10]

This brutal scenario is different, of course, from the impression made by the biblical text. There, the goat is simply "sent forth into the wilderness"; it is presumably free to roam till it dies a natural death. But this manifest meaning is undercut by the bizarre words—*Azazel* and *gezerah*—that disrupt it. The goat is sent to *Azazel* (Lev. 16:8). On one reading, this strange word refers to a harsh, craggy (*az ve-kasheh*) cliff. But on another reading, it evokes the demonic force of Uza and Azael, primeval angels of destruction and sexual violation.

In itself, the word "Azazel" has a freakish quality, exceeding the usual three-letter root. Such anomalous roots are often interpreted as referring to anomalous worlds. Here, Azazel—five root letters—is linked to murderous crags and demonic sexual practices.

This goat is the one chosen by lot from between the two original goats, which, in midrashic reading, are *indistinguishable* from each other. Identical goats whose destiny is declared by the sheer fall of luck. This goat therefore acquires not only a destiny but an identity. Twice described as *chai,* the *living* goat, it is, as we say, *dumb luck* that dedicates it to the destructive energy of Azazel. Differentiated from the sacrificed goat, it is *scapegoated;* the priest consciously displaces onto it the violence of a community. But it differs from the human scapegoat who is usually the object of the irrational and largely unconscious hostility of the group. This goat is willfully assigned its role in a process that is patently arbitrary.

Evil, violence, and disorder are transferred to a demon goat that is then shattered on a cliff. The magical and idolatrous resonances of the ritual challenge traditional commentaries. Ramban, for instance, declares that such rituals involving other powers are in general absolutely forbidden.[11] In this case, however, the goat is sent to the wilderness force that governs places of destruction and desolation and planets that represent bloodshed, war, wounds, blows, disintegration. Ramban catalogs phenomena of disorder, among them the allegorical figure of Esau, man of war, and the animal figures of goat-demons.[12]

What, then, is the religious purpose of sacrificing a goat in this way on the holiest day in the year? Ramban points out that this is specifically *not* a sacrifice to the demon.[13] Unlike the other goat, which is sacrificed to God, the scapegoat is subjected to an anti-sacrificial fate—simply pushed off a crag. But both goats, he remarks, are "stood up alive *in the divine Presence.*" Both fates are acts of obedience to the divine will. Ramban offers a parable of one who makes a banquet in honor of the king and accedes to the king's request to set a place for the king's servant. One is honoring not the servant but the king. Both goats are equally dedicated to God; both die—one in sacrifice and the other in a divinely assigned fate.

The wilderness is a world beyond human agency. The man who has been chosen to escort the animal is given minimal agency: in the biblical text, none at all, and in the Talmudic narrative, the authority to precipitate the animal to its death.

One can readily understand why this ritual of demons and doubles and spontaneous craggy falls provokes objection from the nations of the world. The scapegoat ritual represents all that is troubling to reason and order. This practice, Ramban suggests, will give the other nations good ground for arguing that the Israelites are behaving exactly as pagans do in their ritual practices: that we are, in fact, acting against our own Law in imitating those foreign rituals.[14]

Ramban both acknowledges and repudiates the embarrassing similarity between the Israelite and the idolatrous rituals. The difference lies in the spiritual attitude of the Israelites. In Israelite law, this ritual is a pure act of obedience to the divine will. Like the goats, which are identical and yet, at the decisive moment, so sharply differentiated, the Yom Kippur ritual evokes a pagan world of random cruelty—but with a difference.

After all, this is not a sacrifice. Soon after this account, the Torah will specifically forbid all such goat worship: "They shall no longer sacrifice to the goat demons after which they lust: this shall be an eternal statute for their generations" (Lev. 17:7).

What is recognized here is the lure of such pagan sacrifices—a kind of lust. Goats and bulls and bullocks were worshipped in Egypt and in other cultures of the ancient Near East. The Golden Calf was a homegrown example of that lust that would, in other cultures, be acted out in rituals of orgiastic violence.

These sacrificial rituals to the goat-god are forbidden. But the human fascination with and anxiety about what lies behind them is acknowledged. The scapegoat dies in the land of *gezerah*. This is the world of the divine decree, inscrutable, apparently arbitrary. "*I am God,* who decreed this and you have no right to wonder about these things."[15] In Rashi's version, as we have seen, wondering is not forbidden. The sharp edge of the unfathomable arouses wonder, even as it precludes it.

A quick survey of the biblical use of the word *gezerah* yields some interesting associations. The Psalmist writes of the dead and the desolate: "They are cut off (*nigzaru*) from Your hand" (Ps. 88:6). A sharp

blow of the divine hand has consigned these victims to limbo: undifferentiated, in a mass grave. Alternatively, they are cut off *from* the
saving power of God's hand. Similarly, "I said in my haste, 'I am cut
off from before Your eyes'" (Ps. 31:23). In both cases, the Psalmist's
despair is then converted to hope.

The leper Uzziah finds no place in human society: he is cut off[16]
from the house of God (2 Chron. 26:21). In the book of Esther, Vashti
is the object of a decree (*nigzar aleha*), which is similarly understood
as the atrocious fate of being cut off from human society. Jonah is
thrown into the sea: "I said, I have been driven forth (*nigrashti*)[17] from
Your gaze" (Jon. 2:5). He thinks himself dead.

Finally, the Dry Bones in Ezekiel's vision cry out, "Our bones are
dried up and our hope is lost, we have been cut off!—*nigzarnu lanu!*"
Radical despair reigns here. Dying in exile, the house of Israel feels
herself *cut off from herself,* without even the hope of salvation, which
will always have come too late.

But here, the unmitigated despair of the *gezerah* fate is turned
around in God's response: there will be resurrection. A slow-motion
reintegration of the organs and the breath will be followed by, "And
you shall know that *I am God:* I have spoken and I have acted, says
God" (Ezek. 37:14). The divine response to human despair makes use
of the same expression—*I am God*—as is used repeatedly in Leviticus
to evoke the absolute power of the divine decree. Human consciousness will embrace a sense of divine Presence as counterpoint to the
existential despair of death-in-exile.

In all these examples, *gezerah* evokes a state of irreversible isolation, desiccation. Ezekiel's message of hope to his exiled people
reflects the inscrutable nature of the divine will, for good or ill. In the
scapegoat ritual, the mystery of the *gezerah* plays a central role. The
goat's fate is, in some way, to atone for human sin. Using the religious
language of the time, the Torah describes a procedure that subverts
the pagan beliefs that undergird that language.

SACRALIZED VIOLENCE

We remember the story of Joseph—the original scapegoat. Stripping
him of his famous coat of many colors, throwing him into a wilderness pit, his brothers dip the coat in the blood of a slaughtered

goat (Gen. 37:31). In the symbolic form of his coat,[18] Joseph is cut to pieces.

Why is a goat's blood chosen as circumstantial evidence to deceive Jacob? Rashi answers somberly: "because it is similar to human blood." The similarity of bloods is enacted in the Hebrew words: *damo domeh le-shel adam*. The wordplay on blood, similarity, and the human being suggests a basic identity of human and animal at the level of blood. By way of substitution, the brothers have shed Joseph's blood. Stripping and dismembering him, they enact the wild beast that they later induce their father to imagine (Gen. 37:33).

This is a story of hatred, jealousy, and cruelty. The brothers' irrational hatred is displaced onto Joseph: the narrative makes clear just how irrational their hostility is. Neither Joseph's childish boasting about his dream, nor his father's favoritism toward him, can justify the savagery of their attack. Ghosts of the past haunt this story: Rachel and Leah, the loved and the unloved mothers; the choice of the younger brothers, Jacob and Isaac. If Joseph's brothers had dreamed, what sharp edge of fear and resentment would have haunted their nights?

Violence is endemic in society and in the family. The blood of the victim cries out from the ground. From Cain and Abel, murder is named as a crime. Northrop Frye describes the figure of a typical or random literary victim, the *pharmakos,* who is "neither innocent nor guilty. He is innocent in the sense that what happens to him is far greater than anything he has done provokes. . . . He is guilty in the sense that he is a member of a guilty society."[19] In the mythologies of the ancient world, in the story of Oedipus, for instance, the hero is persecuted and expelled from the community. René Girard comments that the lynching mob as a generative force behind all myth and ritual is characterized by "pure self-righteousness" and by a belief in the pure malevolence of its victim. The collective violence imagines itself as something other than itself, through the image of an animal, for instance.[20]

The community thus purges itself in a paroxysm of what Girard calls "sacralized violence." He sets the Joseph story up against the Oedipus myth. Their similarities mark out the striking difference between them: the Bible clearly expresses an ethical concern that is focused on the injustice done to the victim. The community—Joseph's brothers—are not justified. "The Bible itself," claims Girard, "is perfectly aware of its opposition to all mythological religions. It brands them as idolatrous, and I think that the revelation of scapegoat delusion in mythology is an essential part of the fight against idolatry."[21] Judah's ultimate acceptance of responsibility for the brothers' crime redeems the world in which Joseph and his brothers must live.

Girard's claim of redemption within the narrative is perhaps pitched too high. The human unconscious forces represented by the scapegoat delusion remain forces to be acknowledged, even as they are declared idolatrous. The idols of the old religions, the goats, and bulls, and bullocks linger on in translation, in the purification rituals of Leviticus. The scapegoat ritual of Yom Kippur carries associations with the animal look-alike for Joseph.

An unpublished Yemenite manuscript gives us this midrash:

> The goat had no horns and it said to the brothers, "You are killing two lives"—this teaches that it was female and pregnant. [*Se'ir izzim* indicates *two* goats.] When they came to slaughter it, it cried out in a voice that reached the heavens, so that the angels came down to see, "Joseph lives and I die! Who will tell Jacob?" One of the winds went and told Jacob what the goat said. But in the end, "His heart went numb, for he did not believe them!" (Gen. 45:26).
>
> So the goat cried out, "Earth, do not cover up my blood!" (Job 16:18) and till now, the goat's blood is damp on the earth, until the Messiah comes, as it is written, "I will smelt them as one smelts silver" (Zech. 13:9)—the silver for which they sold Joseph, as it is said, "They sold Joseph for twenty pieces of silver" (Gen. 37:28).

At the moment of slaughter, the goat discovers a human voice and cries out to high heaven against the pain and injustice of existence. As a pregnant female, the outrage is doubled. Her one desire is to be heard by the suffering Jacob, who may appreciate her sacrifice. But Jacob is incapable of absorbing the message. What remains is the sheer residue of damp blood on the earth-surface. The tragic note sings from the midrashic text, at least until the Messiah comes.

W. G. Sebald, one of the great "ghost hunters" who gave expression to the historical conscience of our own age, writes of "the marks of pain which . . . trace countless fine lines through history."[22] He claims as associates all those throughout the ages who have suffered from the violence of the world. Job and the goat of this midrash would be among these associates. The scapegoat ritual, I suggest, subtly invokes this tradition.

"SICK SOULS"

In a classic discussion, William James juxtaposes two philosophical views of the place of evil in the world. Healthy-mindedness, as he terms it, refuses to acknowledge evil as an intrinsic part of existence or as a dialectical element in any "final system of truth":

> Evil, it says, is emphatically irrational, and *not* to be . . . preserved, or consecrated in any final system of truth. It is a pure abomi- nation to the Lord, an alien unreality, a waste element, to be sloughed off and negated, and the very memory of it, if pos- sible, wiped out and forgotten.

Here, we have the interesting notion, fairly and squarely presented to us, of there being elements of the universe that may make no ratio- nal whole in conjunction with the other elements, and that, from the point of view of any system which those other elements make up, can only be considered so much irrelevance and accident—so much "dirt," as it were, and matter out of place.[23]

A different sort of religion would be needed by those who live more habitually with a low "pain-threshold." James calls such suffer- ers "the sick souls," who, in contrast to the "healthy-minded," find that "pity, pain, and fear, and the sentiment of human helplessness" play a significant role in their understanding of the world.[24] These latter, he suggests, offer a more profound and complicated view of the situation.

The anthropologist Mary Douglas cites this passage in the context of her discussion of purity and pollution in human society. Some cultures impose a strict pattern of purity that may result in hypocrisy:

> The moral of all this is that the facts of existence are a chaotic jumble. If we select from the body's image a few aspects which

do not offend, we must be prepared to suffer for the distortion. The body is not a slightly porous jug. To switch the metaphor, a garden is not a tapestry; if all the weeds are removed, the soil is impoverished. . . . The special kind of treatment which some religions accord to anomalies and abominations to make them powerful for good is like turning weeds and lawn cuttings into compost.[25]

"Anomalies and abominations" that are made powerful for good: in the last chapter of *Purity and Danger,* Douglas movingly describes the ritual around such an abomination, the pangolin, the scaly ant-eater, "a hybrid monster, which . . . is reverently eaten by initiates, and taken to be the most powerful source of fertility. At this point, one sees that this is, after all, to continue the gardening metaphor, a composting religion. That which is rejected is plowed back for a renewal of life."[26]

The pangolin is spoken of as a voluntary victim. Its corpse is treated with respect: "[I]f its rituals are faithfully performed the women will conceive and animals will enter hunters' traps and fall to their arrows."[27]

In Douglas's analysis, the Lele pangolin cult invites its initiates to confront their own structures of thought and to recognize them for the "fictive, man-made, arbitrary creations that they are."[28] Strictly pollution-conscious the rest of the year, classifying animal categories for food, the Lele initiates, in the inner cult of all their ritual life, kill and eat the animal that is most dense with contradictions. Douglas suggests that this major anomaly generates "a meditation on the categories of human thought."[29] The mystery of evil and of death will at some point challenge the healthy-minded structures of a dirt-avoiding society. The Lele initiates will "stage . . . a cult of the paradox of the ultimate unity of life and death."[30] The weeds are returned as compost so that the garden may thrive.

RESIDUES OF THE GOLDEN CALF?

The "goat to Azazel" perhaps represents a similar turning from a generally "healthy-minded" view of evil, in which impurity is banned and requires atonement, to a profound confrontation with the paradoxes of life and death. The mysteries and anomalies of death, disintegration, and human evil become the subject of a "meditation": at the edge of the ordered world, in the wilderness, at the jut of a cliff, the goat meets a shattering death. By a deliberately arbitrary casting of lots, the community projects their own misgivings about the world of *gezerah*, of God's inscrutable will, onto the animal.

At this moment, the "healthy-minded" pollution-rituals come to a climax. Evil is eliminated. In Mary Douglas's terms, this may lead the Israelites to confront the limits of dirt-avoidance in the system. But as the goat receives the sins of the people from the hands of the priest, something beyond the union of opposites, of life and death, is enacted. I suggest that this is a moment of tragic irony. The goat with its burden of collective human sin is freed/expelled into the land of *gezerah*. For the people, the goat is perhaps invested with the residue of the Golden Calf, the pathology of Egyptomania that survives, even as it is annually voided in the wilderness.

TRAGEDY IN PLATO, ARISTOTLE, AND FREUD

Tragedy is the literary form with which the goat is radically associated. In Greek, tragedy is the "Ode to the goat."[31] The problem of human evil, of "unnatural" acts that human beings commit, is the subject of Aristotle's *Poetics*. Ultimately, he asks, are such acts containable in a polis (city) governed by reason? He turns to tragedy to test the adequacy of logos (reason) to account for human nature.

Jonathan Lear discusses the thought of Plato, Aristotle, and Freud in relation to this question. "For Plato," he writes, "the ultimate opacity of human destructiveness plays a crucial role in his decision to banish tragedy from the polis."[32] In Plato's conception of human nature, even in the best-governed polis, human destructiveness can only be forcibly suppressed, not eliminated. Tragedy enacts the return of the repressed. It gives the audience an alibi for acting on their own suppressed desire. Tragedy, therefore, is to be banished.

In his later work, Freud picks up on Plato's pessimism: at its worst, human violence constitutes an attack on logos. The repetition neurosis convinced him that there must be a force in human nature that lies beyond the pleasure principle. He called this the death-drive, which is ultimately unfathomable. As Lear puts it, "[I]t remains a permanent possibility for human destructiveness to catch us by surprise; for there must be an element in human violence which remains inevitably surd. These are the moments when we suspect that all this carnage has happened for no reason at all."[33]

"The enduring repetition of surprise," Lear remarks, "may eventually suggest that there is something about human destructiveness which lies beyond logos."[34] In contrast with Aristotle, Plato and Freud have "a more inclusive conception of human nature; and they are willing to countenance the thought that certain forms of human destruction are brute attacks upon logos."[35] Aristotle's account of tragedy suffers from its idealizations of both tragedy and human nature.

For Aristotle, pity and fear are the necessary cathartic emotions of the audience. Lear subtly suggests that the pity felt by the audience makes tragedy "safe for human consumption." Pity is felt for the sufferer who is blind or mistaken and who, in a sense, brings his fate on himself. This "domesticates" terror—and, with it, the eternal *surprise* of such horrifying events. The sense of the unintelligible is banished under such conditions. Aristotle is not willing to countenance the thought that human violence may have no logos at all.

IRONIC DISRUPTION

In the case of the goat to Azazel, on the other hand, the primary emotional reaction of the witnesses to the ritual is a strangely *pitiless* sense of awe, even terror. The drama of the goat has little to do with logos. It is a sober enactment in which human sin is transferred from the body politic to the goat's head, along with the unspoken knowledge of the brutal consummation to come.

This, we remember, is not a sacrifice; it is an act of obedience to a divine decree. It is also the one ritual recourse for sins committed intentionally.[36] Here is the mystery of willful violence, or, as Lear puts it, the "enduring repetition of *surprise*" (my italics). It keeps happening, this hemorrhaging of blood.

Those participating in this ritual are assailed by the unfathomable terror of the situation, but also perhaps by an ironic element in the tragic moment. By this I mean something similar to what Jonathan Lear elsewhere describes as an ironic disruption of daily life.

He understands irony as the recognition of a tension between social pretense and aspiration.

Drawing on Socrates and Kierkegaard, Lear develops his understanding of irony. This is not a matter of already knowing the answer to the question that is asked. Rather, he describes it as the experience of no longer being able simply to live with the available social understanding—the social pretense. "Irony is thus an outbreak of pretense-transcending aspiration."[37] It comes in the form of ironic uncanniness, accompanied by a longing for direction.

Such outbreaks of ironic disruption can happen at any time; one should, he says, learn to "live well" with this possibility. Developing a capacity for ironic experience becomes an ethical challenge. Human excellence depends on developing "a capacity for appropriately disrupting one's understanding of what such excellence consists in. Human flourishing would then partially consist in cultivating an experience of oneself as uncanny, out of joint."[38]

It is in this complex sense that I would describe the Israelite experience of the goat to Azazel as one of tragic irony; and the people's self-awareness at this moment as uncanny, out of joint. A moment of awe and truthfulness and desire for transcendence, which Lear calls aspiration.

COMMANDED TO ASPIRE

From the scapegoat, with its freight of collective impurity, we turn now to the pure music of aspiration: "Be holy, for I God am holy!" (Lev. 19:2).

Like a pool of sunlight in a tangled forest, the demand of holiness moves us from a world of specific taboos, anomalies, and abominations to a blinding moment of aspiration. The difference in tone is unmistakable. From forbidden acts we turn to a positive state of being. How does *being* belong in a legal text so concerned with *doing*?

Rashi relates to this question obliquely in his commentary:

This *parshah* was uttered in an assembly of the entire people, since most categories of law are derived from it. "Be holy!" Be separate from sexual and other sins, because wherever you find caution about sexual sin you also find holiness.

Rashi makes several observations. Structurally, this new *parshah* constitutes a kind of summa of biblical law; for this reason, it was spoken in the presence of the entire people. In this sense, this *parshah* is seminal and central. The concept of holiness is then translated into legal terms: from the positive to the negative, from *being* to *doing* (or avoiding). Holiness indicates extra caution around sexual taboos. Rashi associates this with a concept of holiness as *separation,* a kind of spiritual fastidiousness.

The association of abstinence with holiness is classic. Although holiness is not the same as purity (*toharah*), as a state of being it is constituted by many acts of withdrawal: "One who abstains from committing a sin (lit., sits and does not sin) is rewarded as though (s)he had done a good deed."[39] An apparently passive state of *not-doing* is evaluated on an active register. Clearly, the midrash deals with active resistance to temptation and not with lethargy. Some heroic spiritual movement is taking place.

At the same time, we notice the qualifier, "*as though* (s)he had done a good deed." This resistance is similar to but not identical with active virtue. Holiness belongs in this transitional area, which is constructed by the mind of the Rabbis.

Ramban classically describes "holiness" as the aspiration to go beyond the letter of the law. In the end, the sinews of the law do not provide sufficient nurture for the spiritual life. "One may be a sensualist (*naval*) without stepping outside the law." A gray area that is not forbidden makes space for personal fastidiousness.[40] To navigate this area, one needs the inspiration of an idea like that of holiness. This area is illuminated by the notion of *imitatio dei:* "Be holy, *for I God am holy!*" This is an elitist ethic, which is yet not wholly voluntary. As R. Aaron Lichtenstein, with a fine sense of paradox, puts it, "A Jew is also commanded to aspire."[41]

The ideal of holiness both does and does not translate into specific laws. Perhaps this ideal can be understood in terms of what we have described as experiences of recognition of the tension between social pretense and aspiration in daily life. In Jonathan Lear's terms, these are moments when one can no longer simply live with the available social understanding—the social pretenses—of daily life. A certain *irony* enters into this experience, which both disrupts one's practical identity and, at the same time, expresses a loyalty to the larger meanings of that identity. Such moments are marked by both unease and the yearning that is aspiration.

Ramban seems to speak to this margin between the socially acceptable and the aspirational. This leaves the concept of holiness somewhat undefined: a transcendent and perhaps ironic disruption of daily life, which stands separate from—though it remains linked with—the parameters of law.

Between resembling God and not resembling the pagan nations—Egypt and Canaan (Lev. 18:2–4)—each individual and the entire nation are faced with exhortations and inspirations. What the Torah emphasizes is that it is for this purpose—of being holy—that they were taken out of Egypt in the first place. In an earlier passage, we read:

> For I am God your God and you shall sanctify yourselves and be holy for I am holy. You shall not pollute yourselves with all kinds of insects that crawl on the earth. For I am God who brings you up out of the land of Egypt to be to you as a God, and you shall be holy for I am holy. (11:44–45)

Here is the enigmatic relation between God's holiness and His demand of the Israelites to sanctify themselves. Forging this connection between the human and the divine is the entire purpose of the Exodus. The Exodus, too, is an ongoing project, as evidenced by the present tense, "who *brings* you up out of the land of Egypt." Rashi points this out and quotes R. Ishmael: "If I had not brought them up out of Egypt for any other purpose than that they should not pollute themselves with insects like the other nations, that would have been sufficient!" Bringing them up out of Egypt is an elevation. Separating Israel from its pagan environment is an organic process of elevation.

The Egyptian Exodus had and continues to have a spiritual purpose. Exodus is a fact to which values adhere. In this passage, however, the value of holiness (*kedushah*) is given a minimal meaning, equivalent to abstaining from impurity. This minimal meaning is sufficient to justify the project of the Exodus.

HOLINESS AND ASPIRATION

At the end of the portion of Kedoshim, we find a summary in which the themes of separation, pollution, and holiness are set in a new context: "You shall be unto Me (*li*) holy, for I God am holy; and I shall separate you from the nations to be Mine (*li*)" (Lev. 20:26). Being unto God intimates an undefined connection. Minimal language—*li* (unto Me)—is associated with *being holy,* with divine holiness, and with separation from pagan mores.

Rashi's comment is striking:

> If you separate yourselves from them, then you are Mine! If not, you belong to Nebuchadnezzar and his friends! R. Elazar ben Azaria said: One should not say, I am disgusted by pig-meat, or, I could not bear to wear mixed wool-and-linen clothing! Instead, one should say, I could easily do these things. But what shall I do! My Father in heaven has decreed! . . . One's separation from the ways of the nations should be for My sake. One refrains from sin and accepts the yoke of heaven.

Sexual restraint is motivated by a passionate relation with God. Resistance to sin becomes the energetic enactment of a loyalty: "Of whose party are you?" The moment of resistance to temptation becomes an affirmative moment of identification. When one differentiates oneself from the other nations in the ways of holiness—where the divine decree is at issue—one colors one's being with another desire. This is, in a sense, an erotic moment: a longing to be *unto Me* is realized.

What has emerged is the presence of aspiration. As Jonathan Lear describes it, this is an uncanny experience. An unthinking flux has been disrupted. A gap appears "between pretense and pretense-transcending aspiration." For Lear, we remember, this is also an ironic moment: ironic experience, he claims, is first personal, present tense. It is a sudden shift in perspective.

The term *kedushah* (holiness), then, is linked with the state of *aspiration.* It is utterly serious and radically discomfiting. Questions of value arise. And it affects, in a complex way, one's practical identity.

R. Elazar's aphorism insists on the gap between one's natural desires and the fact of God's decree. He insists on the situation of tension between desire and obedience. Only so can the strangeness and the power of God's desire be seen in its impact on a human life. A choice is to be made. In a sense, the choice is inevitable, not because one has no desire for the forbidden but, on the contrary, because one's desire starkly illuminates the *other* thing: "What shall I do? My father in heaven has decreed!" In a sense, one cannot do otherwise.

LIVING THROUGH COMMANDMENTS

At this point, two possible understandings of the "royal decree" idea have come to light. In one view, the people accept a rigid, authoritarian framework of laws that cannot be justified by ethical or rational thought. The point is sheer obedience, even to the extent of *credo quia absurdum est:* the more absurd the demand, the greater the faith—and therefore the obedience. In the other view, obeying the royal decree becomes an expression of passionate loyalty to the one who decrees. There is an erotic element to the relationship to divine authority. An active tension enters the drama of restraint, once the aspiration is to be "unto Me."[42] "Anyone who accepts the yoke of Heaven and refrains from sinning is rewarded like one who does a *mitzvah* (a good deed)."[43]

This understanding of the divine decree in the context of *being unto Me* casts new light on the divine decree that imposes nonrational laws. Now, the source of the imperial decree is "my *Father in heaven.*" A complex but powerful relationship with God—king and father—stirs the imagination to a possibility of being. The ultimate effect of all the negatives is to develop a state of being that we may call aspirational. What we earlier described as a *romantic* dimension enters the relationship to holiness.

The philosopher Lon Fuller coined the expression "the morality of aspiration." In biblical language, this marks the difference between an ethics of pollution taboos and an ethics of *kedushah* (holiness). The latter ethos provides meaning for the former. *Kedushah,* in this framework, is a movement upward, an energetic state.

William James writes of the "higher kind of inner excitement," which is experienced by those who live with a sense of the divine. In the biblical context, the sense of the divine is closely linked with the taboos that are to be transcended in holiness.

The motive for aspiration is, ultimately, a larger sense of life: "And you shall keep my statutes and My laws: if one performs them, one *lives* through them. I am God" (Lev. 18:5). The purpose of the stringencies of the law is *v'chai ba-hem*—so that you may live through them. A classic rabbinic reading suggests that commandments are to be fulfilled only if life is not endangered by fulfilling them. This becomes an important legal principle.[44] But another reading declares that the purpose of fulfilling the laws is increased vitality. If the laws do not have this enlivening effect, then they should be read otherwise. The nineteenth-century commentator Ha'amek Davar reads and rereads the word *chai* in accordance with his understanding that it sometimes refers to the *fullness* of life. This vitality principle, he suggests, should generate deepened study of apparently unenlivening texts.

One example relates to Genesis 2:7: "Adam became a *living* soul." Sometimes, he writes, "living" means simply "not-dead." Other times, it means living in the fullest way possible for that created being. A human being experiences such wholeness in the development of her intellectual and spiritual capacities. For the Jew, this means the study of Torah and the aspiration toward love of God. Achieving that fullness of life is joy at its most intense. "You who cleave to God your God are all of you *alive* this day" (Deut. 4:4).

Kedushah can be understood as the aspiration toward such vitality. A kind of discomfort is its baseline: a restlessness about all given situations. Here, one is not yet who one wishes to be. One seeks out a deeper and larger way to be.

THE ETHICAL DIMENSION

The sixteenth-century Italian commentator Seforno makes a large claim about the opening commandment: "Be holy!" This, he argues, represents the meta-narrative of Israel from the Exodus to the Giving of the Torah at Sinai, to the Golden Calf, and then to the rituals of purification of Leviticus. From God's words at Mount Sinai, the purpose of the Exodus was defined as, "You shall be unto Me a kingdom of priests and a *holy nation*" (Exod. 19:6). This was to be the history of a *holy* nation, attuned to the possibility of resembling the Creator. Indeed, this was the divine intention from the creation of the first human being: "Let Us make man in Our image and after Our form"

(Gen. 1:26). The ideal of *imitatio dei* underlies the first half of the Ten Commandments.

In this history, as Seforno consistently points out at significant moments in the narrative, the people fall back from the ideal articulated for them at Sinai. The Golden Calf episode represents such a tragic falling away from the Sinai moment of transcendence. "They stripped themselves of their ornaments" (Exod. 33:6); they relinquished their intimacy with the divine; God withdrew from their midst (33:3).

Then, a therapeutic process began to enable a renewed intimacy with the divine. Although this purification of their spiritual being involves the body, these laws governing impure foods and sexual practices are primarily intended to treat the *soul*. The word *nefesh,* used so often in the purification laws,[45] is often translated "soul"; but it more aptly refers to the living human organism, which is a psychosomatic structure—perhaps to be understood as the *ensouled body*.[46] This future body becomes the object of divine desire.

This is Seforno's meta-historical reading of the Israelite narrative and particularly of the Leviticus purity laws. The aspiration to holiness represents a dominant thread of his theology. The purity laws have specific therapeutic aims, but the larger purpose is the fulfillment of a *divine* aspiration. The Jewish people are the bearers of this aspiration. They fulfill, or fail to fulfill, their own version of God's dream.

In William James's terms, the purity laws have a quality of *healthy-mindedness;* they aim to eliminate impurity, disorder. But the holiness ideal brings in the more complex view of evil and disorder as a part of the world's system. The tragic element in human existence creates a need to go beyond systems. Here begins the aspiring movement of the soul.

This aspiration has an ethical dimension that is dedicated, Lon Fuller claims, to the fullest realization of human powers.[47] Unlike other forms of self-development, however, the lives of others depend on such forms of aspiration. In the social world, for instance, when professional excellence is under discussion, the doctor or the lawyer or the teacher views her work with great seriousness because of the impact it has on the lives of others.[48] Aspiration to excellence is not simply a matter of right and wrong, but neither is it dispensable. Using religious language, Fuller remarks, "Sin is a sinking into nothingness."

The play on words eloquently embodies the counterpoint of sinking and aspiring. Without this energy of aspiration, one loses one's life.

TEN THOUSAND HOURS

How, then, is this ideal positioned in relation to the particulars of law? By way of analogy, how do we imagine the relation between the virtuoso musician and the ten thousand hours of practice that have been deemed essential to attain such virtuosity?[49]

Sometimes aesthetic experience provides a grammar for appreciating the position of the ideal of holiness. Ten thousand hours of practice, dense with repetition, train one to overcome the limitations and bad habits of body and soul. Without these detailed rigors of practice, the virtuoso will, in most cases, not emerge. But, *pace* Ericsson,[50] the hours of practice cannot totally account for the "prodigy" of what sometimes does emerge.

By analogy, specific practices and restraints have an important role to play in the pursuit of spiritual excellence. The ideal of holiness is nurtured by the various prohibitions that give it body. But the holy self that the Torah invokes is never guaranteed to appear. There is an *otherness,* a wonder about the holy—as, indeed, Rashi indicates in his translation *perushim*—separate, at a distance. This makes holiness incommensurate with the practices that nurture it.

I think of the Mozart scene in *The Shawshank Redemption*. Set in the brutal atmosphere of a maximum-security prison, the prison yard is suddenly invaded by the sounds of a Mozart aria. The hero, Andy, in a transgressive act that earns him two weeks in solitary, has locked himself in the warden's office and is playing the aria over the hissing speakers of the prison. Everyone, from prisoners to warders, stops in his tracks. Routine is disrupted by the sheer fragile beauty of Mozart's music. Transfixed, every last man stands gazing upward. The experience is one of freedom; pure sound from elsewhere, from another place and another time, is delivered into the "drab little cage" of the prison.

This scene, I suggest, provides an analogy for the uncanny phenomenon of holiness. Being or becoming holy is a function of being moved by a beauty that comes from elsewhere. The *otherness* of the holy evokes a kind of freedom. It is experienced in practices of bodily restraint and spiritual aliveness that help to carry one from one state of being to another, yet unknown. Like classical music, it is usually deemed an elite interest, though its power, it turns out, can be felt by every last man. The practitioner is often marked out as exceptional; but here the Torah commands a whole nation, "Be holy, for I God am holy!"

"BE HOLY!"

What happens when the aspiration to holiness fails to arise? In the enigmatic scene at Meriva, God castigates Moses and Aaron for "failing to sanctify Me before the people's eyes." The consequence of this failure is dire: "Therefore, you shall not lead the people into the Land" (Num. 20:12).

The holiness that failed to happen was the public demonstration, before the eyes of the people, of divine holiness. What would it have required to sanctify God? Rashi provides a classic answer: he should have spoken to the rock rather than striking it. Seeing Moses speak to the rock—the visual impact, "before the people's eyes," of a man speaking to a rock—would have engendered in them a thoughtful response: "They would have said, If this rock that does not speak or hear and has no existential needs nevertheless fulfills God's word, how much more so should I!"

What might have happened—but did not—is an imaginative act. The people might have projected themselves into the rock, recognizing the power of God's word in their own vulnerable lives. Their own human situation would have been illuminated by the miracle of water from the rock. The purpose of the exercise was the impact it might have on *the people's eyes.* Failing to speak, hitting the rock, Moses misses the point; the imaginative process is short-circuited; the double blow of the rod induces no self-reflection in the people.

Moses's failure is a failure to produce in them this movement of aspiration. In other words, he fails to engage their inner world. Speaking to the rock might have created an uncanny moment, a transfigured sense of God's word in their lives.[51]

There is, of course, no knowing what the people might have

thought. Yet such imaginative thinking is crucial if God is to be sanctified in the world. Practical obedience to divine commands requires the larger sense of a divinely connected world.

"Be holy!" is translated by Rabbi Mordecai Yosef Leiner (known as the Mei Ha-Shilo'ach): "Be attuned!" That is, Be attentive to the radiations of the divine that are always waiting to illuminate human life. Being *mezumanim,* attuned in this way, means both avoiding distraction and opening oneself, standing in God's presence, face-to-face, in hope of illumination.

Being holy in this sense would mean clearing space, allowing access to the illumination. D. H. Lawrence wrote of "man in his wholeness, wholly *attending.*" *Kedushah* would then evoke expectation, alertness, aspiration. Rabbi Leiner cites Proverbs 3:3: "Let love and truth not abandon you!"—suggesting the receptive stance of the mystic in a world charged with the divine.

"Be holy!" is immediately followed by a cascade of variegated laws—about life in the family, about the Sabbath, and idolatry, and sacrifice, and social responsibility in agriculture. Punctuated with the statement "I am God," these laws form the superstructure on which many legal categories depend.

At the same time, they themselves constitute the detailed injunctions that flesh out the meaning of the general principle of "Be holy!" An ideal of holiness is grounded in ritual and social practices. The sense of the divine runs like an electrical impulse through the text. Without the detailed practices, the ideal would remain undefined. But without the ideal, without the perspective of the *klal,* all the specifics would lack organic meaning.

OEDIPAL TENSIONS

In order to explore this dynamic of *klal* and *prat* (general principle and particular case), we will look briefly at three examples. The first is "Each person shall fear his/her mother and father" (Lev. 19:3), which immediately follows the imperative of "Be holy!" The second is "You shall not place a stumbling block before a blind person" (19:14). And the third is "Love your neighbor as yourself" (19:18).

Like the others, the injunction "Each person shall revere (lit., fear) his/her mother and father" is briefly phrased, in four Hebrew words, apparently unconnected with what comes before and after. Much commentary proliferates around these four words. What is the difference between *revering* and *honoring* one's parents (as in the Ten Commandments)? Why is the mother mentioned first? Does the word *ish* (person) refer to both sons and daughters? For our purposes, I would like to focus on one Talmudic passage: "What is reverence? One does not stand in his place nor sit in his place, nor contradict his opinion, nor decide a disagreement between him and another person."[52]

The emphasis on the parent's special *place* refers literally to her or his usual seat. But it also evokes oedipal tensions. Where one sits at table has symbolic implications. An apparently innocent act is understood to express a perhaps unconscious wish or attitude. The desire to supplant, which for Freud has murderous undertones, is acted out in harmless gestures.

Contradicting the parent's words, similarly, may not consciously trouble the parent, but it nevertheless constitutes an impingement on the general principle of reverence, which implies holding the parent in high regard, even in awe.

This awe is linked with the taboo that Freud placed at the center of his psychoanalytic thought. *Fearing* one's parents both acknowledges a moment of danger and protects them from oedipal violence. It acknowledges the almost mystical dimension of the parent *as* parent.

Seforno develops this idea: Honoring one's parents is not sufficient, since it is largely behavioral—it includes the duty of feeding and clothing them. But correct behavior may be accompanied by a disparaging attitude. Here arises the idea of reverence—a genuine regard verging on awe in relation to one's parents.

It is in this sense that reverence is expressed in negatives: not standing or sitting in their place, not contradicting them. These actions would represent an impulse to fill the parents' place: that is, to destroy. This unconscious impulse is implicit in the commandment of reverence. In the process, the reverence ideal both inspires the restraints and becomes more fully realized through the confrontation with them.

STUMBLING BLOCKS

We turn now to the stumbling block: "You shall not place a stumbling block before the blind, and you shall fear your God; I am God" (Lev. 19:14).

Once again, a brief and focused exhortation. The literal meaning is clear, forbidding an act of obvious malice against the handicapped. In this case, however, the principle is framed in the negative—following logically from "You shall not curse the deaf." But the verse ends: "You shall fear your God!"—which is, formally, a positive commandment. Rashi comments: Because this is something that no one other than you can know for sure—whether you meant it for good or ill—one could evade judgment by saying, "I meant it well." This is why the text says, "You shall fear your God!"—Who knows your thoughts. Of any issue that is a matter of individual conscience, the Torah says, "You shall fear your God!"

Since motivations are private, they are said to be known only to God. In this case, however, the text cannot be literally referring to tripping up the blind: that could only be malicious. So the verse is interpreted to refer to one who is "blind in a certain matter." It forbids maliciously exploiting the ignorance of others.

Here are some examples of "blind" situations that the Rabbis adjudicate: giving false information; giving bad advice leading to physical or financial loss; acting as an accessory to a crime, even if the other is quite aware of the criminal nature of his intentions, like selling weapons and instruments of violence.[53] Deception is not a necessary feature of this dynamic.

Further examples of this expanded notion of blindness: serving wine to a Nazirite (teetotaler) who is blinded by his desires—one is provoking the other to sin.[54] On similar grounds, it is forbidden to hit one's adult son, since one is provoking him to hit back.[55] Here, again, there is no deception involved and, at least consciously, no malice: the father does not *want* his son to strike back. Nevertheless, a degree of emotional awareness is required if one is to avoid the *stumbling-block* situation.

It is also forbidden to act as witness or even as scribe in a forbidden transaction (where usury is involved).[56] Even though there is neither deception nor provocation, simply participating in a forbidden act comes under the heading of the stumbling block. This is an unexpected text, since there is no blindness and no willful act of malice.

Even more surprising is the law that forbids, on the same grounds, lending to a friend without witnesses. There is no illicit act, and the motivation is friendship. Nevertheless, a temptation has been introduced into the situation; the unwitnessed loan may tempt the debtor to deny his debt.

Finally, the same stumbling-block law is cited as the basis for the duty of marking graves. A priest may unwittingly tread on the grave and violate a prohibition. Here, one is totally passive and yet runs afoul of the stumbling-block law.

In these examples, even where obvious culpability is absent, there remains an issue of *responsibility*. In citing the stumbling-block law, the Rabbis go far afield from the blind man who is being tripped up. None of the immediate moral associations of the original scene remain in the derivative laws. And yet something of the callousness of the biblical words is activated in the more rarefied circumstances of these laws. In any act, or even in abstaining from an act, one may play a potentially destructive role in the organism of the world.

These laws portray a world of violence, greed, and opportunism. The stumbling-block idea urges that one develop not only a conscience but a consciousness of the shadier modes of collaboration with violence. As we have seen, the connection between a father and a son is more complex than one might have thought. The father should be aware of his fraught role in his son's world. Even the friend who kindly lends money should transcend a naïve innocence; he should acknowledge his own nature sufficiently to extrapolate to the other. A witness clarifies the ethical situation and thereby, at least in ethical terms, lightens the debtor's burden.

"You shall fear your God!" sets up an aspirational movement, in which deeper self-knowledge and understanding of the unconscious structure of human relations becomes a trajectory to be pursued beyond one's present grasp.

These cases induce a sense of one's implication with others. In their development from the original stumbling-block scenario, they represent an ethics of aspiration rather than of duty. There is a moral requirement to sharpen one's sense of responsibility beyond the basic knowledge of right and wrong. An acute moral vision may be developed, as in George Eliot's description:

> If we had a keen vision and a feeling for all ordinary human life, it would be like hearing the grass grow and the squirrel's heart beat, and we should die of that roar which lies on the other side of silence. As it is, the quickest of us walk about well wadded in stupidity.[57]

George Eliot exacerbates our imagination of what such a sharpening of empathy might do to us. Ordinary human life, it transpires, is far from ordinary; it throbs with desire and fear. Keener senses might become a fatal gift. But the alternative to such intense awareness is, after all, stupidity.

LOVE YOUR NEIGHBOR?

The particulars of aspiration, then, play out in a world of pain and violence. With this dark assumption, we now approach the heart of the matter: "Love your neighbor as yourself" (Lev. 19:18). Reduced to three words, this is *the* great ethical commandment. From the center of Leviticus, it addresses us with a demand for radical empathy.

How does this commandment of love belong in its context, in a text bristling with negative commandments?

> You shall not go about gossiping among your people; and you shall not stand by the blood of your neighbor; I am God. You shall not hate your brother in your heart. You shall take no vengeance nor bear a grudge against your kinsman. *Love your neighbor as yourself! I am God!* (Lev. 19:16–18)

Suddenly, again, the burst of sunlight in a tangled forest of hatred, vengeance, gossip: the imperative of love. Of these words, R. Akiva says, "This is the great *klal*, the foundational principle of the Torah."[58]

The problem, of course, is that this noble principle is unrealistic. As Ramban and others say, it runs counter to human nature. We will always love ourselves more than anyone else. Ramban therefore limits the meaning of "love" to a concern for the well-being of the other. Perhaps this is the reason for the dative form, "Love *for* your neighbor"—*le-re'acha*. Wish him well, in the same way as you wish yourself well. Even this limited form of love, however, challenges human nature; you will still wish for more blessings for yourself. But, in this commandment, the Torah asks us to attempt to transcend our envy.

At the same time, self-love is acknowledged as a fact of life. Ramban himself remarks, "A human being is partial to himself." *Adam karov le-atzmo.* And R. Akiva famously ruled in accordance with this natural human proclivity: if two people are lost in a desert and one has water sufficient to save one person, one may save oneself: "Your life has precedence."[59]

Freud, too, wrote of this commandment: "[It] is impossible to fulfill; such an enormous inflation of love can only lower its value, not get rid of the difficulty. . . . [This commandment] is the strongest defense against human aggressiveness and an excellent example of the . . . cultural super-ego."[60] Unrealistic, excessive, and ineffective, the superego causes suffering without achieving change. The central expression of biblical ethics becomes the harsh voice that polices one's inner life: a source of frustration rather than inspiration. The commandment, he says, is "unpsychological."

This is not entirely unlike Ramban's comment that the commandment is *haflagah*—an exaggeration, or, in Freud's terms, enormously inflated. Ramban assumes that the commandment cannot be meant literally. He therefore translates the "love" of the commandment to refer to behavioral benevolence. R. Akiva does not cite it in his ruling; but he does maintain that it is "the great principle of the Torah."

YOUR NEIGHBOR?

If we turn our attention from love to "your neighbor," we notice that the word *re'a* is not a specially friendly word. In the immediate context, we read, "You shall not stand by the blood of your neighbor." The neighbor is simply another person like yourself who is in danger and whom you might, at some risk to yourself, save from death. He is not someone you particularly love.

"Your neighbor" is potentially the object of envy (Exod. 20:17), of your oppression (Lev. 19:13), the one on whose territory you might trespass (Deut. 19:14). On the rare occasions where the neighbor is a friend, an adjective is required to make that clear: "Your neighbor who is *like your very soul*" (Deut. 13:7).[61] In a wedding ceremony, the couple arc referred to as "beloved neighbors!"

The *re'a* is, at base, simply one in whose company one finds oneself. This is the other whom we are commanded to love. It is the sheer otherness of the other that gives rise to the commandment. Even the other as your brother is not romanticized: "You shall not hate your brother in your heart" (Lev. 19:17) implies that hatred is not unusual in this relationship. On the contrary, hatred is not forbidden; perhaps, realistically, it could not be forbidden. It is *unexpressed hatred,* hatred in your heart, that is forbidden: "If he has mistreated you, don't pretend to be his friend. . . . But reprove him in the right way."[62] Reading the sequence of commandments, Rashbam creates a therapeutic narrative of effectively expressed hostility. The poison of repressed hatred can lead to murder: "if someone hates his neighbor and lies in wait for him and rises up to strike him down and he dies" (Deut. 19:11).

The English poet William Blake starkly described this dynamic in "A Poison Tree":

> *I was angry with my friend;*
> *I told my wrath, my wrath did end.*
> *I was angry with my foe:*
> *I told it not, my wrath did grow.*
> *In the morning glad I see;*
> *My foe outstretched beneath the tree.*

Blake's "friend" may be the biblical "neighbor" as the object of anger. Telling one's anger relieves pressure; even if it does not lead to murder, repression is an evil in itself. The poison is clearly active in the inner world of the subject. On the other hand, reproving the other is a notoriously difficult art, which the Rabbis advise us not to try if we cannot do it well. And yet in the context of repression it offers a cathartic release.

But if aggression is so prevalent in human relations, what can the commandment to love your neighbor plausibly mean? Here, too, the

Rabbis provide specific examples of how the "general principle" may be applied.

One example refers to the death penalty: the form of execution should be as humane as possible. "Select for the condemned an easy form of death!"[63] This is learned from "Love your neighbor as yourself!" The principle of empathy is at work, even when dealing with someone who seems as distant from oneself as it is possible to be. Assuming "you" are the judge, you must grant the criminal what you would wish for yourself in his place. The neighbor is the quintessential Other in this scenario. Because of this, the commandment of empathy becomes powerful.

Similarly, "It is forbidden to marry a wife without first seeing her—lest he sees something repulsive in her that makes her unattractive to him. For the Torah says, 'Love your neighbor as yourself!' "[64] Physical attraction in marriage is important: this impersonal reality is respected in Jewish law. But the proof text sheds a different light on the situation. The concern here is for the woman: How would you like to be in her position if she marries you and then you are repelled by her? Again, the empathy, or the humanity, is manifested precisely in a situation where male sexual needs put the woman into an object position. The Talmud mitigates this by enlarging the man's moral imagination: she is different from you, but she is also just like you!

The limits of altruism are acknowledged, even as they are (partially) redeemed. Another case: "How is it that a son is permitted [when there is no one else able to do it] to bleed (give medical care to) his father? 'Love your neighbor as yourself!' "[65] The legal question arises because of the risk that the son may slip up and wound his father, which is forbidden. But "Love your neighbor as yourself!" means doing for the other what one would want done for oneself. In my father's place, what would I want?

Again, with all the reverence due to one's father, one is required to have sufficient understanding of one's own nature to extrapolate to the other—who in this case is one's father. In all these cases, the tension of otherness is palpable. It is not just, as Ramban claims, that I wish for the other what I would wish for myself: love as pragmatic benevolence. Rather, the other is someone whom naturally I might find unfathomable, unendurable, intimidating. This very otherness is countered by a movement of *identification:* the other is just like me, in my own sense of internal otherness! My basic vulnerability calls out for a different sense of kinship with the other.

One expression of the paradox is found in the Talmudic parable: How do we understand, "Do not take revenge nor bear a grudge!"? This is like someone who was cutting meat and accidentally cut his other hand. Can you imagine that he would take revenge on his cutting hand by cutting it back with his wounded hand?[66] One's two hands are parts of one body. One should think of revenge as equally absurd. Being part of the same organism affects the relation between the offender and his victim. For one thing, both are subject to unconscious impulses.

ON ONE FOOT

Through a kind of thought game, the Talmud sponsors the idea of a dynamic connection between people who could not be more different. The classic source for this is the famous story of Hillel and the would-be proselyte, who demands of the Rabbi: "Teach me the whole Torah while I stand on one foot!" Hillel answers, "What is hateful to you, don't do to another: that is the whole Torah; the rest is commentary. Now go and learn."[67]

Basing the whole Torah on one principle (like standing on one foot) is Hillel's serious response to what sounds like a provocation in the mouth of the proselyte. Hillel translates the biblical commandment "Love your neighbor . . ." into manageable human terms. Love means not doing to another what you would find hateful for yourself. An impossible positive command is reduced to a plausible and therefore more "rational" negative command.

However, in Rashi's reading, Hillel is also implying that just as you don't like to have your wishes overridden, so don't go against God's wishes. This is the foundation of the whole Torah, which is the divine word: its Speaker becomes the object of our empathy![68] The assumption is that one is humanly sensitive about one's own dignity; God, as your "friend," should appeal to your moral imagination. To imagine God as vulnerable in this way may seem to stretch anthropomorphism too far. For this reason, perhaps, Ben Azzai prefers a different foundational principle: "This is the book of human history on the day God created the human being in the image of God" (Gen. 2:5). Theological dogma is more stable than human psychology. But Hillel's radical theology of ethical sensibility remains to challenge the bounds of common sense.

NOW GO AND LEARN!

Hillel's answer is most striking in its last part: "The rest is commentary. Now go and learn!" The biblical text—or any text—requires interpretation, particularly when a difficult verse, like "Love your neighbor as yourself," is being read. Hillel himself comments on the role of interpretation. This verse, he says, is the basic principle, the basic text—and the rest is commentary. He is giving the proselyte more than information about basic principles. "Love your neighbor" lies at the center; but this text—like all Torah texts—requires of the student a process of interpretation and practice that is called the Oral Torah.

If the proselyte rests content with the "whole Torah" and neglects the detailed examination of context and human experience, he will be the poorer for it. If, on the other hand, he becomes submerged in commentary and forgets the foundation of it all—"Love your neighbor"—then he will have understood nothing at all! If one learns the laws governing the execution of condemned prisoners, or courtship, or bleeding one's father, without attending to the heart of the matter—"Love your neighbor"—one will have entirely missed the point.[69] This the proselyte himself understands, since it is he who challenges Hillel to provide the core text.

What will one have missed? What does the *klal,* the general principle, offer that all the applications lack? Precisely the strangeness, the provocation of the original wording, which cannot be accessed without translation and yet can never be fully translated. When all is said and done, the radical claim "Love your neighbor" eludes domestication: this is its uncanny offering to the reader.

GROUND ON WHICH WE MEET

At heart, the commandment implies, "Love your neighbor—*who is just like yourself!*"[70] The subject is not self-love and benevolence but shared identity. The quality of love may not be the same, but the very being of the other mirrors one's own being. This neighbor—who has every reason to be wary of you; who may need to be protected from your aggression; who may be of a different gender; who may be a man condemned to death, or a revered father—this neighbor is profoundly connected with you. In theological terms, the connection is rooted in the idea that both were created in the image of God. But this idea now needs to be acknowledged in the powerful strangeness of the other's presence.

However, this empathic recognition is not, as Freud scathingly declared, a demand of the superego. On the contrary, being with another means acknowledging one's own inner otherness. One is not being exhorted by the voice of the policeman or the judge; rather, one unavoidably sees a resemblance in the very ground of one's being. Eric Santner writes, "To put it most simply, the Other to whom I am answerable *has an unconscious,* is the bearer of an irreducible and internal otherness."[71] Being with another means "exposure not simply to the thoughts, values, hopes, and memories of the Other, but also to the Other's touch of madness, to the way in which the Other is disoriented in the world."

The encounter creates a shared opening to the uncanny strangeness of the "space we call home." In this vision of things, being just like the other is based on the fact "that every familiar is ultimately strange and that, indeed, I am even in a crucial sense a stranger to myself."[72]

In Santner's discussion, the other is just like you—precisely in the sense that he, too, has blind spots, points of failure, that make him both threatening and unbearable. But precisely here begins "*a specific way of opening to the Other* in the place and time we already inhabit."[73] In our obligations to the Other, we open ourselves also to the idea of God as present within this paradoxical love of the neighbor. That is, within the most concrete dimensions of living in the midst of life we recognize the presence of God, who nevertheless remains absolutely transcendent.

This is love of the neighbor who is just like you in being disoriented in the world. The singular demonic being of the Other becomes the ground on which we meet: what Santner calls the various forms of Egyptomania, the remains of lost forms of life that distort one's being.[74] Here, the Golden Calf is encountered time and time again.

Meeting on this ground, we engage directly with defensive fantasies and allow new possibilities to arise.[75]

OPAQUE RADIANCE

The moment of encounter becomes the moment of acknowledging what it is to be created in God's image. Beyond the idiosyncrasies of internal and external otherness, there remains the *klal gadol,* the great principle, "Love your neighbor—*who is like you!*" Translated into many possible forms of encounter, it yet remains irreducible.

Like the other "great principle"—"Be holy!"—loving the neighbor remains, in all its radiance, somehow opaque. Beyond all legal transactions, it makes a demand that is radical, anarchic, private, and subject to controversy and hypocrisy. Holiness, too, with all its specific applications, is ultimately a personal discipline that resists rigorous evaluation. One aspires to more than can be embodied in formal practice. Like the practice of music, we have suggested, the rules go only so far in accounting for the genius of what can happen. A new world of value, even perhaps a new sensibility, is formed that brings one back to the original yearning as the only satisfactory ground of this future: "This is what I was after all along."[76]

At the heart of all the rituals of atonement, too, there is the principle of the thing—*li'heyot li*—"being unto Me." Being unto God is refracted into a myriad practices and avoidances. Acknowledging the aggressiveness of the human heart, the community works to clear a space for the heart of the matter. This is a cathartic process in which, indeed, the process *is* the encounter with God. And yet, the principles of holiness and of love of the neighbor suffuse the practices of purity with an energy that is, and is not, inherent in those practices.

"You shall revere your God": there are matters that are relegated to the privacy of the heart; there, only the divine can testify to the truth. There, one is free to lie, or to experience the ironic uncanniness of things. The scapegoat is expelled into the wilderness. The Golden Calf is confronted, smashed against the desert rocks. But a sensibility that values truth and love and holiness must infuse all acts of purification if they are to be meaningful. The human heart, the individual conscience validates the practices. At the same time, the behaviors, the *mitzvot,* affect the heart.

This is the hermeneutic circle of religious life. Without a grasp of the whole, how can one engage with the part? Without the part, how can one begin to access the whole? The movement of the two questions perhaps constitutes what we have called aspiration.

A teaching from Sefat Emet:

> Rashi comments on "You shall revere your God": This is said of matters that are left to the individual conscience. The obvious meaning of this is that only fear of God can move one to scrupulous fulfillment of these requirements. But it is also true that fulfilling these commandments brings one to the fear of God. Human behavior and human intentionality have a reciprocal relation to each other. . . . So, both readings are true, as it is written, "The reward of a commandment is a commandment."
>
> And certainly through the depth of fear of God one can come better to fulfill commandments of the private conscience. In turn, the reward for conscientious fulfillment of these commandments is the fear of God that will lead one to the better fulfillment of those same commandments—and so on forever.[77]

And so on forever, concludes Sefat Emet. The energy of aspiration feeds into the acts and is fed by them. This is the dynamic of deepening awareness of the ways in which the parts are implicated with each other. The separate acts, the individual people, so differentiated, subject to conflict, to purification, are nevertheless, from a different perspective, limbs of one body. How, then, can there be revenge, hatred, or oppression?

But both perspectives apparently need to be kept in motion. The world in which "I am holy" and your neighbor is like yourself involves a radical connection between self and other. Separateness gives way to a vision of oneness; separateness dissolves.

In 2001, an experiment was conducted in which the brains of people who were engaged in deep prayer or meditation were scanned using a technology known as SPECT (single photon emission computed tomography). One finding was that certain areas—in the posterior superior parietal lobe—went dark during deep meditative states. "This part of the brain normally feeds us ongoing signals regarding the physical limits of our individual selves in relation to everything else, helping us separate 'us' from 'not us,' with messages such as 'I'm here, not there.'" These signals stopped firing in the deepest meditative states.[78]

This quieting down, it was speculated, allowed the subjective experience of oneness and connectedness that mystics have known through the generations. It constitutes a moment of union with reality. Perhaps learning how to tune down the flow of incoming sensory information helps to achieve "the art of union with reality."[79]

> *With an eye made quiet by the power*
> *Of harmony, and the deep power of joy,*
> *We see into the life of things.*[80]

Perhaps when we come to such moments in the Torah as "Be holy, as I God am holy!" or "Love your neighbor as yourself!" something in us quiets down. Like the moment when we put our hands over our eyes and say, *Shema Yisrael*—"Hear, O Israel, God our God is one!" The sunlit space that is an enclave in the forest is deeply linked by roots and spores to the forest organism, a part of the whole.

6

Emor

An Anatomy of Hatred

Two men get into a fight. One of them blasphemes, he is brought to Moses for judgment, and the case is resolved only when God sentences the blasphemer to death. Since there are only two narratives in the book of Leviticus—the other is of the death of Aaron's sons—it is striking that in both the reader receives a similar kind of narrative shock. In the context of divine revelation, a disruption occurs, an act of violence—in one case, the strange, uncommanded fire;[1] in the other, the fight that generates blasphemy.[2] In both cases, the death of the protagonists ends the disorder they have provoked.

Violence suddenly enters the world. Always there is surprise, the feeling of a world disfigured. Why the blasphemy in the midst of a fight? "The enduring repetition of surprise," Lear remarks, in the course of a discussion about tragedy, "may eventually suggest that there is something about human destructiveness which lies beyond logos."[3] These are moments "when we suspect that all this carnage has happened for no reason at all."[4]

The phenomenon of the unfathomable is intensified in the second story when judgment is delayed: the blasphemer is kept in prison until sentence can be passed "by the mouth of God"—according to Rashi, "because they did not know if it was a capital offense or not" (Lev. 24:12). No one knows what to think, what to say about this act of blasphemy. Never explicitly forbidden until it actually happens, it shocks the reader as much as the other protagonists.

Looking more closely at this strange short story, we notice many anomalies. The blasphemer is described as "going forth"—*vayetze*—from where? He is identified as the son of an Israelite woman—why single her out as such, if not to signal that his status as an Israelite is not as straightforward as it looks? We hear next that he is also the son of an Egyptian man. His hybrid identity is emphasized as the fight breaks out between him and "an Israelite man." In this way, the reader is taken through a series of anomalies. Born of an impossible union between oppressor and slave, the mixed-breed fights the purebred.

Evidently, the "son of the Israelite woman" is the focus of the reader's interest. It is he who "goes forth into the midst of the Israelites" (Lev. 24:10) and it is he—the "son of the Israelite woman," three times described as such—who articulates the divine Name, and curses. Thereafter, he is referred to as "the one who cursed—*ha-mekallel*." He remains unnamed, as do his father and mother and his foe in combat, until he is taken into custody, when his mother is suddenly named.

There is, however, another possibility. Perhaps the story is told from the viewpoint of the "Israelite man," the man of straightforward Israelite identity. It is he who experiences the intrusion into the camp of an outsider, who has "gone forth" from elsewhere. An anomalous presence in camp interrupts the life of the normative Israelite; a fight ensues; and a blasphemy.

Rashi tells the hidden midrashic story:

> The blasphemer had gone forth from the law court of Moses which had ruled against him. When he had come to pitch his tent in the midst of Dan's encampment, he had been asked, "Who are you to camp here?" He had replied, "I am of the descendants of Dan." He had then been told, "But it is written, Each man camps by his flag, according to the insignia of his *father's* house" (Num. 2:2). Then he had gone to court and Moses had ruled against him. So he had risen up and blasphemed. (Rashi to 24:10)

The midrashic narrative explains both the fight and the blasphemy. Since he is of mixed parentage, his situation is complicated. As the son of an Israelite mother, he is an Israelite; but his place in the Israelite camp is regulated by patrilinear principle—according to his father's house. He finds himself disqualified from taking his place in the social, political world—the flags and insignia—of the Israelite camp. Where is he to put himself? In this crisis, he names God and curses.

Why is this disturbing narrative recounted in the book of Holiness?[5] By definition, blasphemy is an abhorrent act—an ugly, obscene use of language. For some commentators, the natural reaction to such an utterance would have been to lynch the offender.[6] Recourse to a court of law introduces doubt into the story: it is, after all, not clear how to evaluate the offense. Only God can decide the matter. But why the uncertainty around this act? Surely words that deface the divine Presence in the world are to be judged most gravely?

An ambiguity seems to attend this offense, which is absent from the closest parallel case—the act of the wood-gatherer who profanes the Sabbath (Num. 15:32–36). However, that act is read by the Rabbis as clearly deserving of the death penalty, without any of the uncertainty that attends our story.[7]

On the one hand, the sin of blasphemy is considered so grave that the words spoken cannot even be mentioned in the text. According to Talmudic law, even the witnesses who must testify to the words by uttering them in court may do so only in private session with the judges; in open court, a euphemism is used; the actual words may not be articulated. The testimony is heard only by the minimum quorum, who respond by tearing their clothes, like mourners after an intimate death. The gravity of the words makes them literally unspeakable.[8]

And yet, the same Talmudic passage excludes the blasphemy of a non-Jew from this mourning response—"else all their clothes will be in tatters!" This is a sarcastic comment on the *commonplace* nature of blasphemies in the non-Jewish world. The horrified reaction to a blasphemy is specific to the Jewish sensibility. In other cultures, such utterance—swear words, for instance, which speak violence against the deity—are trivial, a part of normal speech.[9]

Perhaps because of this ambiguity—blasphemy as outrage or as part of the linguistic order—the case needs to be referred to God Himself. Apparently, the verdict depends on how his identity—Israelite or non-Israelite—is defined. How does God view the profanation of His name? Viewed from the perspective of a normative "son of an Israelite man," the intrusion into the camp of an outsider into the camp—or, worse, of a man of mixed breed—arouses fear and disgust. However, in the Zohar,[10] it is the Israelite man who, by calling his mother a harlot, provokes the mixed-breed to blaspheme. In doing so, he exposes a scandalous story from the past. He therefore bears some responsibility for the blasphemous reaction of the woman's son, who is, after all, defending his mother's reputation. The act of exposing the traumas of the past is, in itself, a grave misuse of language.

But why does the blasphemer attack God rather than cursing the Israelite who provoked his rage? The midrashic plot thickens. The blasphemer's mother, named Shulamit, was the wife of an Israelite taskmaster in Egypt. He was sent on a mission by his Egyptian superior and the latter took the opportunity to enter the Israelite's home and have relations with his wife. In one version of the story, she is declared to be innocent: she thinks she is with her husband. In other versions, she is assumed to be complicit. The son who is born of this encounter is the future blasphemer.

The trauma of such origins—of a rape or act of fraternization between oppressor and oppressed—is linked with the moment when Moses first leaves the palace ("Moses went forth to his brothers to see their sufferings" [Exod. 2:11–12]) and kills the Egyptian overseer who was abusing a Hebrew slave. These two are identified as the adulterous Egyptian father of the blasphemer and the betrayed Israelite husband who is persecuted by the Egyptian. Moses kills the Egyptian for all his abusive behavior "in the house and in the field." "He lifted his eyes to God and said, Is it not enough that the wicked man abused his wife but he is also beating up her husband! Immediately, 'he smote the Egyptian and hid him in the sand.'"[11]

The next day, Moses encounters the two Hebrews fighting. When he intervenes, one of them taunts him: "Who appointed you as an authority or judge over us? Do you intend (lit., say) to kill me as you killed the Egyptian?" (Exod. 2:14). From this reference to killing-by-speech, Rashi notes, "we learn that Moses had killed the Egyptian by *uttering the explicit Name of God.*"

This traumatic history includes sexual abuse, physical brutality, killing, and the violent use of the divine Name. The offspring of this situation is the future blasphemer, the son of the abused mother and of her abuser. Moses has killed the blasphemer's father, and now excludes the son from a place in the Israelite camp. The son defends his mother's honor and curses the divine Name that had been used against his father.

Why tell this story at all? Just as it might have been better in the first place if the Israelite had not confronted the blasphemer, so it might have been better to censor the whole violent story.[12] In a sense, telling the story, even in its stark, repressed biblical form, is itself a kind of blasphemy. However, if in fact the blasphemy happened, the framing of a law is necessary to regulate future cases. The case history precedes and justifies the law; it must therefore be recovered in all its ugliness.

In this case, the violent midrashic narrative, with its linking biblical clues, affects the reader in complex ways.[13] On the one hand, the background narrative may alienate the reader, the unspeakable becoming the unthinkable. But on the other hand, this same narrative may invoke empathy with the human situation of the blasphemer. Complex themes arising from this narrative bear a primal intensity that invites a psychoanalytic reading. In order to discuss these complexities, we will need to go deeper into the thicket. Without articulating blasphemy, we will have to understand it.

BLASPHEMY: GRAVITY OR TRIVIALITY?

It is striking that the law of blasphemy is immediately followed by the law of murder: "Anyone who strikes down a human life shall be put to death" (Lev. 24:17). The natural context of blasphemy, apparently, is murder and violent bodily injury ("As he has done, so shall be done to him . . . An eye for an eye . . ." [chapters 19–20]).

Here, Seforno asks: Why, in this context, do we find—twice—the statement "The stranger is to be treated exactly like the citizen"; once in reference to the blasphemer (24:16) and once in reference to murder (24:22)? An analogy is being suggested: blasphemy is a kind of murder. But who is the victim?

Seforno points to the gravity of blasphemy, raising the possible objection that we have noted—that it is, after all, commonplace in the world and therefore the fact of the blasphemer's mixed parentage might have constituted an extenuating circumstance. After all, Jewish law, even in this passage, assigns different outcomes in different circumstances: whether it is a human being or an animal that has been killed, or injured, or whether it is one's parents or someone else who has been injured. But in these two cases—blasphemy and murder—circumstances make no difference. "*Ka-ger ka-ezrach,* stranger and citizen alike . . . For I, God your God, am the God of both stranger and citizen."[14] In these two cases, there is a gravity that transcends situational difference.

Blasphemy is *both* commonplace and repulsive. But the gravity of the offense becomes clear only after the divine verdict has been delivered. Before that, gravity and triviality hang in the balance, undetermined. If it happens so commonly, perhaps it can be viewed as venial?

How, then, are we to understand the sin of blasphemy? Seforno quotes Isaiah 8:21: "'And it will be when they suffer hunger, they torment themselves and curse by their king and by their god.' This refers to the chronic anger of the poor who are angered by everything that happens to them."[15]

Cursing and blasphemy is an expression of a general exasperation with life. When one is suffering, there is a natural impulse to turn against the authority, whether human or divine, who is seen as the source of oppression.

In a different context, Ramban suggests that the Sin Offering of the repentant leper (*metzora*) is atonement for any expletives (*tifla l'elohim*) he may have uttered in the painful process of his cleansing. Such a minor expletive is natural in the circumstances but needs atonement.

The same expression—*tifla l'elohim*—occurs in Job 1:22. In spite of all his losses at the beginning of his story, "nevertheless, Job did not sin nor did he ascribe anything unseemly to God." The word *tifla* seems to represent a venial offense, a meaningless cry of frustration. When, however, Job is later afflicted with leprosy, the issue of blasphemy appears in full force. His wife urges him to end it all by uttering blasphemy: "Do you still hold fast to your integrity! Blaspheme God and die!"[16] Blasphemy is a kind of suicide or euthanasia. What is undoubted is its destructive effect. Job responds with contempt for his wife's moral and spiritual weakness: "'You speak like one of the *nevalot*—the primitive women. Should we accept only good from God and not accept evil?' For all this, Job did not sin with his lips."

Job's *integrity*, his moral strength, is expressed in his restraint. But

Rashi reevaluates his silence: "but in his heart he did sin." He avoided the sin of blasphemy, which is verbal, castigating his wife for even talking *about* blasphemy. But "in his heart, he did sin." Emotionally, though not verbally, blasphemy has in some way claimed a place in his inner life.[17]

ANATOMY OF HATRED

What, then, is blasphemy in the heart? Hatred is the emotion that motivates both violence in action—the *makkah*—and blasphemy in language. Anger, frustration at injustice, disappointment at one's personal fate—or more generally at the apparent moral chaos of the world—all can be subsumed in the impulse of hatred.

Freud thought of hatred as the ego state that wishes to destroy the source of its unhappiness. In the life of the young child, this refers to the external world that in some way threatens his internal world: "At the very beginning . . . the external world—objects—and what is hated are identical."[18]

"If a person who hates another lies in wait for him and sets upon him and strikes him a fatal blow" (Deut. 19:11). The law addresses the fatal blow of the *makkeh,* but traces it to its hidden root, hatred. Rashi comments: Because of his hatred, he comes to the point of ambush and murder. From here they said, "If one transgresses a light commandment, then one will in the end transgress a weighty one." Like the butterfly effect that triggers chaos, the "light" transgression—hatred—will inevitably find its outlet in murder.

In what sense is hatred a "light" offense? Strikingly, the command against hatred is cited from Leviticus 19:17, a few chapters before the blasphemer narrative. In a powerful passage that deals with hatred and love: "You shall not hate your brother in your heart." This is *unexpressed* hatred; it is precisely *repressed* hatred that has such toxic effects. Better to *rebuke* your brother so as not to bear sin for him in your heart.[19] Repressing animosity is not a virtue; here, it is expressly forbidden. Its pathological potential is evident.[20] However, the call to *rebuke* the other turns out to be, in its way, just as problematic. It is a skill that is easy to get wrong, say the Rabbis. Better not to practice it at all if one cannot do it well.

Seemingly "light," unimportant, the ban on hatred in the heart arises from the One who commands it: "Know who commanded it and let it not be light in your eyes; I am God" (Rashi). The "lightness" is only in human eyes. It gains mass and weight from the divine Presence. "Be as careful with a light commandment as with a weighty one."[21] In this sense, there is no intrinsic difference between the two. Even though hatred does not express itself physically or verbally, it contains the potential for the most violent expressions.

These violent expressions are forbidden. But how can the "lighter" prohibition of "hatred in the heart" be forbidden? If an emotion is inherent, can it be forbidden? In rabbinic thought, the contradiction is only apparent. The assumption is that primal, commonplace destructiveness can, in some way, be managed. Rashbam demonstrates this paradoxical logic, for instance, when he comments on the exhortation against cursing judges: "Many people curse kings and judges when they do not attain their desire; *therefore,* we are warned against this: 'You shall not curse judges.'"[22] The logic is clear: the reason for the prohibition to curse judges is precisely because it is a common practice. *Therefore,* it represents a substantial target for legal intervention!

Again, on this proof text: "This speaks about what really happens in the world. Since kings and judges rule on financial issues and capital offenses, human beings are accustomed to curse them."[23]

Here, again, the logic is laid out with empirical clarity: cursing kings and judges is such a common practice because they have the power to rule on existential issues—capital punishment and financial damages. Since one stands to lose one's property or even one's life in the wake of such rulings, anger, resentment, and despair are a natural reaction to losing one's case. The curse is an expression of hatred of authority and of those who wield it. Its grounding in a common resentment ties emotion and behavior together. Implicitly, this bundle of hatred and cursing is understood to be a "natural" human response, which Torah law prohibits.

THE VIOLENCE OF THE LAW

It is the violence of the law that, in the first place, elicits the forbidden curse. However, the same expression, "cursing the *judges* (*elohim*)" has two meanings. Rashi offers both meanings: "This is an exhortation against blasphemy, as well as against cursing judges." *Elohim* is a name

for God, as well as for the powerful forces that police the world. Forbidding blasphemy acknowledges the same human reaction against
power that restricts, condemns, and punishes human desire. Hatred
is the violent and helpless response to the violence of the law. In
Freud's terminology, it is the *id*—the primal aggressive instinct—that
hits out blindly at those who oppose it. The id, as Bruno Bettelheim
has remarked, is simply the *it* of a human being—that child part that
will brook no opposition.[24]

As the legal theorist Robert Cover puts it, the legal world, the organized violence of institutions "places bodies on the line."[25] A society
builds a legal world on coercion; "the judges deal in pain and death."[26]

The biblical legal world shows an awareness of this in the injunction not to leave the body of an executed criminal hanging overnight.
"You shall indeed bury it the same day, for the hanged man is a curse
against God" (Deut. 21:23).[27]

Rashi reads this strongly. Leaving the body hanging overnight subjects it to disfigurement and is, in itself, a profanation of God:

> This is an insult, an act of contempt for the King, since the hu-
> man being is created in the divine image. This is like identical
> twins, one of whom becomes a prince while the other is jailed
> for robbery and hanged. Seeing him, people say, "The prince has
> been hanged!" Every *curse* (*kelalah*) in the Torah is an expression
> of taking *lightly* (*kal*) or insult.

God's presence in the world is vulnerable to slights and insults. The
blasphemer has done something to deface that presence; his hanged
body, too, evokes the "twin" in whose image he was created. The violence of blasphemy is played out in the punishment: both diminish
the impact of the divine. If the blasphemer must be hanged, the disgrace of a human body must be kept to a minimum. Immediate burial
is required.[28] The Name of Heaven—the *Shem shamayim*—is not to be
doubly desecrated.

"You shall not profane My holy name, and I shall be sanctified in
the midst of the Israelites; I am God who sanctifies you, who brings
you out of the land of Egypt to be God to you" (Lev. 22:32–33). The
purpose of the Exodus is the human sanctification of the divine. This

involves a certain heroic attachment to ideals of beauty and dignity. The act of blasphemy is, essentially, an explosive act of disfigurement of the divine, and therefore of the human image. It undermines the purpose of the Exodus, which is a continuous process of realizing that beauty: God *brings* us out of Egypt, in order to become our God. Exodus in the present tense is an ongoing process that is undermined by human acts of violence.

Profanation, like cursing, makes a hole in the midst of things. *Le-chalel*—to profane—is rooted in the idea of a cavity;[29] *le-kalel*—to curse—likewise, is to make light of the weighty. But the devaluation of values is most clearly intimated in the specific term for blasphemy—*va-yikov et Ha-Shem,* which Rashi, following the Targum, translates as *u-farish*—"he *articulated clearly* the divine Name, which is called the *Shem meforash*—the explicit Name that he had heard at Sinai. And he cursed it."[30] There are two stages to blasphemy—the very articulation of the Name that is almost never to be articulated, followed by the curse.

Articulating the Name itself raises the basic question of disclosing what is meant to remain covered, implicit. This is an act of devaluation of the Name that was publicly heard, in the divine voice, at Sinai. Otherwise to be shrouded in mystery, its privacy is violated by the blasphemer, even before he actually curses. Ironically, Rashi emphasizes that this Name was heard by the blasphemer at Sinai—who then ravages what had been revealed. There had been a singular moment of disclosure that he now vulgarizes in order to demolish its power.

In view of this, it is striking that this whole case is then treated as a mystery that requires divine explanation—"to be explicated through the mouth of God." It is the divine mouth that must pronounce judgment and reduce the mystery to human dimensions of meaning and action. The world of law, with all its violence (the death sentence), is the decoding of an enigma, immediately and for the future: "Anyone who articulates the divine Name shall be put to death . . . the stranger and the citizen alike, when he articulates the divine Name" (Lev. 24:16).[31]

Blasphemy is thus an expression of aggression toward God, as the authority, the King-Judge, whose judgments threaten human life. In the Talmudic narrative, the blasphemer has experienced Revelation at

Sinai and therefore knows the secret Name of God. With this knowledge, he has become part of the collective of Israel. But the traumas
of his past disrupt any stable identity. He cannot pitch his tent in any
part of the camp. Displaced from the public social world, with its
powers and institutions, he is also intimately *homeless*. He lashes out
against God, who has shaped his fate in a way that threatens his most
basic sense of self.

TANGLES OF THE LAW

Is his mother a harlot? What did she know during her encounter with
the Egyptian? Is her son a *mamzer*—the declassed offspring of an act
of adultery? Or, since this adultery took place before the Torah was
given at Sinai, is he simply *ke-mamzer*—*like* a *mamzer*? The label matters; it will have significant effects on his life. His mother's state of
consciousness during one particular night has drastic implications for
the fate of her son. Is he, in fact, even Israelite? Commentaries argue
over the issue. Since his mother is Israelite, he must be, too. Why,
then, is he described in rabbinic sources as *having become an Israelite*?[32]

Ramban discusses these issues in his commentary on the beginning of the narrative. On the one hand, he notes that this man, with
his particular history, actively chose to adhere to his Israelite background. He "went forth . . . *into the midst* of the Israelites." He vol-
untarily leaves one possible world to enter into another. This means
that he *converted* to the Israelite religion. Ramban understands this
to mean that he committed himself to the religion *in the same way* as
Israel in general entered the covenant at Sinai, through circumcision
and immersion and the sprinkling of blood.

This extraordinary reading credits the blasphemer with having
made a choice that now identifies him as a member of the Israelite
people. He follows his mother, and is therefore a part of her people.
And yet he is described in rabbinic sources as a *ger*—an outsider; his
Egyptian paternity and the outlaw status of the *mamzer* remain a blot
on his identity and fate. Alienated, angry, he fights the Israelite insider
and attacks the deepest meanings of his own best moment at Sinai.

He finds himself caught in a tangle of the law. Neither clearly inside
nor outside, his marginality deprives him of any sense of home. In
this state of confusion, *vayikov et Ha-Shem—he simplifies* meaning by

articulating it in its most violent form. To articulate in this way is to reduce a complexity, killing it by spelling it out.

Of course, this is what law does when it categorizes, pinning the butterfly into a page of words. In a sense, it is analogous with what Moses did when he killed the blasphemer's father by uttering the explicit divine Name. But a corollary of this is that the divine Name is vulnerable to the hostility of those who articulate it. It can be spoken in many ways, for sanctification or for defilement.

Moses uses the Name to destroy the Egyptian persecutor and (perhaps) rapist. This is an act of ultimate violence on Moses's part. It is his first reaction to the field of violence that is Egypt. Words about smiting, blows, killing abound, in describing both the Egyptian ethos and the divine response. The Ten Plagues—*makkot*—are the most obvious example of the language of violence that describes both Egyptian evil and divine punishment.

In this stark drama, Moses plays a central role. His hand brings down plagues, splits the Sea, and smashes the Tablets of Revelation. In the end, it strikes the rock at Merivah, effectively bringing his life and mission to an end.[33] The cycle of violence is perpetuated in the private world of traumatic experience.

Like the blasphemer, Moses is the outsider who has "gone forth"— *vayetzei* (Exod. 2:11): he has left the palace to see his brothers' sufferings. The Israelite slaves are his brothers, but does he know that they are his brothers? Or is their family relationship known only to narrator and reader? If we read this moment with a sense of dramatic irony, then Moses is caught in a crisis of uncertainty about his own identity. In the eyes of his people, too, he remains somehow unknown, difficult to place. "Moses the man who brought us up from the land of Egypt—we don't know what has happened to him!" (Exod. 32:1). "And no one knew his [place of] burial" (Deut. 34:6).[34]

Moses's mother nurses him, hides him, and places him in the river of death. Then, she resumes nursing him, as the adoptive child of another woman. After that, like many a biblical mother, she disappears from the scene. The blasphemer's mother, however, is named—just at the crisis of the story, when he is apprehended for his blasphemy. She is called Shulamit, daughter of Divri, which the midrash reads, "[S]he was a prattler (*dabranit*) who greeted all comers with Shalom!"[35] In this derogatory midrash, she insists on her place in the world. But a tragic history issues from her: a son without a place in the world who, in fighting to defend her name and his integrity, blasphemes. He gives voice to a scream of rage. Behind the scream lie what Elizabeth Hardwick has called "the human collisions [of the past] that are, finally, our biographies."[36]

STATES OF VULNERABILITY

The case of the *ger,* the stranger, is the emblematic representation of such states of vulnerability. No less than thirty-six times, the biblical text reiterates its concern for the stranger, "for you yourselves were strangers in the land of Egypt." The ground of this empathy is shared experience: your experience of this form of suffering should sensitize you to the similar situation of others.

However, commenting on Exodus 22:20, "You shall not vex the *ger,* the stranger, for you yourself were a stranger in the land of Egypt," Rashi chooses to emphasize a different moral: if you vex him, he can vex you back, by saying, "You too came from strangers! Don't point out a blemish in your friend when you have it yourself!" In Rashi's Talmudic source,[37] one is forbidden to cause the stranger emotional distress by referring to his pagan background, by talking about his parents and his past way of life. This extends to harassing a Jew who has changed his life by becoming observant. One may not distress him by referring to his past life.

The understanding is that the *ger* has skeletons in his cupboard, secret sources of embarrassment about his previous lifestyle. It is not empathy that Rashi is invoking but the knowledge that the most authentic insider carries a similar sense of inner *out-of-jointness,* a private history that haunts his inner world.

The Talmud uses a strange analogy: "One who has in his family someone who hanged himself will not be referring to hanging, even in a casual way ('Hang this picture for me!')." The sense of shame, of a "kernel of indignity," as Santner puts it, has a place in everyone. It is precisely this "kernel" in oneself that can make one unkind to the Other, who carries his "touch of madness" all too obviously.[38] For Santner, the demand to "Love your neighbor as yourself" means to endure the Other in his sometimes compulsive way of being. Like you, he *has an unconscious;* he is the bearer of an irreducible and internal otherness. In the abrasive encounter with him, one encounters one's own destitution, one's compulsive attachments to a social world that validates one's being. In Rashi's words, "he can vex you back": he can remind you verbally of your embarrassing "kernel of indignity," of the ways your investment in dignity serves a defensive purpose. "One who rejects the blemish of another rejects his own blemish."

In such an ethical demand, shame—the reference to the "blemish"—plays an ambiguous role. On the one hand, it is forbidden to shame the other verbally, by referring to his past life. On the other hand, the sense of shame can deepen the spiritual life of the outsider. Standing at the margins can make one aware of and help to release one from the defensive postures of the insider.[39]

THE READER'S AMBIVALENCE

In this connection, we may remember the encounter between Moses—who, we remember, refers to himself as a *ger* (Exod. 2:22)—and his father-in-law, Jethro. Moses recounts the history of the Exodus, a salvation history of the most resonant kind. "And Jethro rejoiced—*vayichad*—at all the goodness that God had enacted for Israel in saving them from the hand of Egypt" (Exod. 18:9). Moses's story is the first exercise in narrative to be narrated within the biblical text *about* the Exodus: effectively, it is the first fulfillment of the commandment to *tell the story.*[40] Rashi's comment focuses dramatically on the effects of a story:

> "Jethro rejoiced": that is the plain meaning of *vayichad.* But the midrash reads this: His flesh broke out in goose bumps (*chidudin chidudin*—sharp pins and needles) in his grief over the destruction of Egypt. So we say, "For ten generations, be careful what you say to a *ger* (a stranger)."

The visceral response of Jethro is not pure joy. The story of Israel's salvation is also the story of Egypt's defeat. Jethro is positioned to hear both stories, since he has a midrashic history of association with

Pharaoh and his people.[41] The story arouses in him a conflict of identifications: "his flesh broke out in goose bumps" vividly represents his divided loyalties—as well as providing a strong wordplay on *vayichad.*

A story has the power to arouse empathy in the reader or the listener. But its power may also lie in its ability to evoke deep ambivalences. While the law will cut through these ambivalences with its decisive readings, the narrative will allow full play to the inner world of the reader/listener.

Perhaps the story of the blasphemer, too, may be considered as a way of telling the story of the Exodus. For its traumas are also part of the history of all those who emerged from the violent field of Egypt. Perhaps for this reason, the story of the blasphemer is given in both the stark mystery of its biblical form and in the traumatic elaborations of its midrashic form. The effect on the reader is complex and, I suggest, ambivalent. There is repulsion and empathy, alienation and identification.

Within the story itself, storytelling plays a central role. The secret history of the blasphemer is revealed to him with devastating effect. His mother's name is revealed to the reader, with its derogatory implications about her uninhibited ways of speaking. As we have noticed, this reading of her name is in itself a kind of shaming. And the divine verdict indicates an authoritative reading of the events that have until now been undefined. Now a clear story can be told to insider and outsider alike: a story that leads to a death, in which the whole community is involved.[42]

THE AXE FOR THE FROZEN SEA

In this sense, a powerful story is by its nature both traumatic and potentially redemptive:

> I think we ought to read only the kind of books that wound and stab us. If the book we are reading doesn't wake us up with a blow on the head, what are we reading it for? . . . We need the books that affect us like a disaster, that grieve us deeply, like the death of someone we loved more than ourselves, like being banished into forests far from everyone, like a suicide. A book must be the axe for the frozen sea inside us.[43]

Breaking through defense mechanisms, the story that is worth reading has about it something indecent but necessary. This particular story about forbidden speech acts sheers close to reenacting the blasphemy. Like the procedure in the law courts, it avoids the explicit words, the actual names, by at first using generic terms—an Israelite, the son of an Israelite—and by avoiding repeating the words of the curse. But once the court has been cleared, in the presence of the judges alone, the witness utters the words, and all tear their clothes. An act of mourning—for a death, a destruction. Who, or what, has died? In reading the story, something similar transpires. Beyond the public words, there is the dangerous hidden story, which the reader constitutes for herself/himself. The words must be spoken, but they may not be spoken. With each story, something is mourned.

THE BLEMISH OF STRANGENESS

In the laws forbidding harassment of the stranger, what is the position of the reader? The answer is clear: the laws are addressed in the second person to the reader. We are the potential harassers. We are those who may torment the stranger, the widow, or the orphan.

In the story of the blasphemer, too, the Torah addresses us. I have suggested that the subject of this story is, precisely, the *insider,* the Israelite man. He is the one whose ordinary life is interrupted by the turbulence that the stranger brings with him. The *ger,* the stranger, carries associations with the *gargir,* the rootless organism, a globule, a shriveled olive, for instance. Stripped of the envelope of language and culture, the *ger* appeals, demands, intrudes. His otherness arouses a defensive solidarity in the citizen. Even the ways in which the Other is recognized as sharing a common humanity can work against him: he is similar to me, yet uncannily different, impossible to assimilate into my story.

The outsider is evocative in ways that can be unbearable. In our narrative, the outsider has some of the associations of the *ger,* some of the *mamzer*—which can be read as *moom zar,* the blemish of strangeness. Something in his presence brings out cruelty—the *achzar,* which can be read as *ach-zar,* only strange. Cruelty often arises from the sense that others are *only* foreign. What we share with others, our common humanity, ultimately finds no place in our reaction.[44]

The blasphemer, before he utters his attack on the divine Name, carries a full load of irreparable stigma. The midrash offers an other-worldly prospect of redemption:

> "And there went forth the son of an Israelite woman": We find (Eccles. 4:1), "But I returned and considered all the oppressions." Daniel the Tailor interpreted the verses as applying to bastards (*mamzerim*). "And behold the tears of such as were oppressed." If the parents of these bastards committed a transgression, what concern is it of these poor sufferers? So also if this man's father cohabited with a forbidden woman, what sin has he himself committed and what concern is it of his? "And they had no comforter [but] on the side of their oppressors there was power." This means, on the side of Israel's Great Sanhedrin which comes to them with the power derived from the Torah and which removes the bastard from the fold, in virtue of the commandment, "A bastard shall not enter the community of God" (Deut. 23:3). "But they had no comforter." Then God said, "It is My task to comfort them."[45]

The *mamzer* is the extreme case of the oppressed who, because of their parents' misdeeds, become victims of the law. Those who administer the law are identified as the oppressors: their power to exclude is backed by a clear Torah text. In this situation, God recognizes the opportunity to be the sole comforter of the oppressed.

The inexorable power of the law is a function of *this* world, which is our world. The end of the midrash (not quoted) presents the un-alloyed splendor of the world to come. God, too, has been in exile with the *mamzer* in this world—rather like the midrashic tradition of God's being in exile with the Jewish people in their sufferings. Ul-timately, the divine Presence that suffers with the oppressed of this world will bring redemption to light.

Two languages meet in this midrash: the language of law, in which the fate of the *mamzer* is written in stone, and the language of conso-lation and redemption, where God is set against the legal hegemony of the Sanhedrin. In this kabbalistic vision, the intrinsically broken world throws up phenomena of human suffering that only divine reframing can redeem.

A HOLE IN THE DOOR

In all this, we, the readers, to whom the Torah is addressed, are positioned rather uncertainly between the two worlds: we are citizens of the ordered world, set to protect our dignity against deranging strangeness, while in some sense God joins the *mamzerim* in exile from *our* world. In another sense, of course, we are affected by the rhetoric of the midrash to realign ourselves with God.

The Sages, the Sanhedrin try to make moral sense of situations where the victim is punished. When they reveal the name of the blasphemer's mother, and when they decode her name to implicate her in the adultery, they are perhaps trying to harmonize the moral disorder of the narrative. If the mother did not realize that it was not her husband who was with her, the *mamzer* situation, in all its harshness, is created without her moral agency. Such a notion is ethically unthinkable. She must, therefore, on some level have been aware of the true situation.

In a similar sense, there is no language to give ethical meaning to the fate of the blasphemer. In the technical tangle of the blasphemer's situation, the position of the blasphemer is constructed as untenable. How can the reader position herself in relation to such a fate? As the midrash implies, there is no comfort within the system of law for such tears as his. Here, God is conspicuously absent; the midrash recognizes this when it uses the God language of consolation and redemption to describe another, ultimate world.

The sufferer who blasphemes, however, *bores a hole* (*vayikov*, he cursed) in the meaning-structure of this world. The Zohar translates: "He made a hole in the door"—a violent puncture in the available words of the culture. His aggression pierces the divine Name that killed his Egyptian father. His words blast the world apart. In a sense, this is an understandable reaction to the slings and arrows of outrageous fortune, as well as to the oppressions of the law. It is a conscious attack on meanings that deny him his place in the world. Pure hatred spews from him, such as the witnesses find it hard to repeat, even within the court of law.

The words that cannot be repeated resound mutely through the narrative. Those who heard them place their hands on his head before stoning him. They, too, are traumatized by what they have heard;

they are secondary victims of the violence. Perhaps they, too, have had destructive thoughts? Otherwise, why are they fated to hear such obscenity?[46] One sees and hears that which can be taken into one's inner world. The witnesses' hands on the blasphemer's head express a wish for their own atonement.[47]

The hatred that shoots out of the narrative must affect the reader whose own inner life is unconsciously engaged. Roland Barthes discusses a similar experience of looking at a photograph and suddenly being affected by some detail that *pierces,* ruptures, punctuates the meaning of the photograph. He calls this the *punctum,* the sensitive point, the wound, the "little hole . . . the accident which pricks me (but also bruises me, is poignant to me)."[48] The language of the photograph is disrupted by this detail—it has been "pricked."

The words "He articulated the Name and he cursed it" affect us like a *punctum* of this kind. The (repressed) story leads up to this point, but it can be part of no continuum. The blasphemer is jailed, awaiting divine interpretation: how to think, what to do about the unthinkable? The destructive effect of the utterance remains enigmatic.

ATTACKING ONE'S OWN MIND

In the classic compendium of the laws given in the Torah, *Sefer Ha-Chinuch,* we find this:

> The blasphemer *empties himself* of all goodness when he utters these evil words. All the beauty of his soul turns toxic, and he becomes like an animal, since the faculty that distinguishes him from the animal and makes him human—language—has been used for destruction, removing him from any form of understanding. He has become like a disgusting roach, or worse. This is why the Torah warned against this, for the good God desires our good, and every utterance that bars us from the good runs counter to God's desire.[49]

In this reading, the blasphemer is the real victim of his own blasphemy. The power of language has been mobilized to diminish the goodness of the world. Physically destroying another person is one expression of hatred. Cursing is a verbal form of the same aggressive impulse. And blasphemy, aimed against the divine Name, *empties out* the good contents of one's inner life. In the imagery of this passage, the blasphemer is *eviscerated* of all that makes him human.

Psychoanalytic thinkers like D. W. Winnicott, Melanie Klein, W. R. Bion, and Jonathan Lear discuss the self-destructive impulse. Lear, for instance, speaks of acts of mental self-disruption. Such acts are neither good nor bad; they exist before good and bad, caused by a buildup of mental pressure, which is itself a result of the disruptions in a life. What the disruption is *for,* he suggests, depends on what happens next. The tragic possibility is that one may use these outbursts to *attack one's mind.*[50]

Lear cites Freud's famous anecdote in which he observes his grandson playing the *fort-da* game. The child would throw a wooden reel tied to string over the edge of his cot so that it disappeared into the cot. At the same time, he would keep saying *o-o-o-o,* which the family decodes as *fort* (*gone*). He would then reel it back by the string with a joyful *da* (*there*). Disappearance and return, the painful motif of his mother's absence and the joy of her return, become a game. Lear writes: "The game is prompted by a rip in the fabric of life. If we are trying to respect the child's point of view, we cannot even say that the game is prompted by loss. For it is only after the game is installed that the child will begin to have the concept of loss or absence. . . . The outcome of the game is to convert what would otherwise be a nameless trauma into a loss."

Lear describes the child as in the process of developing courage. If, on the other hand, the child were to get stuck repeating *o-o-o-o* and never get to *da,* he "might begin to use these outbursts to attack his own mind. For the child would never be able to get a thought together if each attempt to do so was interrupted by an outburst of '*o-o-o-o.*' . . . This would be the beginning of a massively self-destructive, self-annihilating character."

In his other cap as philosopher, Lear then makes a large distinction between the world of psychoanalysis and that of Aristotle. "There is no place in Aristotle's ontology," he declares, "for such a character." For Aristotle, all possible varieties of human beings are oriented toward the good, however mistaken one's notion of the good may be. The self-destructive character, on the other hand, is not directed toward any good; it is involved "in a primitive attack on the capacity to form motivation."[51] Rather than getting to the *da,* he simply blows his experience apart.

Is there any place in biblical or rabbinic thought for the self-destructive character? Taking the blasphemer as a test case, one could identify him as one for whom the "accidents" of his life have been simply *too much:* the sexual and genetic disorders of the past have disrupted his real position in the world.

There is a buildup of pressure. The wound of loss has not constituted itself into any kind of meaning. It is, in Lear's terms, a *nameless trauma.* In this situation, the blasphemer attacks the good itself—the divine Name that he heard at Sinai, along with the whole Israelite people. He is not *motivated* to this: he is *pierced* by the *punctum* of his own narrative. The story he hears about his past tells him that the divine Name was articulated by Moses to kill his father. He responds to the nameless impact of that which, for him, cannot be assimilated to meaning or purpose.

In this narrative, the Torah and the midrash evoke an extreme scenario through which to confront the question of God's goodness. Lear describes the possibility of attacking "the good," or "one's own mind," or "the capacity to form motivation." The primal nature of this attack seems to place it before and beyond the realm of choice. *Sefer Ha-Chinuch* seems to assign responsibility to the blasphemer who "empties himself of all goodness." For readers of the Torah, the question must arise: If the blasphemer is condemned to death, he is presumably responsible for his act. But the presumption is troubling.

AN EXCESS OF DEMAND

Let us return to the particulars of the story. The outsider/insider, son of a double, illicit and violent past, socially excluded from his chosen world, spiritually blemished and shamed, becomes an emblem of the sometimes unbearable constriction of a human destiny. Commentaries note that this was a unique case of miscegenation and its tragic outcome. The larger normative history of the Israelites in Egypt proclaims itself clear of any similar blemish. This story would not then represent a recognizable situation: it would be a singularly grotesque event. However, normative lives in every generation have, on occasion, known such disruptions, more or less repressed. Otherwise, why would the Torah tell the story?

In a further turn of the screw, the Zohar identifies the "Israelite man" who fights the outsider as the son of Shulamit's husband by another wife! That is, the combatants are *quasi*-brothers, one the son of Shulamit and the Egyptian, the other the son of Shulamit's husband in a second marriage. They have no shared parent; an adultery and a remarriage stand between them and brotherhood. The network of connections only serves to highlight the isolation of the blasphemer. The buildup of pressure finds its outlet in his self-destruction.

In attacking the divine Name, the blasphemer attacks his own mind. For the power of language is such that *anything at all* may be said. Words may be combined in infinite sets. Each such set has its own power to create or destroy. "The limits of my language are the limits of my world," Wittgenstein wrote. If Shulamit goes around pattering, *Shalom! Shalom!* to all comers, she is reducing the possibilities of peace to a patter. In the face of the disruptions of a life, babbling the word prevents her from engaging with the "game of loss."

This game, playful as it may be, involves work. Aggression breaks out between the two *quasi*-brothers. From this aggression, and the legal verdict that ensues, peace cannot emerge. Rashi makes a skeptical comment about the possibility of legislated peace: " 'If there is a fight between people and they go to court for a ruling' (Deut. 22:21), in the end, they will inevitably go to court. Learn from this that peace does not emerge from aggression!" Rashi is observing that recourse to the law is no way of achieving peace. Law speaks a different language from that of peace. As we have seen, it practices its own forms of violence.

Blasphemy is a manifestation of extreme linguistic power. Human words have power to create worlds and destroy them, and anything at all can be said. Pushing this power to the point of self-annihilation would, paradoxically, mean reducing language to a repeated moan— *o-o-o-o*. The game of loss, in Lear's metaphor, can be well played only by keeping the *da* somehow in motion, in conversation with the *fort*. Alternations of absence and presence demand courage and the capacity to think.

The option of blasphemy must be condemned by God—"by the

mouth of God." It is not the law court that can decide this, but the God who has, in a sense, addressed the human being with a rip in the fabric of his life. God's word alone can acknowledge what is excessive about human life. Trauma contains what Freud calls "an excess of demand."

At points in life, one is addressed by something that is sensed as "indigestible." One can't do anything with what has presented itself; one can't translate it into a workable project. To be traumatized is to experience every attempt at naming, at interpretation, as leaving a *remainder*.[52] Something that resists language remains of the unfathomable impact of the past.

This understanding of trauma sheds light on the blasphemer's explosion of hatred; or on the Israelite's experience of being "interrupted" by the outsider with his "excess of demand"; or on the reader, who is called on by the narrative to open up to the pressures of its demand. When the divine word condemns the blasphemer, it comes to resolve an enigma that human law cannot resolve. How can one think about the choice to blow apart one's world when one's mind cannot provide complete understanding of its ruptures?

By placing the blasphemer in the same context as the murderer, condemning both to death, God implicitly frames both acts as acts of violence against the divine image. To kill another, or oneself, or to attack the divine Name—which is bound up with one's own mind—is a matter of grave metaphysical import. As Lear puts it, "[i]t is an attack on any attempt to orient oneself toward the good."[53]

LOVE AND HATE

At the same time, aggression is an essential part of human creativity. D. W. Winnicott challenges us to engage with the ambivalence of love and hatred: with the "destructiveness that is personal, and that inherently belongs to an object that is felt to be good—in other words, that is related to loving."[54] Destructiveness that we acknowledge as ours requires integration, which means taking "full responsibility for *all* feelings and ideas that belong to being alive." The price of failing to integrate aggressive feelings is, precisely, "the loss of the destructiveness which really belongs to ourselves."

For Winnicott, if we avoid this responsibility, we have to project the hatred outside ourselves. The ruthlessness of one's own primitive impulses is difficult to tolerate. But if one cannot reach this part of oneself, constructive activity is "false and worse than meaningless."[55] On the other hand, constructive and creative experiences make it possible to get to the experience of one's own destructiveness—which generates the "capacity to enjoy ideas, even with destruction in them."[56] The paradox centers on getting to that place of acceptance of one's own destructiveness that makes integration possible.

We recall the rabbinic commentary on Deuteronomy 6:5: "You shall love God your God with *all your heart*." The word for "heart" is spelled with a double *beit* (*levav*, rather than *lev*), to indicate that one loves God with both one's natural inclinations—the good and the evil impulses.[57]

Love of God, like any love, deploys opposite forces, the good and the evil inclinations. Or, in Winnicott's terms, the constructive and the destructive impulses. Without the "evil impulse," the aggressive impulse, say the Rabbis, no hen would lay an egg.[58]

In Winnicott's discussion of destructiveness and its roots in early infant development, self-recognition is the condition for integration. The rabbinic understanding of love of God includes owning the reality of one's "evil inclination." Here, the two commandments of loving God and loving one's neighbor intersect. Intrinsic to the fulfillment of loving one's neighbor is the reality of hate. ("You shall not hate your neighbor in your heart.") Hate is not to be repressed but acknowledged and, in some way, managed. The *fort-da* game ("Gone! There!") names the loss and plays with it. Inventing the game requires that "[the child] tolerate mother's absence. . . . For we can think, in any realistic sense, only when we can think about absent objects."[59]

If the existence of destructive instincts in oneself—toward others or toward God—is denied, then murder or blasphemy may provide an outlet for an unbearable tension. The child who, in Lear's terms, is unable to get a thought together turns against his own mind. This is, essentially, a suicidal position: what the *Sefer Ha-Chinuch* described as an *emptying out* of one's human ability to understand what has happened to one.

Suicide itself, like murder, is forbidden, "for He made the human in the divine image."[60] The biblical verse is a powerful matrix for the prohibition of suicide, since it is framed by the relationship of God with the human being: destroying or damaging the image affects the divine prototype. God's own self is intimately invested in the human being. Murder compromises that investment, as does blasphemy in its implications for the human self.

This information is transformative. In a famous passage in the Ethics of the Fathers, we read. "Beloved is the human being who was created in the image of God; exceeding love appears when one is made to know that one was created in His image" (*Pirkei Avot* 3:18). To be made aware of one's divine origins is an expression of "inordinate love"—of exceeding or even excessive love. The mishnah emphasizes the mystery of the process of self-awareness. Coming to *know* about one's own divine origin involves some act of grace.

The mishnaic statement is more than a description of origins: it is a claim about human capacity, ultimately about human nature. It is, one might say, a provocation—a call to deepen one's imagination. It requires a creative response to the *too-muchness* of human life. What is it to play with the paradoxes of this self-awareness? To think about the conflicting impulses within oneself? What would it mean to be unable to think in this way? To annihilate oneself so that such thinking becomes impossible?

THE SLAP ON THE MOUTH

"R. Chanina said: Slapping the jaw of an Israelite is like slapping the jaw of the Shechinah!"[61] The side slap with the back of the hand is an insulting attack on the speech of the other. Striking someone on the jaw is equivalent to breaking his flow of speech, and this is equivalent to doing the same to God. A slap of this kind shames rather than injures the other. Rabbenu Bachya cites this Talmudic adage in the context of the prohibition of striking someone dead, which, as we have noted, is juxtaposed with the offense of blasphemy. The blasphemer is, in effect, attacking himself, annihilating his own power of speech, his own ability to think-in-speech. His attack on his own mind is like silencing the voice of God.

But being slapped on the mouth is, according to a famous midrash,[62] the foundational experience of every human life. The newborn infant, just emerged from her mother's womb, is slapped on the mouth by an angel; the slap makes her forget her previous life within the womb, where a light burned that revealed the whole world and where she knew the entirety of Torah. It wipes her mind clear of its primal knowledge. Thereafter, the new human being will relearn what has been forgotten.

The angel's slap is the *punctum* of this scenario. Why the gratuitously violent gesture? In Maharal's reading,[63] the slap performs a double task: it makes the infant forget the entire Torah and it opens her mouth to language. What is created at this moment is the complex being of body and soul that is the human. Before this, the infant was pure soul/intellect, knowing the whole Torah. Now, as she enters the physical world and becomes fully embodied, her creation is completed.

The slap on the mouth, which elicits language, creates her as the embodied soul that we identify as human. Now, she becomes a living-speaking-bodily being that by definition cannot know the entirety of Torah. Using the Talmudic expression *makkeh be-patish*, Maharal invokes the potter's tap on his vessel that signifies its completion. A blow has become a slap and then a tap—and a new creation comes into being.

Moses, Maharal suggests, is the exceptional human being who has never been slapped by the angel, and therefore lacks facility with language. Somehow uncompromised by the physical, Moses is "not a man of words," as he declares of himself. This apparent disability allows him to retain an oceanic knowledge of the entirety of Torah.

The entirety of Torah—*kol ha-torah kulah*—is the primal nonverbal knowledge that is withdrawn with the angel's slap. What is it to know that entirety and then to forget it? A midrash on the Song of Songs provides us with an enactment of this:

> When Israel heard the words, "I am God your God," the study of Torah was implanted in their hearts so that they learned without ever forgetting. They came to Moses and said, Moses our teacher, set an intermediary between us, as it says, "You speak with us and we will hear! For why should we die?" (Exod. 20:16). What is to be gained by our disappearance? So they returned to being learners and forgetters.
>
> Then, they said, Moses is flesh and blood and will pass away; so his teaching will pass away. Immediately, they came back to Moses and said, Moses our teacher, would that He would be

revealed to us a second time! Would that he would kiss us with the kisses of his mouth! Would that the study of Torah were implanted in our hearts as it once was! He answered, This is not for now but for the world to come, as it says, "I have placed my Torah in their midst and I shall write it upon their hearts!" (Jer. 31:32)[64]

This is a story of dangerous knowledge and its forgetting. In order to survive the totality of knowledge, the people ask to become limited and human—that is, "learners and forgetters." Like a perforated sieve, the human being cannot retain her learning: it is gained and lost. In three timeframes, the midrash portrays the dialectic of totality and limitation, ecstasy and safety, remembering and forgetting. In the midst of Revelation, the people ask for a less intimate, less consuming encounter with God. Returned to a state of lowered consciousness, they yearn for what they have lost, what they have "forgotten." But they remain diminished, with their desire acknowledged but deferred to the end of days. Instead of the kiss, they have the Oral Torah, which allows them to speak, interpret, play with loss and recovery. In terms of the national experience of Revelation, the midrash plays out the "slap on the mouth" that opens the mouth and closes off totality.

RECONSTRUCTING THE PAST

If this is the human situation, the blasphemer is the one who insists on using language to blow apart all human structures. Traumatized by a disrupted life, he disrupts his own ability to *think* about loss. In doing this, he is himself shattered. His attack on the divine Name signifies his annihilation of himself.

In articulating and cursing the ineffable, that which cannot be spoken, he *pierces* the boundaries of existence. We have noticed that the Zohar translates *Vayikov:* "he bored a hole in his door." Mei Ha-Shilo'ach[65] offers a poignant reading of the blasphemer's position: "He wanted to open up the depths of what has been deferred to the world to come. He wanted God *retroactively* to purify human acts, revealing them as *always having been without sin.* This would reconstruct him as unambiguously an Israelite. No vestige of his mother's adultery would remain, and he would be an Israelite like any other." In effect, the blasphemer wishes for divine grace to save human beings from the effects of their own actions. This, however, is not God's will: He wants human beings to act and to bear responsibility for their acts.

Mei Ha-Shilo'ach ends by referring to the opening word of the narrative: *Vayetze*—"He went forth"—and to a midrashic reading: "He went forth—he repudiated—the previous commandment, about the showbread in the Tabernacle. 'Is it the custom of a king to eat stale bread!' "[66] He meant to mock the idea that only through specific rituals at specific times (on Shabbat), and within specific spaces (the Sanctuary), and through specific people (the patriarchs or the Israelite people) can human beings experience the divine influx into the world. He insisted that God can save at any time, in any place, and through any human agent.

THE BLASPHEMER'S FANTASY: THE GOLDEN CALF

In this mystically inflected reading, the blasphemer will not accept the notion of a limit to the influx of the divine into the world. In boring a hole in the boundaries of language, he insists that anyone, in any place or time, can channel divine salvation. The commandments that focus on specific moments, scenes, and soul agents of redemption are derided as constrictions of the divine impact on the world. Essentially, they limit *what can be said.* He wants to create a world in which anything at all can be said.

Perhaps another way of saying this is that he wants a world without ambiguity and without conflict. The stale bread that he mocks represents all that bears the weight of time and space. Why not serve the King a fresh loaf at any time and place?

It is true that we can say anything at all. It is also true that we can imagine anything at all. Each language speaks the world in its own way. The future tense, the optative mode, the conditional form, tells of the unboundedness of language. George Steiner writes of the "counterfactual" human capacity:

> We can say any truth or any falsehood. We can affirm and negate in the same breath. . . . To speak, either to oneself or to another is . . . to invent, to re-invent being and the world. . . . Man alone can construct and parse the grammar of hope. . . .

But the unboundedness of discursive potentiality has its negative . . . [it] entails the logic of nullity and of nihilism. . . .
Limitless as language potentially is, it acquires validity only
inside closed speech systems. It is for this reason that ritual,
liturgical, canonic codes of saying, as in prayer, in sacramental
formulations and sacred or revealed texts, strive to close, to
circumscribe word and world by means of taboo, of reiteration,
of apocalyptic finitude. *Each blasphemy, in turn, re-affirms the
open indeterminacy of language.*[67]

In the imagery of Mei Ha-Shilo'ach and the Zohar, the blasphemer
affirms the open indeterminacy of language by blasting open the door
of the closed speech system. He will clear the closed space created by
his mother's adultery. Nothing will have ever happened that could
blight the future existence of a *mamzer;* no lust or cruelty will have
been irreparable in its ability to haunt the generations. The fantasy of
the blasphemer, his hatred of the limitations of the law, is, in a sense,
entirely plausible:

Here resides the true sense in depth of the Judaic prohibition
on the enunciation of the name, or, more strictly speaking, of
the Name of the Name, of God. Once spoken, this name passes
into the contingent limitlessness of linguistic play. . . . In natural
and unbounded discourse God has no demonstrable lodging.

But "the polyglot is a freer man." The blasphemer's dream, as it is
imagined by Mei Ha-Shilo'ach, is a vital human dream. Against this
dream stands the persistence—through time and space and human
agency, through sin and its tendency to recur—of divine desire for
human action. The fulfillment of the dream, as we have seen with the
divine kiss of total knowledge, is deferred to a future time and place.
And also, perhaps, to poets:

No one is a poet unless he has felt the temptation to destroy
language and create another one, unless he has experienced the
fascination of non-meaning and the no less terrifying fascination of meaning that is inexpressible.[68]

In the thinking of Mei Ha-Shilo'ach, a similar fantasy underlies the sin of the Golden Calf.[69] In his Hasidic commentaries, the Calf represents the desire to evade the uncertainties of time by a onetime total revelation of the ways in which God runs the world. The desire is for a key to understanding the mystery of divine interaction with the world. Such a revelation—embodied in the Calf[70]—would relieve human beings of the need for *prayer*. For prayer expresses, with every day that passes, the changing forms of our situation and vulnerability.

The Golden Calf episode follows immediately on the teaching about Shabbat. Significantly, Shabbat holds something of this total quality: it evokes time out of time and the end of days. Then no prayer will be needed in the light of ultimate truth. But that light—of divine omnipotence that leaves no space for human action—is not for now. The Golden Calf, the *Egel*, is "that which is *not yet*." The time is not ripe. The hope for such a time is out of joint with our world of human agency.

For Mei Ha-Shilo'ach, then, the cardinal sin of the Golden Calf—the sin of prematurity, of apocalyptic desire—is the generic sin of the wilderness journey. It is a desire to disable the specific religious language of the Israelites, to bore a hole in the door, and to allow the totality of the divine to saturate reality. But even the desire for this cannot yet be authentic. Even our yearning is formed in the language we speak now.

RESENTMENTS

Apocalyptic desire overlooks—or denies—the endemic discontent of this world. Organizing human dreams is the persistence of that human experience that Mei Ha-Shilo'ach calls *tar'omet*—resentment, or rage. The extreme situation of *tar'omet* is that of the "blemished priest," who may not carry out his priestly functions because of some physical defect. This case is discussed in our *parshah:* "He may eat of the bread of his God, the Most holy as well as the holy; but he may not enter behind the curtain or approach the altar, for he has a defect" (Lev. 21:22–23). Mei Ha-Shilo'ach enters into the subjectivity of the blemished priest, whose prevailing state must be one of *tar'omet*—resentment.[71]

Qualified by heritage and desire to serve as priest, he is barred
by his congenital defect. Why must he be distanced from his spiritual destiny? Mei Ha-Shilo'ach assumes that such a priest must be
embroiled in personal/metaphysical questions—like the Talmudic
rabbi whose ugliness is the target of unkind comment: "Go ask questions," he retorts, "of the Artist who made me!"—somehow sublimat-
ing or skirting his personal bitterness.

In the reading of Mei Ha-Shilo'ach, this bitterness of the blemished
priest is addressed by the Torah: "he may eat of the bread of his God."
In his inner being, he will lack nothing; he will be nurtured by his own
intimate connection with God. He should not be enraged by the fact
that he is barred from the priesthood, for his situation is his specific
way of serving God. In abstaining from following his spiritual desire,
he is fulfilling the divine will, just as much as in any positive act.

The blemished priest may react to his delegitimization with
tar'omet—baffled anger at the physiological fatality of his life. Mei
Ha-Shilo'ach tries to neutralize the bitterness by reframing the priest's
situation. In his creative reading, "eating the bread of his God" gives
the priest his own inner connection with God. Despite, or perhaps
because of, his functional limitation, he is given a personal religious
language to express his devotion to God.

Tar'omet appears in the commentary of Mei Ha-Shilo'ach[72] in a
more general form at the very beginning of the parshah: "Say to the
priests, Aaron's sons, say to them, 'No one shall pollute himself for
any dead person among his kin' "(Lev. 21:1). Here, "the priests" refers
to any servant of God who is caught on the horns of a dilemma. He
believes that nothing happens by chance in this world; that divine
providence is always at work. Precisely such a person can fall into
tar'omet, resentment at the mysterious fatality of what God brings
about. It is, paradoxically, only the believer who can experience this;
the nonbeliever regards misfortune as simply the work of chance. The
believer lives in a meaningful world and is therefore prone to feeling
personally betrayed by the God with whom he is deeply engaged.
Resentment becomes an occupational hazard of faith.

Given this complex situation, God warns the "priest" to avoid
the defilement of such resentment: it pollutes the soul (the nefesh).
Divine justice is called into question when one experiences loss or
absence—expressions of middat ha-din, the unfathomable divine

attribute of severe justice. For this Hasidic master, the problem is psychological as well as theological—a matter of the health of the soul. To encourage the "priest," therefore, he advises the friend to *whisper* that he rid himself of bitterness of this kind. Even when God speaks in a language of deprivation and loss, even then His intention *ba-omek*—deep down—is for the good.

In this passage, Mei Ha-Shilo'ach speaks in the most general way of the besetting sin of the "servant of God." When the dogma of providential meaning collides with the unfathomable violence of life experience, *tar'omet* is a natural response. The relevance of this to the situation of the blasphemer is obvious. As the Zohar puts it: he blasphemes against the Name *which he has heard at Sinai.* The conflict arises from the fact that, with his congenital defects of parentage and identity, he nevertheless stands *inside* the language of revelation.

In this situation, the counsel that the Torah offers is based on the repeated expression *Emor:* "*Say* to the priests . . . and *say* to them." *Saying,* as opposed to *speaking,* is translated in the Zohar as "in a whisper." Whispering is an intimate way of evoking a common language. Only in this way can one hope to address the grievances that arise from a sense of betrayal. Where strident proclamations of faith may further alienate the sufferer, the whisper is the only possible mode of communication. The message is both seductive and traumatic: it addresses the troubled "priest" with an intensity that captivates, but the message cannot be fully comprehended.

Cruel and incomprehensible events befall a person. They are taken most personally by the believer, who strives to discern divine meaning in whatever befalls him. To whisper is to acknowledge the mystery of the elemental: a world where divine love may, despite our pain, prevail. The whisper lends depth to the relationship and to the ongoing conversation.

For the blasphemer, there is no such intervention. Alone with the starkness of his frustration, he insists on breaking the boundaries of language. At the opposite extreme from the whisper, here is the supersonic scream of hatred. Here, in this "unbounded discourse," as George Steiner says, "God has no demonstrable lodging."

KICKING DOWN THE SUKKAH

The theme of *tar'omet* is the focus of Mei Ha-Shilo'ach's discussion of the blasphemer. He *"kicks out"* at his fate; his anger prevails, and he blasphemes.

The reference to *kicking out* is taken from a Talmudic passage: In the future, pagans will be given the commandment of Sukkah, of dwelling for seven days in booths. Then, if God brings the sun out of its sheath, the pagan will kick out at his *sukkah* (booth) in sheer frustration at not being able to fulfill the commandment. By contrast, the believer will accept God's will with equanimity.[73]

The issue of *tar'omet* becomes the touchstone of authentic religious desire. The Sukkah commandment is to "leave your fixed abode and stay in a temporary abode." Mei Ha-Shilo'ach reads this as the spiritual requirement to suspend one's rigidities of ego and allow oneself to be drawn after the divine will.

We remember Jonathan Lear's analysis. After the *o-o-o-o* of loss or absence, what *happens next*? If the child cannot move from the *fort* (gone) to the *da* (there), he may begin to use these outbursts to attack his own mind. "This would be the beginning of a massively self-destructive, self-annihilating character." The move to *da,* on the other hand, establishes a game that "converts the rip in the fabric of experience into an experience of loss. . . . Inventing the game, the child thereby creates the capacity *to think* about mother's absence. . . . This is courage-in-the-making."[74]

"GO TO YOURSELF!"

In this crisis, the traumatic event, the rip in the fabric of life, plays an essential role. The moment of self-disruption is the necessary response of the child to the loss of the mother. In the thinking of Mei Ha-Shilo'ach, the moment of *tar'omet* plays a similarly critical role in the history of the soul.

The clearest manifestation of this is in his commentary on Abraham's *Lech lecha* moment: "Go forth from your land, your birthplace, and your father's house" (Gen. 12:1).[75] He reads this famous command literally, as "Go *to yourself!*" He glosses God's words: "No external ob-

ject can be called *life*—the essence of life you will find in yourself!"
He cites the famous midrash about the traveler who sees a castle on
fire.[76] The traveler asks, "Who is the lord of the castle?" The lord of the
castle gazes out at him and says, "I am lord of the castle."

The lord's gaze is turned *upon the traveler—alav*. (The usual idiom
is *elav, at* him.) Mei Ha-Shilo'ach reads this as turning the traveler's
attention to *himself*, to his own turbulent question. The castle on fire
represents the world of idolatry in which Abraham lives; he alone is
sufficiently troubled by the disorder of the world. Can anyone be in
charge when the fires of lust and greed burn unchecked? Abraham is
troubled to the depths (*hir'im be-nafsho*); he is seized by *tar'omet*, by
baffled anger at the chaos of the world. Can there be a Creator? "Who
created all these things?"[77]

God gazes *upon* him and replies, "Look *at yourself*! No one else has
a problem with this! From the *tar'omet* of your heart, you can imagine
that there surely is a Creator who has aroused your heart and soul to
such a question!" Gazing upon Abraham, God lets him become conscious of his own unique turmoil, which is his unique self.

What Mei Ha-Shilo'ach describes is the moment when a self is
born. This is the moment when one is addressed by God, called by
name, interrupted in one's unawareness. Instantly, a fraught relationship forms: What do You want of me? This is the moment of
revelation—of self and of God. The content of revelation—the laws,
the ethical instructions, the narrative—will follow.

For Mei Ha-Shilo'ach, the disruption of a life—the sense of violent
anarchy in the world—is met by an inner storm. Like the child who
throws the spool beyond reach and cries out, *"Fort!—Gone!"* Abraham
enacts the rip in the fabric of his life. God's role as lord of the castle is
simply to draw his attention to the power of his own question, which
constitutes its own answer. The heart of the matter is the reflexive
movement inward.

It is striking that R. Zadok Hacohen, the disciple of Mei Ha-
Shilo'ach, expresses a similar idea in more radical form. When God
gazes upon Abraham—*alav*—He is really saying, " 'You yourself participate in the being of the lord of the castle! Everyone else sees what
you see, but no one else reacts with your passion (*ro'esh*)! Because of
your tumult, you can reach out to the truth that there is a lord of the

castle and seek Him out. Your quest originates in Me; the place of My presence is in your heart!' This is the meaning of 'I am lord of the castle.'" The I of God is identified with Abraham's unique selfhood.

God directs Abraham to his own *tar'omet,* to his inner passion at the apparent absence of God. Abraham's inner world is in itself the answer to his question: not simply because God has aroused him to his quest, but because Abraham's heart, in all its turbulence, is the very place of God's presence.

In the theology of Mei Ha-Shilo'ach, we might say that the "priest," the servant of God, first identifies himself as such when he becomes aware of his own *tar'omet.* It is his inevitable protest at what is missing that marks him out as a servant of God. But this disruption is healed when he opens himself to the whisper of hope.

Once one has invented the game of loss and recovery, the original *tar'omet,* the disturbance, the rip in the fabric, is resolved, invisibly mended. Or perhaps a trace remains, to haunt the work of the priest. With all his courage, his willingness to hear the whisper that tells of a hidden order of goodness ("God's wish is always, *deep down,* to do good"), perhaps his response holds a tension between the two impulses, love and hate. "You shall love God with your whole heart" means loving Him with both impulses, constructive and aggressive. We notice that Mei Ha-Shilo'ach leaves the priest's response unheard. A complexity, an excess, remains.

For "deep down," *ba-omek,* evokes unconscious depths, not entirely fathomable. Even Moses bears some remote resemblance to the blasphemer: he, too, comes of hybrid parentage, biological and virtual, Hebrew and Egyptian; he, too, calls himself a *ger* (Exod. 2:22); he, too, carries resources of anger and violence within him; he, too, resists God's call, at least at first. The fact that he cannot decide the blasphemer's fate may indicate that he is in some way implicated in it.

Perhaps the reader of the blasphemer narrative senses this complexity. Perhaps that is why the narrative remains so disturbing. Like Moses's narrative to Jethro, it arouses visceral reactions in the listener. One's skin prickles. The narrative calls one by name. "You shall love God, your God" invites the whole self to respond.

7

Behar/Bechukotai

The Order of Intimacy

SABBATICAL AND JUBILEE YEARS

"God spoke to Moses at Mount Sinai, saying, 'Speak to the Israelites and say to them, When you come into the Land which I am giving you, the Land shall rest in a Sabbath for God'" (Lev. 25:1–2).

The laws of the Sabbatical year, known as the *Shmittah* year, date back to the Revelation at Sinai. This is specifically acknowledged in the opening verse of the Torah section—perhaps in the context of the national expectation at this moment that entry into the Land would soon ensue.[1] The prospect of *land,* in its agricultural sense, opens an entirely new vista for the recently liberated people. After centuries in the foreign land of Egypt and months in the wilderness, the prospect, as a nation, for the first time, of being *landed* faces them with a difficult demand: every seventh year, the land is to *rest,* to lie unworked, restored to God in its state of nature.

This demand, as it turns out, accompanies the people for all the forty years of their wilderness wandering. Rooted in the Revelation itself, it evokes the foundational notion of the Sabbath. The weekly Sabbath event—the seventh day of rest—is extended and amplified over an entire year of rest, every "week of years."

Failure to observe the sabbatical laws is attended with the penalty of exile—of losing the Land. "Then the Land shall compensate for its sabbatical years throughout its days of desolation while you are in the land of your enemies; then shall the Land rest and compensate for its sabbatical years" (Lev. 26:34). A terrible irony inhabits this sentence: Failing to observe this year of land rest will result in an endless condition of "rest" while the people are displaced to alien lands. The midrashic tradition calculates the exact arithmetic of exile—seventy years of exile to make up for seventy lost Sabbatical years. We will return to the ironic implications of this concept of land rest.

In addition, there is the law of the Jubilee year: every fiftieth year, the land returns to its original owners. Slaves, too, are liberated, both in the seventh year and in the fiftieth year, in the latter more definitively. Other laws, apparently unconnected, appear here: the individual is urged to assist the poor by giving loans; charging interest on loans is forbidden. Idolatry is forbidden.

Many of these laws invoke empathy for the disadvantaged who have been compelled to sell themselves or their lands. A motif of socioeconomic concern seems to drive this group of laws.[2] However, the theological language that undergirds these passages is unmistakable: The Sabbatical year, like the weekly Sabbath, is "for God." "For Mine is the Land—you are strangers and residents with Me!" (Lev. 25:23). A cosmic metaphysical ethic connects these laws of property with other seemingly unconnected laws, like the one forbidding idolatry (26:1).

ALIENATIONS

An intriguing narrative passage in the Talmud links many of these laws by setting them in chronological—and catastrophic—sequence:

> R. Yose ben R. Chanina said: Come and see how terrible are the consequences of violating the provisions of the seventh year. A man who trades in seventh year produce must eventually sell his movables, for it is said, "In this year of Jubilee you shall return every man to his possession," and in juxtaposition to this, "and if you sell anything to your neighbor, or buy of your neighbor's hand"—which refers to what is acquired from hand to hand.
>
> If he disregards this, he eventually sells his estates, for it is said, "If your brother falls into poverty and sells some of his possessions." He has no opportunity to amend his ways before he sells his estates, for it is said, "If your brother falls into poverty and sells some of his possessions."
>
> He has no opportunity to amend his ways before he sells

his house, for it is said, "If a man sells a dwelling house in a walled city." (Why state in one case, "if he disregards this," but in the other case, "He has no opportunity"? R. Hun said: Once one has committed a sin and repeated it, it is permitted to him. "Permitted to him!" How can you think so? But say, it becomes to him *as though* permitted.)

It is not brought home to him before he sells his daughter, for it is said, "If one sells one's daughter to be a bondswoman," and though the sale of his daughter is not mentioned in this section, yet it teaches us that one should even sell one's daughter and not borrow on usury. What is the reason? His daughter makes a deduction and goes free, whereas his debt grows ever larger.

It is not brought home to him until he borrows on interest, as it is written, "If your brother falls into poverty and his hand is subjected to you," in proximity to which is stated, "Take no usury of him or increase."

It is not brought home to him until he sells himself, as it is said, "If your brother falls into poverty with you and sells himself to you." And not only to you but to a proselyte, as it is said, "and sells himself to the proselyte." And not only to a righteous proselyte but to a resident alien, as it is said, "or to the resident alien." "The family of a proselyte" means a heathen. When it is said, "to an offshoot," it refers to one who sells himself to the service of the idol itself![3]

The first misstep leads to an avalanche of disasters. A relatively minor offense, called "the *dust* of the sabbatical laws"—trading in seventh-year produce—has grave consequences: one is compelled to sell one's movable property, one's estates, then one's home, one's daughter, oneself to a fellow Israelite, to a proselyte, to a resident alien, to a heathen, and finally even to the service of the idol itself!

What is remarkable about this narrative of woe is that the stages of catastrophe are in some cases also offenses against Torah law. Selling himself as votary to idolatry represents the lowest point of his trajectory, even in legal terms. Similarly, lending money for interest is forbidden. And, stage by stage, the saga is punctuated with the expressions "if he disregards this" and "he has no opportunity to mend his

ways," which indicate that he is increasingly drawn into negative behavior that he comes to experience as legitimate. He enters a world
of fatal apathy; a minor offense has the power to induce a deepening
condition of spiritual stupor, as well as financial paralysis. "He has
no opportunity to amend his ways" emphasizes the helpless tenor of
his experience.

It is striking that a history of serial misfortunes blurs into a history
of serial misdeeds. Proof texts from our *parshah* are cited to provide
the structure of events; but they are quoted out of context, so that
their meanings are inflected. The rabbinic narrative becomes one of
disregarded moral responsibility. The Torah laws apparently target the
rich *buyer* of land and slaves. However, in this rabbinic morality tale,
the impoverished *seller* who has fallen on hard times becomes the protagonist. Due to his own fecklessness, he is forced to strip himself of
everything that gives him meaning and identity. He is held to account
for the progressive *loss of himself.* He is reproached for his increasing
alienation from himself, which culminates in his selling himself as
an officiant in the worship of idols—that *alien service* (*avodah zarah*).
He has, in a word, *exiled* himself from himself.

The slippery slope begins with a minor offense—trading in the
produce of the seventh year. Then, relentlessly, forbidden acts/
misfortunes escalate. Why should a minor misdeed drag in its wake
such dire consequences? The taboo on trading in the produce of the
seventh year contains implicit meanings that emerge under the scrutiny of rabbinic law.

We observe, for instance, how Rashi calls on the midrash to open
up the meanings of a related detail of the narrative. "'If your brother
falls into poverty': This teaches you that one is not allowed to sell
one's estate unless in dire poverty" (Lev. 25:25). In Rashi's source,[4] this
reads, "How do we know that one is not allowed to sell one's estates
in exchange for liquid assets, so as to buy an animal or furniture or a
house? One is allowed to sell one's estates only in dire poverty."

Here, the biblical text is read with attention to the first clause:
"*Only* when your brother falls into poverty—that is, he is in need of
bread—may he sell his ancestral land." A general principle emerges:
the reasoned calculation by which one fills one's purse with cash to
buy, for instance, a home or furniture, is outlawed. Fields cannot be
exchanged for houses; nor can houses be exchanged for furniture.

One may not trade in a major resource for possessions of a lesser order. This is not only injudicious; it is forbidden.

SHIFTING THE SUBJECT

As we have seen, the biblical text clearly calls on the kinder nature of the rich relative to redeem the property of "your brother," who is the victim of misfortune. In the midrash, however, it is the impoverished victim of fate who is seen as subject to the terms of the law.

Similarly, we read just before this, "The land shall not be sold into perpetuity" (Lev. 25:23). Rashi comments: "This prohibits the buyer from holding on to the property in the Jubilee year, when land should return to its original owner." As long as the Jubilee year is observed, sale of land is never in perpetuity. The buyer must yield the land to its ancestral owner.

Ramban, however, raises another possibility. Since our text speaks of *selling* the land, rather than *buying* it,[5] it seems that the text is primarily addressing the seller, urging him to avoid colluding in any way with the buyer by implying that the sale will, after all, be effective in perpetuity. Such a stipulation will only make it harder for the buyer to relinquish his property in the Jubilee year. It is preferable to calculate the price on the basis of the number of productive years until the Jubilee.

Ramban understands this prohibition, then, as *advice* to both buyer and seller: "Between you, observe the law of the Jubilee, and don't be resentful about it, for the Land is Mine, and I do not want it to be sold in perpetuity, as it may be in other transactions."

Colluding to transgress the law of the Jubilee year is forbidden, even though the prohibition is legally ineffective. In Ramban's reading, it is forbidden largely because of the resentment that the buyer will feel at having to restore the estate to its original owner. Here, it is the seller who is the primary addressee—perhaps because he is motivated to make unrealistic promises in order to raise the price of the property.

Once again, we see how the moral and legal spotlight moves from its obvious target—the wealthy buyer—to the seller. Or, at least, to the commercial relation between the two of them. Their language is to be informed by the Jubilee consciousness—of the "mobility" of the land, of its return to its proper state, and of the theological underpinning of the whole transaction.

The land is "not yours": *you* refers to the seller who is asked to position himself and his claims on the periphery of a reality where God is at the center. This reality, perhaps ironically, is grounded in *land,* the most solid foundation for all reality. In a few words, the sense that "my land is *mine*" is shifted. One cannot dispose of the land to perpetuity. It is, after all, *Mine* in a different sense: it is *His,* and therefore it will revert to me whether I want it or not. My subjectivity is subjected to Another. I am a stranger, a resident on His piece of ground.

In the slave-master relationship, we can glimpse yet another example of this shift in subjectivity. At the end of a section dealing with the laws of the Jubilee in regard to the liberation of slaves, as well as with the possibilities of redemption of slaves before the Jubilee year, we read: "For Mine are the Israelites as servants: they are My servants, whom I liberated from the land of Egypt—I am God, your God" (Lev. 25:55).

The syntax is obviously like that of the verse about God's ownership of the Land. God claims the whole people as His "slaves," emphatically repeating the claim ("they are My slaves") and adding a historical explanation: I liberated them from Egypt and, therefore, as Rashi puts it: "My contract is prior to any social arrangement." In this case, God's claim is not merely that He can dispose of His land as He wishes; here, God's claim logically undermines the whole human system of Hebrew slavery. A more radical declaration, "They are My slaves," loosens the hold of the master on his slaves. There is perhaps an irony in the fact that the concluding verse of the section on the Hebrew slave, with all its terms and conditions, radically subverts the whole institution.

LISTENING OUT

We have seen several examples of the midrashic tendency to shift the moral focus of the biblical laws from the privileged to the impoverished protagonist. Typecast for the role of victim, he becomes the subject of the narrative. His slave state, which is tolerated in the biblical text, is read as ultimately untenable. God is present in this turnaround of social convention. We began with a narrative about the cascade of misfortunes that befalls one who trades in the produce of the seventh year. The victim turns out to bear responsibility for many decisions along the way: in his trajectory, he increasingly allows himself to lose himself. This is not a matter of blaming the victim; rather, it makes of the victim the moral subject of the story.

Perhaps the most vivid example of this shift in viewpoint is a classic midrash about the slave who refuses to go free in the seventh year:

> R. Yochanan ben Zakkai expounded: Why should the ear be singled out from all bodily organs? God said, The ear that heard at Mount Sinai, when I said, "Mine are the Israelites as servants—they cannot be servants to other servants!" And nevertheless went and acquired a master for himself—that ear shall be pierced with an awl.[6]

The slave who wants to remain with his master has his earlobe pierced with an awl into the doorpost of the house. The midrash questions: Why is the ear made to suffer? And answers that this Hebrew heard God's voice at Sinai proclaiming His exclusive "ownership" and *nevertheless* sold himself into slavery. The ear is the offending organ, the seat of rebellion.

The slave who refuses to go free is, in a sense, freely asserting his wish to give up his freedom. However, there is a radical dissonance between God's declaration at Sinai and the slave's subjecting himself to another human being. As in our first midrashic narrative, this decision becomes not just a misfortune but an expression of alienated identity.

It remains strange that the ear is marked out in this case: many things were heard at Sinai; why does the ear not suffer for other offenses? In fact, this verse about God's ownership was *not* heard by the people at Sinai. They heard only the Ten Commandments (in most views, not even all of them).

However, there is another version of this midrash, also in the name of R. Yochanan ben Zakkai. Here, a different—and surprising—proof text is brought:

> Students asked R. Yochanan ben Zakkai, Why does this slave have his ear pierced rather than any other bodily organ? He answered, The ear that heard at Mount Sinai, "You shall have

no other gods before Me" and nevertheless went and broke off
the yoke of the kingdom of heaven, accepting the yoke of flesh
and blood—that ear shall be pierced.[7]

In the Jerusalem Talmud, R. Yochanan refers to the second of the
Ten Commandments, "You shall have no other gods before Me"—
which was, indeed, heard at Sinai. In this version, the taboo against
selling oneself into slavery is identified with the sin of idolatry. Only
a free human being can accept divine authority in his life. Acquiring
a master for oneself is read as an active rejection of that personal
responsibility to God. Entering into a spurious contract with a human
master violates the prior contract. This becomes clear in the act of
confirming one's slave condition for all time (i.e., till the Jubilee year).[8]

The moment of accepting "the yoke of the kingdom of heaven" is
classically understood as the moment when one utters the words of
the *Sh'ma* prayer: "*Hear,* O Israel, God our God, God is One." Hearing is the posture of receptivity. There are certain situations when
one is exempt from uttering these words. The bride and groom on
their wedding night, for instance, are exempt, since one cannot serve
two masters. An impassioned emotional state precludes the total sub-
mission to divine authority. The issue is one of personal freedom to
accept the yoke of heaven.

"I love my master," says the slave who refuses to go free. In terms
of the passage from the Jerusalem Talmud, this is idolatry: he is projecting his sense of divine power onto another human being. Abandoning his responsibility to God, he is also denying his own power.

Sefat Emet offers a challenging reading of the problem of the slave
who will not reclaim his freedom.[9] Even in the best case, where the
slave claims that it is *spiritually* better for him to be with his master
(Deut. 15:16), where perhaps surrendering his autonomy better enables
him to fulfill his religious duties, nevertheless, "Israelites were created
to be alert and ready to *hear* the word of God." At Mount Sinai, the
Israelites had declared, "We will *do* and we will *listen!*" *Doing* alone,
fulfilling one's duties, is not sufficient for an aspiring soul. *Listening*
implies an ardent attention to what *else* God may say. This attitude
Sefat Emet calls the attitude of the *hasid*—the one who wants to transcend rote behavior, to *listen out* for God's voice. This is the posture
of freedom.

The slavish desire of the slave encapsulates, for Sefat Emet, the continual hankering of the liberated people to return to Egypt. The fantasy is that life as a slave in Egypt was conducive to a conscientious fulfillment of commandments! But such nostalgia violates the revelation of the ear. Loving one's master, one cannot truly love God. Again, even if one feels that one loves God better in the context of having a master and a slave wife, that the situation of slavery is conducive to the religious life—nevertheless, the character of the Israelite is to *listen out,* to reattune himself constantly to the voice of God.

Strikingly, Sefat Emet becomes a kind of devil's advocate for the recalcitrant slave. Making the best case for him, he reaches bedrock—the aspiring character of the Israelite soul. This slave has violated his *ear,* his innate capacity for *listening out.* Therefore, his ear is marked.

Once again, laws that in the biblical text are addressed to the master are reread as applying to the fallen condition of the Hebrew slave. As we saw in the original *slippery-slope* narrative, slavery represents not only a misfortune but also a series of choices made by someone who has become deaf to God's voice. An unexpected perspective focuses on the drama of the one who ends up as a slave: he is not simply a victim but the protagonist of his own story. We are interested not only in ameliorating harsh social conditions but in the inner life of someone in free fall—less and less capable of orienting himself in relation to the divine. Or, in other words, to his own true self.

The Hebrew slave has heard without *listening.* In Freudian language, he suffers from repression. The God who liberated him from Egyptian slavery is not heard with any enthusiasm. Other gods, other fantasies, preoccupy him.

TRANSFERENCE HEROICS

Acquiring a human master in one's life is idolatry. The ban on idolatry is, in fact, the next topic after slavery: "You shall not make idols for yourselves" (Lev. 26:1). Rashi points out the connection: "One who sells himself to a heathen should not say, 'Since my master is a libertine, I will be like him; since my master worships idols, I will be like him.'" Rashi then proceeds to quote a briefer version of the slippery-slope narrative. Close to the lowest point in his trajectory, the slave sells himself to a heathen. Rashi is indicating the logic of the sequence: a series of junctures, in which the protagonist might have reversed his fall, but did not—or could not.

In this account, slavery essentially means imitation, assimilation to the world of the master. Losing one's autonomy becomes an alibi for a perverse desire. Perhaps there is a masochistic pleasure in relinquishing autonomy. Although the Hebrew word is the same, the condition of *service* to God is very unlike that of *slavery*. Even the rabbinic exhortation to *imitatio dei*—"Just as He is compassionate, so you be compassionate"—is quite different from the slavish imitation of idolatrous practices.

"[P]ersonality," says Otto Rank, "is shaped and formed according to the vital need to please the other person whom we make our 'God.'"[10] Identifying oneself with the powerful other, one hopes to enlarge one's own being. "Transference heroics," as Ernest Becker names this dynamic, is a combination of genuine aspiration and the concern for safety and control.

Becker's important book *The Denial of Death* discusses this issue of transference heroics at great length and in some depth. Fear of both life and death figures large in his presentation. He cites Albert Camus on the fear dimension that leads to "acquiring a master": "Ah, *mon cher*, for anyone who is alone, without God and without a master, the weight of days is dreadful. Hence one must choose a master, God being out of style."[11]

In another dimension, however, transference sees in the other the self-transcending life process that offers the larger nourishment it needs. Martin Buber calls this "imagining the real."[12] One creates the reality one needs in order to discover oneself.

Transference, then, is not simply fantasy projection. It reflects both fear of life and death and *life-enhancing* illusion. To acquire a master for oneself and imitate his idolatry is an expression of transference in its fear dimension. Accepting the yoke of the kingdom of heaven, on the other hand, represents one's yearning for an enlarged life. To identify with divine compassion is, precisely, to imagine the real. The spell cast by persons is a caricature of the complex act of imagination involved in a relationship with God.

LETTING GO

In this sense, slavery becomes an enactment of human fear, with the master replacing the God who is "no longer in style." In other words, these midrashic passages about slavery lead inexorably to idolatry. This reflects the larger history of the Israelites that leads them to worship of the Golden Calf. Throughout their wanderings in the wilderness, those who were slaves in Egypt hanker repeatedly to return; fear generates a fatal nostalgia.

Achieving *release* from Egypt has become impossible. Birth into a larger world involves the trauma of *letting go:* what Otto Rank called the "trauma of birth." This is the paradigm of all other traumas of *emergence.* A key to this level of release is the ability to *listen* to what lies beyond the straits of fear.

What God offers is a difficult liberty.[13] The meaning of the *Shmittah* year is inherent in its name. The word *shmittah* means release, remission, the relaxing of tension:

Every seventh year you shall practice *remission* of debts. This shall be the nature of the *remission:* every creditor shall *remit* (lit., relax his hand) the due that he claims from his fellow; he shall not dun (lit., pressure) his fellow or kinsman, for the *remission* proclaimed is of God.[14]

Letting go of what is mine is the basic posture of *Shmittah.* The hand opens, it does not clench itself, it relaxes its tension. In the long passage that follows, the physical imagery of clenching and relaxing is repeatedly evoked. Hand and heart both are bidden not to harden, to tighten against the impoverished kinsman. Generosity means releasing hand and heart, so that a full giving can happen. Your eye, too, the way you look at your poor neighbor, needs to soften: clear the evil in your glance and in your heart (Deut. 15:9–10). Do not refrain from giving and let your heart not resent the act of giving.

A phenomenology of *openness* emerges from these images. The grip of the ego is a force to be reckoned with. Rigid emotional muscles have the power to abort blessing. Letting go is the genius of the *Shmittah* year: "You shall truly open your hand for your brother, your poor and needy kinsman!" (Deut. 15:11).

This movement governs the remission of debts, the willingness to offer financial help to the poor, but especially the act of releasing slaves. It is clearly the master who is being addressed and exhorted to relinquish the slave—*tishlechenu chofshi,* repeated four times, is the active impetus of release. But even in the extreme case where the slave refuses to leave and where he clearly feels a strong bond with his master, the ceremony of the pierced ear expresses the biblical sense of disapproval of this kind of bond. Rabbinic interpretation, as we have seen, emphasizes the fantasy nature of the slave's attachment.

The slave may remain with his master only when there is something like genuine reciprocity in the attachment. The ceremony of the pierced ear can be performed only where there is a balanced emotional situation. One-sided affection, or if one of the two is sick, or if the master is unmarried or childless—in all these cases, the slave may not remain in the slave relation.[15]

In other words, even in the best scenario, where the master-slave relationship is permitted to continue, this is an undesirable situation. Even in the best case, pinning the slave's ear to the doorpost is a shameful procedure. It cannot be performed in the Jubilee year, when all slaves are definitively released.

Once again, the focus of the biblical laws is clearly on the master, who is required to overcome his natural reluctance to *let go.* The slave, even in his refusal to go free, is seen as a third person in the interaction of God and the master.

Nevertheless, if we look at the discussion of the issue in *Sefer Ha-Chinuch,*[16] we notice that the moral spotlight is enlarged to include both master and slave.

Psychologically, the focus is on *arousing* the master, strengthening his motivation to release his slave in the Jubilee year. Arousal is necessary because he is in a kind of stupor of possessiveness. An alternative world, disrupting the normalcy of the conventional world, needs to be imagined. This is "very difficult." But the difficulty is then extended to include the slave: he, too, has to overcome his resistance. The mitzvah, the obligation for slaves to go free, needs to be fulfilled, regardless of the desire of both master and slave. It represents the divine desire for *everything*—land and slaves—to return to its primal state.

Slaves are released on Rosh Hashanah, the New Year, ten days before the shofar sounds on the Day of Atonement. During this transitional period, the slave lives as a free man in his master's house, eating and drinking, with a crown on his head.[17] This enactment—in other cultures it is called *saturnalia*—invokes a state of apocalyptic reversals. Perhaps a kind of shock therapy for the sickness that is slavery. But the reversal of social conventions is stark, even grotesque. There is a violence in the abrupt upending of relationships.

GOING WILD

When the shofar blast resounds throughout the Land, what does it proclaim?

> You shall sanctify the fiftieth year. You shall proclaim liberty (*dror*) throughout the Land for all its inhabitants. Each of you shall *return* to his estates and each of you shall *return* to his family. That fiftieth year shall be a jubilee for you: you shall not sow, neither shall you reap the aftergrowth or harvest the untrimmed vines, for it is a jubilee. It shall be holy to you: you may only eat the growth direct from the field. Each of you shall *return* to his estates. (Lev. 25:10–13)

The world regains the equilibrium it has lost over the previous forty-nine years. The jubilee is a more radical version of the release or return of the *Shmittah* year. To the basic concept of *Shmittah* is added the final release of Hebrew slaves and the *return*—twice repeated in this short passage—to one's ancestral lands. There is a repeated reference to holiness, as well as to the proclamation of *dror,* here translated "liberty." The specific holiness of the Jubilee year begins at its very beginning, ten days before Yom Kippur when slaves and property are freed from their alienated state. Liberty, as we have seen, begins before the actual movement of return.

However, *dror* is also understood to refer to freedom of movement to live (*dar*) and trade wherever one wishes.[18] This suggests that the Jubilee liberation, aside from returning slaves and land to their original proper condition, also initiates a kind of disorder, even chaos. Living and trading wherever one likes indicates a laissez-faire dimension of the Sabbatical year.

In the Sabbatical year, the basic weekly pattern of *work-rest* is elaborated in terms of the land. *Shmittah,* letting go, is characterized by not-sowing one's land, by not-pruning one's vineyard, by not-harvesting produce from either source. This could be called *neglecting* one's property, or desisting from the purposeful activities that for six years have nurtured growth and prosperity. Does this agricultural state of things not represent a *regression* from the general civilized human impulse to develop, to be productive?

After six days of intensive creativity, God *rests—shavat—*which means He *desists* from creativity. The weekly Sabbath is distinctly unproductive: on this day, human resources are consumed and not replenished.

In the Sabbath year, too, the progress narrative is relinquished. Nothing is improved, developed. This does not mean that one starves: one eats of one's field, but on equal terms with one's servants, with resident aliens, and with animals: "The Sabbath of the land shall be to you a source of food, to you, your male and female slaves, the hired and bound laborers who live with you, and your cattle and the beasts in your land: all its yield will be a source of food" (Lev. 25:6–7).

Rashi comments: "Although I have forbidden it to you, I have not forbidden it for food or other beneficial purpose." The balance is striking: the land is forbidden to you—except for personal, immediate consumption, on a par with others. The issue is one of ownership: there is to be no exclusive ownership of the land. Your access to its resources is for survival in the moment. You may not comport yourself as the *ba'al ha-bayit,* the owner of the house—a certain arrogance of the legally entitled is to be relinquished; it becomes meaningless. This includes long-term planning, the activity of investing in the future that characterizes private ownership.

Rashi emphasizes that it is God ("I have forbidden") who is behind this abandonment of the field. The paradox of this commandment is that, on the one hand, one may not cultivate one's estate; but on the other hand, the *field* and what survives in it determines what one may consume in the *house.* One may not store food in one's house if there is none left in the field; or keep food for one's domestic animals if there is none in the field for wild animals. The domestic economy of the *house* is thus subjected to the needs of the *field.*[19]

Perhaps most strikingly, one may not trade, as we have seen, with the fruits of the field. In direct contrast to the character of the six years, when "you shall *gather in* your produce (to the threshing floor)," *gathering-in* is forbidden in the seventh year (*shmittah*) and in the fiftieth year (*yovel*). Which means that "you shall eat *from the field*" (Lev. 25:11).[20] The direct connection with the field prohibits trading—the exchange system that offers larger satisfaction of many needs and pleasures.

Whom does this benefit? One possibility is that this cessation of productive labor and of trade is for the good of the land itself, which is improved by lying fallow. Or perhaps it is for the good of the poor and needy who gain equal access to agricultural produce? However, whether the poor benefit from the abandoned fields is a moot point. The poor may in fact suffer most in an unproductive economy. And the biblical text clearly declares that these periods of cessation are to be "a Sabbath *for God*," not essentially for the land or for the well-being of society. The religious character of these laws is emphasized. These swathes of time—the Sabbath day, the Sabbath year, the Sabbath of Sabbaths (the Jubilee year)—are all sanctified in their very inertia.[21]

DILIGENT INDOLENCE

The issue of trading was, we remember, the first misstep in the slippery-slope midrash. The Hebrew word *sechorah* is rooted in the notion of "going round and round," of circulation. In the *house*, the human province dominated by the will to thrive, goods are prepared for market (i.e., on the threshing floor): in the market, they are exchanged for the products of other fields. Resources circulate, people circulate, ideas circulate; the exchange of goods, of slaves, of communication creates a sense of cultural as well as agricultural vitality. Today, for instance, this is approximated by the prosperity of the town where a music festival—or the Olympic Games—takes place. Increased trade and cultural exchange feed off each other.

The ban on *sechorah*, then, cannot represent a general critique of this universal practice. For six days, six years, forty-nine years, *sechorah* is the way of the turning world. More than that, under the general heading of *work*, it may even be the privileged mode for normal life—a positive commandment.

"Six days you shall work and you shall do all your work . . . and the seventh day shall be *shabbat* (cessation) for God your God; you shall do no work" (Exod. 20:9–10). This does not merely tolerate the work of the six days;[22] it says, You are obliged to work during the six days. "Rabbi says, This is a separate edict. Just as Israel are commanded to keep the Sabbath, so are they commanded about work."[23]

A dialectic is at play between work and nonwork. In line with this, the Rama notes that it may be permitted to set sail on the day before the Sabbath, even though this will mean sailing on the Sabbath, if one is traveling *on business* (i.e., trading). In some views, work, trading, constitute a positive obligation during the six days of the week.[24]

Reading in this way enhances the positive value of trading, of the civilized practice of increasing productivity and exchange—the values of the *yishuv*, of human settlement. "When the Sanhedrin [the High Court] was in session, trade and commerce thrived in the world."[25]

Psychologically, too, work enhances vital energy. Keeping busy has a survival value in itself. Rabbinic statements advise that artificial forms of labor should be invented, so as to occupy oneself.[26] "Great is work that warms up those who engage in it." R. Yoshayahu used to move his furniture around on the Sabbath eve, if he had no useful labor to perform. Mental health concerns are associated with idleness: the court may intervene to divorce a couple if the husband will not let his wife work! *Batalah*, the boredom of not working, can be fatal. Work, or trade, makes one feel purposeful, alive; the workaholic can attest to the dangers of this dynamic when it becomes compulsive.

At the same time, the meaning of the Sabbath overlaps with the notion of *batalah*. Essentially, the word "Shabbat" itself holds negative connotations. It refers to cessation; even idleness and boredom may be part of the character of the day. Unplugged from one's usual productive activities, one is left in a kind of vacuum. It is this state that is to be "for God."[27]

The seventh year, in the same way, is a kind of energy void, which is sanctified, "for God." Like the Sabbath day, it stands in a dialectical relation to the work years. On the one hand, there is the vigor of productivity, the purposeful use of energy and resources, the hopefulness of creating a better future; but there is also a ruthlessness, a drive to exploit resources, to regard the world in an instrumental way. On the other hand, there is *not working*, which is also learned from God. It is associated with holiness. But it goes against the grain of human nature, it involves waste and even destruction of resources; in the radical case of the Jubilee year, it requires the "arousal" of a dormant sensibility. It exposes one to the dread of emptiness. In other words, the Sabbath modality is not natural to human beings.

The poet John Keats provocatively describes the condition of the artist as one of "diligent indolence." A secular version of the Sabbath modality, this can be the experience of any "Man who has arrived at a certain ripeness in intellect." "How happy is such a 'voyage of conception,' what delicious diligent Indolence!" A state of minimal external stimulation, of meditative idleness, it yields comparison with the flower rather than with the bee: "It has been an old Comparison for our urging on—the Bee hive—however it seems to me that we should rather be the flower than the Bee." One needs little to nurture such receptivity: certainly not the industrious and officious "urging on" to increase productivity. Subtle interactions become possible in such a state. Keats describes these as "taking hints."[28]

Celebrating effortlessness, Keats celebrates *batalah*—indolence, not working, a kind of receptive void. The Sabbath phenomenon, in one of its aspects, builds such an experience into the life of the Israelite—every week, every seven years, every fifty years. A different kind of creativity may grow out of this *void* time, if it serves the sacred and turns toward study and reflection.

TWO ORDERS: DURATION AND INTIMACY

However, the particular note of waste and destruction that seems to be part of the Shabbat modality is absent from Keats (although he seems to feel guilty about "wasting time"). This aspect of the *Shmittah* and the Jubilee years offers resistance to romanticization: these periods are times of loss, wasted opportunities and personal frustration. The human instinct to *make something* of one's resources, to invest and develop and ensure continuity, is systematically thwarted. These are times of *tohu*, of emptiness and void that return us to the world of God before Creation.

Georges Bataille writes powerfully about the religious notion of sacrifice that, he claims, enacts the anguish of the individual in a world of *things*. As we have noticed, he claims that the basic condition of one's worth in such a world is *duration*: How long and effectively can one last?[29] "[Man] is afraid of death as soon as he enters the system of projects that is the order of things."[30] Against this system stands what Bataille calls "the intimate order that is not reconcilable with the order of things."

Between the two orders, man engages in both the "order of things" and the intimate order, which involves sacrifice and the *defeat of individuality*. On the one hand, work and the fear of dying, which are interdependent;[31] on the other, the disappearance of duration, which "uncovers a ground of things that is dazzlingly bright."[32] To sacrifice is to relinquish and to give: it relinquishes the world of real things, of productivity, for a world of "consumption that is concerned only with the moment.... To sacrifice is to give as one gives coal to the furnace."

The moment of sacrifice has a violent dimension; even if it does not involve blood, it is "abrupt," it runs counter to the normal tempo of consciousness.[33] Sacrifice in Bataille's thinking answers to the concept of the *olah* offering, the burnt offering that is totally consumed. But more generally it evokes a core dimension of the Shabbat idea that transports one to a different temporality.

We have noticed that *Shmittah* and Jubilee begin to be practiced only after the conventions of land ownership have been established. It is at the point where one can point to one's own property and know it as one's own that the counter-principle of *Shmittah* becomes relevant. Work and the existential anxiety that is associated with it are replaced by no work and its different anxieties. The land is *betelah* and *chareivah*, void and ruined.[34] It is returned to its primal and sacred condition—and, mystically, to its ultimate condition: no longer a thing, an instrument for human projects.

For this reason, failure to observe these commandments is punished more gravely than other prohibitions: "Exile comes to the world for the *Shmittah* of the land."[35]

Exile is the fate of those who neglect the imperative of *Shmittah*. Letting go of property and of the impulses of ownership that tie one to life and continuity protects one from the catastrophe of exile. Exile is the grotesque shadow that haunts these laws—as though the periods of *cessation* constitute homeopathic doses of that catastrophe.

Bachya reads the dialectic in the text: "The secret of *Shmittah*," he writes, "is that 'your field,' 'your vineyard,' 'your harvest' will, after the interval of reversion to God's ownership, return to being indeed *yours,* in a fuller way."[36] The Shabbat time-out is blessed by God, which means that the day after is invigorated *la'asot*—to work and productivity.

Suspending the world of things for a day or a year preserves an essential balance between the instrumental use of land/slaves/money and the world of intimacy that is normally invisible. In a sense, this is a balance between power and powerlessness failure to maintain this balance results in exile: "If you wish to avoid exile, exhort them about *Shmittah* years and Jubilee years—'You shall observe my Sabbaths!' "[37] The plural form refers to all versions of the Sabbath principle.

SINISTER LIBERATION

The prophet Jeremiah describes with particular ferocity the historical connection between the violent manifestations of exile and the violation of the Sabbatical years. The king, Zedekiah, has induced his people, under solemn oath, to free their slaves; Nebuchadnezzar calls off the siege on Jerusalem; the masters promptly break their oath and force their slaves to return:

> Therefore thus says God: You have not listened to Me, to proclaim liberty (*dror*), each one unto his brother and each one unto his neighbor: Behold, I proclaim for you a liberty (*dror*), says God, unto the sword, unto the pestilence, and unto the famine; and I will make you a horror unto all the kingdoms of the earth. (Jer. 34:17–18)

Failure to liberate slaves is ironically met by "liberation" from God's protection against the horrific destructions of exile. The people's treachery is, at root, a profanation of God's name (v. 16), a breach of their covenant with God to liberate their slaves. The religious dimension of the *Shmittah* laws is placed at the center; failure to release their slaves releases the people from divine protection. Rashi writes: " 'I proclaim for you a liberty': from *Me,* since I am no longer your master to protect you. So you shall be prey to the sword and to famine."

To assert one's own ownership over others is at the same time to disqualify oneself for that relationship with God that is called "accepting the yoke of the kingdom of heaven." There has been a betrayal of the "listening" faculty. The people become *hefker*—un-owned, alienated from spiritual reality. If they refuse to loosen their grip on their slaves, they find God's grip loosened from them.

THE TERROR OF STANDING UPRIGHT

In *Dearest Father*, Kafka renders his nightmare vision of "the sphere system of violence" that is the choreography of power. The figure of his father sits at a table: "I walked round it in circles, feeling myself throttled by it. And around me there walked a third, feeling throttled by me. . . . And so it went on, right out to the circling of the constellations, and further still. *Everything felt the grip at the throat*" (my emphasis).[38]

A terrible inversion of the Ptolemaic system of the spheres, all harmony and beauty. In a letter to Felice, Kafka interprets a dream of hers: "Had you not been lying on the ground among the animals, you would have been unable to see the sky and the stars and wouldn't have been set free. Perhaps you wouldn't have survived the terror of standing upright."[39]

The "terror of standing upright" is Kafka's visceral experience of the utilitarian social world of will and work. Only by lying on the ground among the animals is it possible to be set free. Seeing the sky and stars holds the immense benefit of relinquishing one's *thing* position in a world of *things*.

Kafka's language here is religious (set free, redeemed—*erlost*), even as he inverts conventional religious imagery. Horizontal, not vertical, is the position of redemption. Surrendering power over the animal, Kafka voices something of the *Shmittah* sensibility.

The *Shmittah* is offered as a periodic immunization against exile. The cycle of terror and guilt is broken. Releasing one's throttlehold on others, one feels exempted from human hierarchies of power. Resuming one's place in those hierarchies, one will perhaps bear one's power with a difference.

"AS A DRIVEN LEAF": HALLUCINATIONS

For Jeremiah, the benign power of God represents an alternative to the human power world. The solemn covenant with God is a pact

between the weaker partner and the One who offers protection. To
break this bond when danger recedes is to revert to the automatism
of a closed system of fear.

Once God's protection is withdrawn, a devastating biblical description (Lev. 26) of the terrors of homelessness ensues. This is the section
of Leviticus known as the *Tochachah*, the *Rebuke*. We remember the
midrashic slippery-slope narrative—one who fails to observe the law
forbidding trade in the *Shmittah* year is finally sold into heathen slavery. Here, in the original biblical text, the Torah renders the national
fate in similar rhetoric: It is a matter of stages: each phase increases
in horror, as the people fail to pay attention to the meaning of their
misfortunes. The phase of exile is described thus:

> "And you I will scatter among the nations, and I will unsheathe
> the sword against you. Your land shall become a desolation and
> your cities a ruin. Then shall the land make up for its Sabbath
> years throughout the time that it is desolate and you are in the
> land of your enemies; then shall the land rest and make up for
> its Sabbath years." (Lev. 26:33–34)

The seventy years of exile answer to the number of missed Sabbath years.

Rashi offers a psychological reading:

> "Your land shall become a desolation": Since you will not soon
> return to it, and on that account "your cities shall be a ruin."
> That is, they will *appear to you* a ruin. For when a man is exiled
> from his house, or from his vineyard, or from his city, knowing
> that he is ultimately to return to it, it *appears to him* as though
> his vineyard or his house were not ruined.[40]

The catastrophe here is the hopeless state of the exiled. Long exile
with no prospect of return devastates the imagination, which projects
its desolation onto the object of yearning.

Even the survivors will be traumatized to the point of hallucination:

> As for those of you who survive, I will bring faintness into their
> hearts in the land of their enemies. The sound of a driven leaf

shall put them to flight. Fleeing as though from the sword, they shall fall though none pursues. (Lev. 26:36)

Rashi: "A driven leaf": Like the sound of one leaf rustling against another. Or, like the sound a door makes against the doorpost.

The misery of the exiled unbalances the mind. Even if they are not actually persecuted, they suffer from paranoid fantasies—"fleeing *as though* from the sword." Rashi exercises his imagination to convey the hollow sound of the rustling leaf, or the bang of a door loose on its hinges. We are left to imagine how these sounds might resound in the mind of the troubled exile.

This depiction of mental disorder takes us to the lowest point of exile. The inner reality of exile signifies the radical loss of selfhood. Such alienation is reflected in the midrashic narrative in the reference to being sold as a slave to heathen rituals—*avodah zarah*, "alien worship."

The driven leaf imagery haunts us. Perhaps the slippery-slope midrash meant to imply that the failure to observe *Shmittah* in the first place is an expression of a compulsive, paradoxical *sanity*. To trade in the fruits of the *Shmittah* year is, after all, one might say, to be extremely sensible. But this commonsense act betrays precisely that anxiety about work, duration, and death that makes one clutch at the world of things. As Bataille puts it, this anxiety obscures the "ground of things that is dazzlingly bright," which is uncovered precisely in the Sabbath moment. The *Shmittah* year acts as a homeopathic dose of exile, not only from home and land, but from a socially coherent sense of self. The Sabbath experience is a form of temporary madness.

We are touching here on the core of selfhood. Twin impulses reign here: the desire to be the *ba'al ha-bayit,* the master of the house, who knows what belongs to him/her, who invests resources into improving the world, husbanding the fruits of the land so that there may be a future; and the ability to let go, to loosen one's grip, to relinquish, to consume resources in one uncalculated moment. Under the first impulse, work is driven by fear and sacrifice is anguish; under the second, the suspension of the work modality means the experience of the sacred, the passion of being part of a larger reality.

In the *Shmittah* year, one passes from one world to another, almost from one self to another. Temporary exile from the conventional boundaries of self paradoxically protects one from the radical alienations of exile.

DRAWN AFTER GOD

Once the original covenant at Sinai has been disrupted by the Golden Calf, the *Shmittah* laws become the basis of a new covenant with God. On the verge of entering the Land, the conditions of possession and dispossession are set forth. Loyalty to this pact will suffuse the people's relation with God.

In this sense, the *Shmittah* laws answer to a new reality: now *landed* after their wilderness wandering, their sense of the divine must undergo a change from the literal *wild(er)ness* in which they had first known God.

Jeremiah offers the classic description of this primal time and space: "I remember for you the affection of your youth, your bridal love: how you went after Me in the wilderness, in a unsown land" (Jer. 2:2). The "unsown land" is the spiritual condition in which the Torah can be given. As Sefat Emet observes, the Torah cannot be accessed "unless one *suspends* (*mevatlin*) the things of this world and is drawn to trust in God alone."

In this teaching, the Hasidic master acknowledges the extreme difficulty of this moment. He regards the *Shmittah* year as a literal reenactment of the wilderness experience: the unsown land approximates that foundational historical moment. A shift of focus happens when one relinquishes one's compulsive sanities, and when one knows the startling experience of being *drawn after* God. As the *thingness* of the world disappears, one uncovers a "ground of things that is dazzlingly bright." Like the honeymoon time of wonder, that wilderness period could only be a temporary aberration from the rhythms of the "real" world. But built into those rhythms is the Sabbath experience, which restores the radical sphere of lost intimacy—every week, every seven years, every fifty years.

What is the "ground of things" that is uncovered? In his parting song, Moses recounts his people's spiritual history: "He found him in a desert region, in an empty howling waste" (Deut. 32:10). Rashi comments:

He found them (Jacob's sons) to be faithful to Him in the desert land, when they accepted His Torah, His sovereignty and His yoke, something that Ishmael and Esau had refused to do. . . . "In the empty howling waste": that is, in a land of drought and desolation, a place of screeching monsters and ostriches; even there they were *drawn* (*nimshechu*) after their faith and did not say to Moses, "But how can we go out into the wilderness, a place of drought and desolation?" Just as it is said, "I remember for you the affection of your youth, your bridal love, when you went after Me into the wilderness, into an unsown land." (Jer. 2:2)

Rashi emphasizes the death-valley terror of the wilderness. In this mythic wasteland, he indicates what they *don't* say: "How can we go forth into this deathly place?" The heroism of the honeymoon, in this reading, lies in the people's *suspension* of normal concerns about the future, about survival. They find themselves *drawn* into a terrifying primal intimacy with the divine. Rashi calls this attraction *faith* and links this death-valley description with Jeremiah's paean of praise, thus transforming the Deuteronomy passage into a heroic spiritual history.

THE GROUND OF THINGS

Of course, there are other midrashic traditions that focus on the many occasions when Israel does protest against the starkness of the wilderness: "What shall we eat? What shall we drink?" But Rashi chooses, even against the grain of the biblical text, to focus on the honeymoon tradition. He speaks of the beginning of the journey, before Sinai, before the marriage ceremony; and finds there a stark passion that can be invoked later within the practices of married life—on Shabbat, in the Sabbatical year and the Jubilee year.

This heroic passion is played out within "the void of a howling wilderness" (*betohu yillel yeshimon*). The compressed despair of this phrase is filled out in Rashi's commentary, "a place of the howling of jackals and ostriches."[41] Exotic animals are the source of the unearthly wail of the wilderness. But they in their turn are projections of the people in this space.

The *yelalah* is the howl of hopelessness. It is the cry of the void (*tohu*). Against this, Isaiah affirms meaning: "Not for emptiness did God create the world: He formed it to be cultivated (lit., settled)" (Isa. 45:18). The worlds of meaningful work and of wilderness void stand in stark opposition.

We remember King Lear's desolate cry on the death of Cordelia: "Howl! Howl! Howl! Howl!"[42] And the prophet Hosea describes his people as "wailing upon their beds" ("They did not cry out to Me sincerely, as they lay wailing upon their beds" [Hosea 7:14]). This is the ululation (*yelalah*) of despair.[43]

"Even there," says Rashi, "even in the howling negation of the wilderness, the people were drawn after faith." Even there, or perhaps precisely there. When the world has lost its plenitude, its purposeful energy, something new may be born. The fact that this wilderness, in its very emptiness, was the birthplace of Israelite history suggests that it constitutes the ground of things.

OPENING THE HAND

The *Shmittah* year invokes this ground of things. In the passage on "letting go" in Deuteronomy, we have noticed the repeated expression *pato'ach tiftach*—"you shall indeed open up your hand" (Deut. 15:8 and 15:11). The doubled verb for "opening" also invites interpretation.[44] In the context of the *Shmittah* year, it means unstinting generosity in offering gifts and loans to the released slave:

> You shall let him go free from you. And when you let him go free from you, you shall not let him go empty-handed. You shall indeed furnish him out of the flock, threshing floor, and vat with which God your God has blessed you. Be very aware that you were slaves in the land of Egypt and God your God redeemed you, therefore I command you in this way today. (Deut. 15:12–15)

Letting go of one's property means releasing the clenched heart and hand. This requires much practice. It runs counter to a natural "wickedness," or "stinginess" of heart and eye (Deut. 15:9–10). For instance, one should not stint on loans during the intervening years, out of calculation that the *Shmittah* year is approaching when all loans will be remitted. "You shall indeed open your hand."

Poverty as a social inevitability (Deut. 15:11) suggests that acts of charity—*tzedakah*—cannot be motivated only by good intentions of transforming social reality. In a radical teaching, R. Nahman speaks of *tzedakah* as the act of *breaking one's own cruelty!* When one encounters true destitution—that is, the situation where one's money will not in any sense *redeem* the victim from the poverty cycle nor will it redeem the world from its pain—refusing charity is called *cruelty.* The charity that gives only to the worthy poor has a dimension of this cruelty. The hand opens only when the poor can be redeemed.

In R. Nahman's teaching, the opening of the hand is a foundational movement—an exercise in developing compassion. Facing unredeemable despair, the hand clenches shut. The moment of opening, like the gradual opening of the birth canal in R. Nahman's meditation, involves pain and the counterpressure of contraction. What is to be born is the compassionate self.[45] This self cannot be born unless the cruelty is acknowledged; in this sense, only the compassionate self can truly give *tzedakah.*

The site of this birth is holy ground. This is where God is present. It is where God commands, in the first person: "*I* command you—You shall indeed open your hand!" In the service of God, beginnings are difficult. Something has to open, a passage has to widen. In this process, the practice of *tzedakah* becomes a sacred enactment.[46]

IMPOVERISHMENT, COMPASSION

The issues we have been discussing can be addressed from many different vantage points. There is the practice of the Sabbatical year, with its transcendence of instrumental concerns. Releasing the slave and forgiving debts become expressions of a primal movement for which the wilderness, exile, and the deathly void provide biblical and midrashic imagery. There is the practice of *tzedakah:* there is the experience, particularly, of a first birth.

Ultimately, there is simply a dynamic of human experience that requires what the poet Louise Glück calls *impoverishment.* In an essay by that name, she recounts her own experience of the seasons of dryness in which no poem flows. Her first such experience was devastating, a two-year silence in which she seemed to have lost herself. In her psychic inertia, she knew a desolate emptiness, a "sense of having nothing." Panic and helplessness were eventually followed by speech of a different caliber than ever before. "Some work is done through suffering, through impoverishment, through the involuntary relinquishing of a self."

The alternative to a life with such silences, she says, is "a life made entirely of will and ultimately dominated by fear. . . . The deft skirting of despair is a life lived on the surface, intimidated by depth, a life that refuses to be used by time, which it tries instead to dominate or evade." Addressing a class of graduating students, she urges them:

> Realize, then, that impoverishment is also a teacher, unique in its capacity to renew, and that its yield, when it ends, is a passionate openness which in turn re-invests the world with meaning. . . . [An intensity of awareness] is impoverishment's aftermath, and blessing: what succeeds temporary darkness, what succeeds the void or the desert, is not the primary gift of the world but the essential secondary gift of knowledge, a sense of the significance of the original gift, the scale of our privilege.[47]

Unconsciously, the self engineers its own defeat. To regard this as a blessing must be a retroactive recognition; it cannot diminish the actual rawness of the experience. The Sabbatical year comes as such a moment of impoverishment, which is also divine commandment and divine Presence. In the face of despair, something is demanded of us: a willingness to open, to soften, to let go, not to manipulate reality or force the future. So a real future may emerge, deepened by compassion—the secondary movement of the soul.

NOTES

INTRODUCTION

1. See Exodus 25:8: "They shall make Me a sanctuary and I shall dwell in their midst."
2. See Tanchuma Yashan, *Tissa* 3.
3. *Shemot Rabbah* 51:6.
4. *Shemot Rabbah* 48:7.
5. *Ein mukdam u-me'uchar ba-torah.* "The Torah does not necessarily reflect the chronological order of events." In general, the French school of commentary, led by Rashi, maintains this approach. The Spanish commentators hold to the *p'shat* position.
6. *B.Megillah* 13a.
7. *Shemot Rabbah* 51:6.
8. The Hebrew for "sacrifice" is *korban,* an act of achieving intimacy with the divine.
9. *J.Ta'anit* 4:5.
10. *B.Shabbat* 88b.
11. See Rashi.
12. See, for example, God's indictment, "They have speedily turned aside from the way I have commanded them: they have made themselves a molten calf, they have bowed down to it, and sacrificed to it, and *they have said,* These are your gods, O Israel, who brought you up from the land of Egypt!" (Exod. 32:8). Both Ha'amek Davar and Meshech Chochmah point out that the climax of the indictment is what the people have *said* rather than what they have done. Their mental life is the heart of the matter.
13. *Shemot Rabbah* 42:6.
14. *B.Shabbat* 88a. The heretic mocks the Israelites: "*Amma paziza*—You are a rash people who have put your mouth before your ears!"
15. Sefat Emet Shemot, 121.
16. According to a famous midrash, one of the first questions one is asked on the Day of Judgment is, Did you hope for redemption? *Tzippita l'yeshua?* (*B.Shabbat* 31a).
17. *B.Kiddushin* 22b.

18. George Eliot, *Daniel Deronda* (New York: Penguin, 1995), 787.

19. Sigmund Freud, *Civilization and Its Discontents,* in *The Standard Edition of the Complete Works,* trans. James Strachey, vol. 21 (London: Hogarth Press, 1953–74), 120.

20. George Eliot, *Middlemarch* (New York: Bantam Classic, 2008), 194.

21. Eliot, *Middlemarch,* 211.

22. Jan Assmann, *Moses the Egyptian: The Memory of Egypt in Western Monotheism* (Cambridge, MA: Harvard University Press, 1997), 72. It was Assmann who coined the expression "Egyptomania," which we will discuss later.

23. Assmann, *Moses the Egyptian,* 112.

24. See Rashi: "I did not know that this calf would emerge!"

25. See Seforno to Exodus 32:19.

26. Sifra to Leviticus 9:7.

27. See chapter 2 in this volume.

28. Gaston Bachelard, *On Poetic Imagination and Reverie; Selections from the Works of Gaston Bachelard,* trans. Colette Gaudin (Indianapolis, IN: Bobbs-Merrill, 1971), 19–21.

29. See *Shemot Rabbah* 43:1.

30. See chapter 1 of this volume.

31. Eric Santner, *On the Psychotheology of Everyday Life: Reflections on Freud and Rosenzweig* (Chicago: University of Chicago Press, 2001), 45.

32. Santner, *On the Psychotheology of Everyday Life,* 82.

33. *B.Menachot* 99b. See also *B.Shabbat* 88a. Only with the later event of the Purim story did the people "fulfill what they had already accepted." The original revelation finally "registers" with them when it modulates to the mode of "Oral Law"—becomes internalized by interpretation and transmission.

34. Rosenzweig Lehrhaus letter, cited in Nahum N. Glatzer, *Franz Rosenzweig: His Life and Work* (New York: Schocken Books, 1953), 243.

35. *Likkutei Moharan* II, 4:2.

36. Louise Glück, *Proofs and Theories: Essays on Poetry* (Hopewell, NJ: Ecco Press, 1994), 134.

37. *B.Gittin* 43a.

38. The proof text cited in the Talmud is from Isaiah 3:6: "Let this ruin, stumbling block, be under your hand." The Talmud reads this as referring to the Torah, which *is* the ruin, the stumbling block (*machshelah*).

1. VAYIKRA

1. *B.Yoma* 4b.

2. *B.Niddah* 16b.

3. *Vayikra Rabbah* 1:7.

4. *Midrash Ha-Gadol* to Leviticus 1:1.

5. *Vayikra Rabbah* 1:5.

6. *Vayikra Rabbah* 1:6.

7. Tanchuma Yashan 60:4.

8. See *Mei Ha-Shilo'ach,* vol. 1, on *Vayikra.* He cites Isaiah 65:24: "Before they call, I respond." The human being makes "space in his heart, clearing it of other desires." Then, God responds to the unvoiced human desire.

9. See David Stern, "Midrash and the Language of Exegesis," in *Midrash and Literature,* ed. Geoffrey H. Hartman and Sanford Budick (New Haven, CT: Yale University Press, 1986), 122.

10. See, for example, Tanchuma Terumah, 8.

11. In general, the commentators who adhere to *p'shat*—to the contextual reading of texts—adopt the first approach, while those who are drawn to *d'rash*—to the multilayered, a-chronic reading—adopt the second approach.

12. Tanchuma Yashan, *Tissa* 3.

13. *J.Ta'anit* 4:5.

14. Cf. Numbers 7:89. Rashi reads *middaber* in the same reflexive way.

15. Rashi to Exodus 33:8.

16. Ex. 43:1.

17. Eric Santner, *On the Psychotheology of Everyday Life: Reflections on Freud and Rosenzweig* (Chicago: University of Chicago Press, 2001), 45.

18. Santner, *On the Psychotheology of Everyday Life,* 10.

19. Santner, *On the Psychotheology of Everyday Life,* 15.

20. Rosenzweig shifted radically at this time from his decision to convert to Christianity. ("I will remain a Jew.") He also changed his career path, from the academic pursuit of philosophy to the teaching of Jewish thought in his own newly created *Lehrhaus.*

21. Santner, *On the Psychotheology of Everyday Life,* 82.

22. Quoted by Santner, *On the Psychotheology of Everyday Life,* 119.

23. *Shemot Rabbah* 43:7.

24. Quoted by Santner, *On the Psychotheology of Everyday Life,* 90, n.5.

25. Quoted by Santner, *On the Psychotheology of Everyday Life,* 91, n.5.

26. The commandment is literally at the center of Leviticus 19 (v. 18).

27. The obligations range from ethical guidelines on choosing a wife to laws dealing with proper treatment of condemned prisoners. See chapter 5 in this volume.

28. *B.Brachot* 32a. This "rereading" is generated by God's dismissive "Let Me be, and My anger shall burn against them" (Exod. 32:10), which Moses interprets as an invitation *not* to let God be! In the words of the Talmud, he "catches God by the garment and says, 'Master of the Universe, I shall not let You be until You forgive them!'"

29. *B.Brachot* 7a.

30. "Calling" is traditionally assumed to signify the doubled use of the name. God's first invocation of Moses, at the Burning Bush, was in this form

(Exod. 3:4). It expresses *chibah,* that form of intimate relationship that comes to its apex in the *Vayikra* moment.

31. See Jonathan Lear, *A Case for Irony* (Cambridge, MA: Harvard University Press, 2011), 11–12. Lear uses Kierkegaard's thoughts on irony as the basis of his discussion.
32. See Lear, *A Case for Irony,* 16.
33. Lear, *A Case for Irony,* 22.
34. Paul Ricoeur, *Interpretation Theory: Discourse and the Surplus of Meaning* (Fort Worth: Texas Christian University Press, 1976), 44.
35. Ramban to Leviticus 4:2.
36. The punishment would be *karet,* excommunication.
37. The English translations hint at culpability.
38. See Leviticus 4:23. And *B.Kritot* 11b; *B.Yevamot* 88a.
39. Leviticus 4:13,23; 5:23.
40. See Ha'amek Davar on Leviticus 4:13. Cf. Zecharia 11:5: "Those who kill them do not acknowledge guilt."
41. Jacob Milgrom, *Leviticus 17–22: A New Translation with Introduction and Commentary* (New York: Doubleday, 2000), 1425.
42. The fine is 20 percent over the amount owed.
43. Jonathan Lear, *Love and Its Place in Nature: A Philosophical Interpretation of Freudian Psychoanalysis* (New York: Farrar, Straus & Giroux, 1990), 65–66.
44. See Gur Aryeh on this verse.
45. This is called *mit'assek.* See *B.Kiddushin* 81b; and Rashi there: "Anyone who has a heart to mourn should mourn such a happening!—one had no intention of swallowing and yet one is held responsible."
46. See, for example, 1 Samuel 25:7.
47. Tanchuma Vayikra, 6.
48. Jonathan Lear, *Happiness, Death, and the Remainder of Life* (Cambridge, MA: Harvard University Press, 2000), 129.
49. Lear, *Happiness, Death, and the Remainder of Life,* 173.
50. See Leviticus 5:17–18.
51. *B.Krittot,* chapter 6, mishnah 3.
52. Rashi on *B.Chulin* 41b.
53. Jorge Luis Borges, "Funes the Memorious," in *Labyrinths,* ed. Donald A. Yates and James E. Irby (Harmondsworth, Middlesex, UK: Penguin Books, 1970), 87–95.
54. George Eliot, *Middlemarch* (New York: Bantam Books, 1985), 238.
55. Shoshana Felman, *Writing and Madness* (Ithaca, NY: Cornell University Press, 1985), 240.
56. *B.Temurah* 16b. In other versions, three thousand laws are forgotten.
57. *B.Menachot* 99b; *B.Shabbat* 87.
58. See Rashi's last comment on the Torah, on Deuteronomy 34:12. In his

midrashic reading, these last words evoke Moses's earlier account of his smashing of the Tablets ("And I smashed them *before your eyes*" [Deut. 9:17]).

59. *B.Menachot* 99b.

60. *B.Eruvin* 54. See Rabbi Yitzhak Hutner's essay on the virtue of forgetting in his collection on Hanukkah 3:3.

61. See David Stern, "Midrash and the Language of Exegesis: A Study of Vayikra Rabba," in *Midrash and Literature,* ed. Geoffrey H. Hartman and Sanford Budick (New Haven, CT: Yale University Press, 1986), 122.

62. This is the way Rashi often translates the term *va-yinachem:* "He changed his mind, regretted, was consoled." See, for example, Genesis 6:6.

63. *Vayikra Rabbah* 2:1.

64. See Deuteronomy 7:7.

65. *B.Ketubot* 110b.

66. See *Vayikra Rabbah* 1:14.

67. Quoted in Santner, *On the Psychotheology of Everyday Life,* 15.

2. TZAV

1. Tanchuma Shmini 3.

2. Strikingly, Rashi reads Moses's original response to the angel's call at the Burning Bush, "Here I am!"—as "ready for kingship, ready for priesthood!" (Exod. 3:4). Moses is prepared for the largest destiny.

3. This was practiced by delivery into the hand of a leather glove to symbolize bestowal of dignities.

4. Franz Rosenzweig, *The Star of Redemption* (Notre Dame, IN: University of Notre Dame Press, 1985), 405.

5. See Exodus 12:42.

6. The literal meaning refers to careful supervision to prevent the dough from rising; but the Mechilta puns on *matzot/mitzvot* teaches the virtue of alacrity in keeping the commandments.

7. *Bereishit Rabbah* 84:11.

8. The messianic implications of the Night of Watching are significant. See, for example, *Shemot Rabbah* 18:12, and the proof text, "The sentinel (*shomer*) said, Morning comes and also the night" (Isa. 21:12). The midrash tells of the anguish of the woman whose husband has gone over the seas and of the "sign" that keeps a sometimes fragile hope alive.

9. Eric Santner, *On the Psychotheology of Everyday Life: Reflections on Freud and Rosenzweig* (Chicago: University of Chicago Press, 2001), 115.

10. Meshech Chochmah to Exodus 32:7.

11. Song of Songs 1:12.

12. *B.Shabbat* 88b.

13. *Shemot Rabbah* 42:8.

14. Emmanuel Levinas, "A Religion for Adults," in *Difficult Freedom: Essays on Judaism,* trans. Seán Hand (Baltimore: Johns Hopkins University Press, 1997), 21–22.
15. See note 13.
16. Santner, *On the Psychotheology of Everyday Life,* 9.
17. Santner, *On the Psychotheology of Everyday Life,* 82.
18. Neither the loss nor the recovery of the clouds is mentioned in the Torah.
19. In *B.Sukkah* 11b, there are two views: the booths in the wilderness were literally huts, as we have them now; or else they were the Clouds of Glory that we symbolically represent in our booths.
20. Michael Eigen, *Flames from the Unconscious: Trauma, Madness, and Faith* (London: Karnac Books, 2009), 12.
21. D. W. Winnicott, *Human Nature* (London: Free Association Books, 1988), 101–2.
22. D. W. Winnicott, "Fear of Breakdown," in *Psycho-Analytic Explorations,* ed. Clare Winnicott, Ray Shepherd, and Madeleine Davis (Cambridge, MA: Harvard University Press, 1989), 92.
23. Winnicott, "Fear of Breakdown," 94.
24. Emily Dickinson, *The Poems of Emily Dickinson,* ed. R. W. Franklin (Cambridge, MA: Belknap Press of Harvard University Press, 1999).
25. Rambam, Laws of Lulav 8:12-15.
26. See also *B.Sukkah* 11b and Rashi's reference to juggling torches.
27. See Victor Turner, "Metaphors of Anti-structure in Religious Culture," in *Dramas, Fields, and Metaphors: Symbolic Action in Human Society* (Ithaca, NY: Cornell University Press, 1974), 272–99, for an analysis of the "anti-structural" ethos of the poor and the outcast. This becomes a "value-bearer," representing *communitas,* which embodies the value of sheer humanity.
28. *J.Sotah* 4:1.
29. Rav Yitzhak Hutner, *Pachad Yitzhak,* Sukkot 9:6.
30. Wordsworth, "Intimations of Immortality from Recollections of Early Childhood."
31. *Midrash Ha-Gadol* 40:38.
32. *Shemot Rabbah* 51:4.
33. *Shir Ha-Shirim Rabbah* 2:11.
34. Among the spices used in the Tabernacle is *galbanah*—pungent, bitter-smelling.
35. Quoted—and disputed—by Ibn Ezra to Exodus 34:1.
36. *Pirkei Avot* 3:18.
37. Rashi on Leviticus 9:23.
38. See Rashi to Leviticus 9:23.
39. *B.Sukkah* 2a.
40. We refer to this anxiety in the Grace after Meals on Sukkot: "May the Merciful One raise up for us again the Sukkah of David which is *falling.*"

41. Scrupulosity is characterized by a distressing, obsessive quality and is associated with guilt. I am suggesting the slight margin that separates this from conscientiousness in the fulfillment of the priestly role.
42. See Ramban 12:31. See also Sifre 128. They are already free, as Pharaoh has "liberated" them.
43. See, for example, his commentary to Exodus 27:20.
44. *J.Pe'ah* 1:1.
45. *J.Yoma* 1:1.
46. Cf. Wordsworth, "Intimations of Immortality": "Fallings from us, vanishings; / Blank misgivings of a Creature / Moving about in worlds not realized." See note 29.
47. Wordsworth, "Intimations."
48. Tanchuma Pikudei 11.
49. See *B.Baba Metzia* 87a; Rashi to Genesis 21:7.
50. *Be-kirba:* See Rashi: "She looked into her inward parts and said, Shall these innards—*kirvayim*—carry a fetus, shall these shrunken breasts fill with milk?"
51. The scoffers' gossip includes the idea that the baby is a "foundling from the market." See Rashi to Genesis 21:7.
52. *Shemot Rabbah* 52:3.
53. "The last day" refers to the proof text of the midrashic passage: the description of the "woman of valor" in Proverbs 31:25.
54. *Shemot Rabbah* 52:3.
55. *B.Brachot* 31a.
56. Psalms 126:2.
57. *B.Brachot* 31a.
58. Milan Kundera, *The Book of Laughter and Forgetting* (New York: Penguin Books, 1981), 61–62.
59. See Santner, *On the Psychotheology of Everyday Life,* 48. A performative utterance "indicates that the issuing of the utterance is the performing of an action—it is not normally thought of as just saying something." J. L. Austin, *How to Do Things with Words,* ed. J. O. Urmson and Marina Sbisà (Cambridge, MA: Harvard University Press, 1975), 6–7.
60. Santner, *On the Psychotheology of Everyday Life,* 115.
61. Rosenzweig, *The Star of Redemption,* 179.
62. Santner, *On the Psychotheology of Everyday Life,* 84–85.
63. Levinas in Santner, *On the Psychotheology of Everyday Life,* 85.
64. Emmanuel Levinas, *The Levinas Reader,* ed. Seán Hand (Cambridge, MA: B. Blackwell, 1989), 207–9.
65. Giorgio Agamben, *Remnants of Auschwitz: The Witness and the Archive* (New York: Zone Books, 1999), 68–69.
66. See Catherine Clément, *Syncope: The Philosophy of Rapture* (Minneapolis: University of Minnesota Press, 1994), 1. Whirling dervishes, the tango,

physical spasms like hiccups, laughter, coughing induce an "absence of the self," a "cerebral eclipse."

67. Rosenzweig in Santner, *On the Psychotheology of Everyday Life,* 84.
68. *Vayikra Rabbah* 11:9.
69. Mechilta d'Rabbi Ishmael, Yitro, 9th month.
70. See Shmuel Lewis, *Ve-lifnei kavod anava,* 133. Lewis associates this midrash with Victor Turner's concept of *communitas,* and with the anti-structural dynamic created by social groups that have no place in the hierarchies. He points out that this midrash is found with a different wording, in which God's presence dwells "upon him." This suggests that the humble are the recipients of the Holy Spirit (*ruach ha-kadosh*).
71. Or Ha-Chaim on Exodus 25:8.
72. On the literal level, the camp surrounds the Tabernacle, God's dwelling, with the tribal flags ranked on all four sides around the center.
73. The word for "sign"—*ot*—is linked, by wordplay, with the desire—*ta'avah*—of the people. God's position among the angels becomes the object of human desire. See *Bamidbar Rabbah* 2:2.
74. Levinas, *The Levinas Reader,* 209.
75. Rashi on Song of Songs 3:11. The verb *le-chabev* carries an active charge: to cherish her, to be increasingly aware of his love.
76. Rashi on Song of Songs 3:11.

3. SHMINI

1. *B.Megillah* 10b.
2. See Rashi to Leviticus 9:1.
3. The expression *ranen* finds a home in the book of Psalms and to a lesser extent in Isaiah—where it appears in exhortation and prophecy, and where it enacts precisely the gesture of sacred song.
4. Sefat Emet Vayikra, 114.
5. Rashbam to Leviticus 9:24–10:2.
6. Rashbam compares this to Elijah's command at Mount Carmel: "Do not set any fire" (1 Kings 18:25). There, too, it was important not to preempt the miracle of divine fire, out of sheer impatience.
7. Sifra Milu'im 22. Cited in Meir Yitzhak Lokshin, *Perush Ha-Rashbam al Ha-Torah* (Jerusalem: Horev, 2009).
8. Christopher Bollas, *The Shadow of the Object: Psychoanalysis of the Unthought Known* (Free Association Books, 1991), 146.
9. Rashi to Leviticus 9:23.
10. Meshech Chochmah (to Lev. 9:7) suggests that, in a sense, the people are implicated in Aaron's sin. They caused him to sin, so his expiation sacrifice is to atone for them as well, as agents in his sin. The death of Nadav and Avihu is punishment for their father's sin and for the whole people, who are then commanded to "weep for the burning" (10:6).

11. See Rashi to Exodus 32:5: "Aaron saw that it [the Golden Calf] had a spirit of life in it . . . that the work of Satan had succeeded."
12. William Shakespeare, Sonnet 129.
13. Sifra to Leviticus 9:7.
14. Psalms 51:5.
15. Georges Bataille, *Theory of Religion* (New York: Zone Books, 1989), 37.
16. Bataille, 40.
17. Bataille, 43–44.
18. Bataille, 46.
19. Bataille, 4448–49.
20. Bataille, 52.
21. Bataille, 50.
22. See Rashi to Exodus 3:10: "your words will be *effective* in freeing the people from there."
23. Gaston Bachelard, *Air and Dreams: An Essay on the Imagination of Movement* (Dallas, TX: Dallas Institute Publications, 1988), 2–3.
24. Eric L. Santner, *On the Psychotheology of Everyday Life* (Chicago: The University of Chicago Press, 2001), 45.
25. See Jan Assmann, *Moses the Egyptian: The Memory of Egypt in Western Monotheism* (Cambridge, MA: Harvard University Press, 1997), 72.
26. See Seforno and Ha-amek Davar to Deuteronomy 1:27.
27. *J.Ta'anit* 4:5.
28. See note 8.
29. See Edward Greenstein, "Deconstruction and Biblical Narrative," in *Interpreting Judaism in a Postmodern Age,* ed. Steven Kepnes (New York: New York University Press, 1996), especially 44–45.
30. Bataille, *Theory of Religion,* 47.
31. *Shir Ha-Shirim Rabbah* 1:52.
32. Julia Kristeva, *Black Sun: Depression and Melancholia* (New York: Columbia University Press, 1989), 41.
33. Kristeva, *Black Sun,* 5.
34. See Exodus 7:22—*chartumei mitzraim be-lateihem.*
35. *B.Yoma* 75a.
36. R. Leiner is not alone among Hasidic thinkers in emphasizing the *chissaron.* But his linking of this with prayer goes to the heart of religious experience.
37. Bollas, *The Shadow of the Object,* 146.
38. Jonathan Lear, *Love and Its Place in Nature: A Philosophical Interpretation of Freudian Psychoanalysis* (New Haven, CT: 1998), 179.
39. Jonathan Lear, Introduction to Hans W. Loewald, *The Essential Loewald: Collected Papers and Monographs* (Hagerstown, MD: University Publishing Group, 2000), xxxii.
40. Adam Phillips, *The Beast in the Nursery* (New York: Pantheon Books, 1998), 13.

41. *Vayikra Rabbah* 20:5.
42. Phillips, *The Beast in the Nursery*, 13.
43. Quoted in Adam Phillips, *On Kissing, Tickling, and Being Bored: Psychoanalytic Essays on the Unexamined Life* (Cambridge, MA: Harvard University Press, 1993), 19.

4. TAZRIA/METZORA

1. Writing in the time of the coronavirus, such a classification becomes strangely imaginable. The virus lingers on surfaces, transfers through the air to the lungs, and manifests in fever and breathing difficulties.
2. See Samson Raphael Hirsch, *The Pentateuch,* trans. Isaac Levy (London: Isaac Levy, 1959), Genesis 2:21.
3. Ramban on Leviticus 13:47.
4. Jorge Luis Borges, *Selected Non-Fictions* (New York: Viking, 1999), 231.
5. Michel Foucault, *The Order of Things: An Archaeology of the Human Sciences* (New York: Pantheon Books, 1971), xv.
6. *C'na'anim* is used as the parallel expression to *sochrim*—traders, in Isaiah 23:8.
7. See the discussion of this tension in, for example, Beit Yaacov, *Bereshit* 2.
8. *Vayikra Rabbah* 16:2. The ending is a classic pun on *metzora/motzi ra.*
9. *Anaf Yosef* to *Vayikra Rabbah* 16:2.
10. See Alshich to Psalms 34:13.
11. *Pri Zaddik,* 5, 125–26.
12. *B.Gittin* 43a. This is based on Isaiah 3:6: "This stumbling block shall be under your hand."
13. *R'sisei Layla,* 13.
14. *B.Baba Batra* 12a.
15. For a Hasidic understanding of this, see, for example, Beit Yaacov, *Tissa* 68: the light of the second set of Tablets makes more impact on Moses's face, precisely because it follows the Golden Calf and the fracturing of the first Tablets.
16. *B.Menachot* 29b.
17. See *B.Temurah* 16a. When Moses dies, three hundred laws are forgotten, till Otniel ben Kenaz reconstructs them on the basis of *pilpul*—the "playful" connection of fragments.
18. *B.Menachot* 99b.
19. Leviticus 10:10.
20. Rashi to Leviticus 10:10.
21. See the comment of Ha'amek Davar on the expression *bein . . . u-vein.*
22. *B.Shavuot* 18b.
23. Kenneth Burke, *Language as Symbolic Action; Essays on Life, Literature, and Method* (Berkeley: University of California Press, 1966), 9.
24. Burke, *Language as Symbolic Action,* 10–12.

25. Burke, *Language as Symbolic Action*, 65.

26. Burke, *Language as Symbolic Action*, 449.

27. The expression *chituch ha-dibbur* (lit., the incision in language) conveys articulation, a clear-cut verdict—the place of *separation*.

28. Jeremiah 15:19.

29. *B.Gittin* 43a.

30. Mordecai Yosef Leiner, *Mei Ha-Shilo'ach*, vol. 1 (Brooklyn, 1991), 36a.

31. It occurs eight times in the Scriptures.

32. *B.Arachin* 16b.

33. *Galmud* is derived from the root *g-l-m*, meaning raw, shapeless material.

34. *Eichah Rabbah Petichta*.

35. Maimonides, *Laws of Tzora'at*, 9:2.

36. See *B.Baba Kama* 40a.

37. *B.Mo'ed Katan* 5a.

38. *B.Sanhedrin* 104b.

39. Iain McGilchrist, *The Master and His Emissary: The Divided Brain and the Making of the Western World* (New Haven, CT: Yale University Press, 2009), 58, 250. Even mental representation, without direct sense stimulus—imagining—activates some of the same neurons.

40. Cited in Stephen Frosh, *Hauntings: Psychoanalysis and Ghostly Transmissions* (London: Palgrave Macmillan, 2013), 69.

41. *B.Chulin* 60b.

42. Frosh, *Hauntings*, 86.

43. Frosh, *Hauntings*, 114.

44. *Torat Kohanim*.

45. *Mei Ha-Shilo'ach*, vol. 1, 36a.

46. See, for example, *Mei Ha-Shilo'ach*, vol. 2, 8 on Genesis 1:27.

47. Paul Ricoeur, *History and Truth* (Evanston, IL: Northwestern University Press, 1965), 322–24.

48. Sefat Emet, *Vayikra*, 139.

49. Primo Levi, *The Periodic Table* (New York: Schocken Books, 1984), 33–34.

50. *Likkutei Moharan* 1:282.

51. Psalms 37:10.

52. Ricoeur, *History and Truth*, 323.

53. Lear, Introduction to *The Essential Loewald*, xxix–xxxi.

54. Lear, Introduction to *The Essential Loewald*, xxxi–xxxii.

55. *Bereishit Rabbah* 13:2.

56. See Richard Powers, *The Overstory: A Novel* (New York: W. W. Norton, 2018). In one section, Powers discusses the communication methods trees use to warn of predators and to lure allies.

57. See Genesis 24:63: "Isaac went out to meditate/*pray* in the field." The midrash understands this specifically as the original *minchah* (afternoon) prayer.

58. See Jeremiah 26:18.
59. *Concise Science Dictionary* (New York: Oxford University Press, 1996).

5. ACHAREI MOT/KEDOSHIM

1. Rashi to Leviticus 16:1.
2. See chapter 2 in this volume.
3. *B.Yoma* 60a.
4. *Chukah* (statute) is derived from *chakak,* to engrave.
5. See Esther 8:8: "The written text that has been written in the king's name and sealed with his ring *cannot be withdrawn.*" The word *gezerah* is not used but the notion of implacability is thoroughly conveyed.
6. 1 Kings 3:16–23.
7. *B.Yoma* 67b.
8. See, for example, Rashi's comments on the beginning of the *Akedah* narrative. The midrash attributes to Abraham a tendency to *hirhurim* around the divine command to sacrifice his son. Rashi adopts this line of thought, without criticizing Abraham. See Avivah Gottlieb Zornberg, *Genesis: The Beginning of Desire* (Philadelphia: Jewish Publication Society, 1995), 93–95; and Zornberg, *The Murmuring Deep: Reflections on the Biblical Unconscious* (New York: Schocken Books, 2009), 173–78.
9. *B.Yoma* 65b.
10. *B.Yoma* 87b.
11. See also Maimonides, *Guide for the Perplexed,* 3.
12. *Se'ir* is a goat and also the name of Esau's territory.
13. See Ramban to Leviticus 16:8.
14. See Leviticus 18:3.
15. *B.Yoma* 67b.
16. *Nigrazti* is used here—possibly a case of reversed letters but identical meaning. Rashi quotes contemporary grammarians who relate the word to *garzen*—axe—and link the various forms of *nigzarti—nigrazti—nigrashti.*
17. See previous note.
18. *Va-yishalchu* (Gen. 37:32) is translated by Seforno, "They cut it up with daggers." See also Thomas Mann, *Joseph and his Brothers* (New York: Knopf, 1948), 373–74: "cutting into very little pieces his trust, his whole notion of the world . . . Desperately he tried to protect the garment and keep the remnants and ruins of it still upon him. Several times he cried out: My coat! My coat! And even after he stood naked, still begged them like a girl to spare it."
19. Frye, quoted in René Girard, *Oedipus Unbound: Selected Writings on Rivalry and Desire* (Stanford, CA: Stanford University Press, 2004), 100.
20. Girard, *Oedipus Unbound,* 101.
21. Girard, *Oedipus Unbound,* 112.

22. W. G. Sebald, *Austerlitz,* trans. Anthea Bell (New York: Random House, 2001), 14.

23. William James, *The Varieties of Religious Experience: A Study in Human Nature* (New York: Collins, 1960), 142.

24. James, *The Varieties of Religious Experience,* 144.

25. Mary Douglas, *Purity and Danger: An Analysis of Concepts of Pollution and Taboo* (London: Routledge & Kegan Paul, 1966), 164.

26. Douglas, *Purity and Danger,* 168.

27. Douglas, *Purity and Danger,* 170.

28. Douglas, *Purity and Danger,* 171.

29. Douglas, *Purity and Danger,* 174.

30. Douglas, *Purity and Danger,* 177.

31. There is a suggestion that a goat was given as a prize for the best tragic play of the season.

32. Jonathan Lear, *Open Minded: Working Out the Logic of the Soul* (Cambridge, MA: Harvard University Press, 1998), 174.

33. Lear, *Open Minded,* 181.

34. Lear, *Open Minded,* 186.

35. Lear, *Open Minded,* 187.

36. Throughout the year, *unintentional* sins are atoned by the Sin Offering and the Guilt Offering.

37. Jonathan Lear, *A Case for Irony* (Cambridge, MA: Harvard University Press, 2011), 20.

38. Lear, *A Case for Irony,* 37.

39. *B.Makkot* 23b.

40. The area of *lifnim mishurat ha-din* ("contextual morality"—see note 41) itself forms part of the halachic system. Its proof texts are "And you shall do the right and the good" (Deut. 6:18). See Ramban *ad loc.* Also *B.Baba Metzia* 30b, 83a; Rambam, *Hilchot De'ot* 1:5.

41. See Aaron Lichtenstein, "Does Jewish Tradition Recognize an Ethic Independent of Halakha?" in *Modern Jewish Texts,* ed. Marvin Fox (Columbus: Ohio State University Press, 1975), 72.

42. See Rashi to Leviticus 20:26.

43. *B.Makkot* 23a.

44. An important legal implication is that one may violate all commandments when life is at risk, with the exception of the three cardinal prohibitions.

45. See, for example, Leviticus 11:44–45.

46. See Franz Rosenzweig's use of the term *Beseelung,* or ensoulment, in *The Star of Redemption.* Franz Rosenzweig, *The Star of Redemption* (Notre Dame, IN: University of Notre Dame Press, 1985).

47. Lon Fuller, *The Morality of Law* (New Haven, CT: Yale University Press, 2000), 5.

48. See David Luban, "Natural Law as Professional Ethics: A Reading of Fuller," *Social Philosophy and Policy* 18 (2000): 176–205. *Georgetown Law Faculty Publications and Other Works.*

49. See Malcolm Gladwell, *Outliers: The Story of Success* (New York: Little, Brown, 2008). This notion is based on the research of Anders Ericsson, who claimed that the hours of practice are the major factor in achieving excellence.

50. See note 49.

51. Agnes Callard discusses a form of rationality she calls "proleptic." "Proleptic reasons are provisional in a way that reflects the provisionality of the agent's own knowledge and development: her inchoate, anticipatory, and indirect grasp of some good she is trying to know better." Agnes Callad, *Aspiration: The Agency of Becoming* (New York: Oxford University Press, 2018), 72.

52. *B.Kiddushin* 31b.

53. Maimonides, *Laws of Murder,* 12, 14.

54. *B.Pesachim* 20b.

55. *B.Mo'ed Katan* 17a.

56. *B.Baba Metzia* 75b. All the examples in this section are taken from Nehama Leibowitz, *Studies in Vayikra/Leviticus* (Jerusalem: World Zionist Organization, 1980), 173–78.

57. George Eliot, *Middlemarch* (New York: Bantam Classics, 2008), 238.

58. *J.Nedarim* 9:4.

59. *B.Baba Metzia* 62a.

60. Sigmund Freud, *Civilization and Its Discontents* (New York: Penguin Books, 2002), 79.

61. See also the description of Jonathan and David's relationship.

62. Rashbam to Leviticus 19:16–17.

63. *B.Ketubot* 37b; *B.Sanhedrin* 48a.

64. *B.Kiddushin* 48a.

65. *B.Sanhedrin* 84b.

66. *J.Nedarim* 9:4.

67. *B.Shabbat* 31a.

68. See Rashi to *B.Shabbat* 31a.

69. See Rav Eliyahu Dessler, *Michtav Me-Eliyahu,* vol. 2, 142.

70. See Dessler, *Michtav Me-Eliyahu,* vol. 1, 37–38.

71. Eric L. Santner, *On the Psychotheology of Everyday Life: Reflections on Freud and Rosenzweig* (Chicago: Chicago University Press, 2001), 82.

72. Santner, *On the Psychotheology of Everyday Life,* 6.

73. Santner, *On the Psychotheology of Everyday Life,* 91.

74. Santner, *On the Psychotheology of Everyday Life,* 45.

75. Santner, *On the Psychotheology of Everyday Life,* 101.

76. Agnes Callard, *Aspiration: The Agency of Becoming* (New York: Oxford University Press, 2018), 76.

77. Sefat Emet, *Vayikra, Kedoshim,* 155.

78. See Elizabeth Lloyd Mayer, *Extraordinary Knowing: Science, Skepticism, and the Inexplicable Powers of the Human Mind* (New York: Bantam Books, 2007), 65–66.

79. Evelyn Underhill, cited in Mayer, *Extraordinary Knowing,* 66.

80. Wordsworth, "Tintern Abbey," July 13, 1798.

6. EMOR

1. Leviticus 9:24–10:2. See chapter 3 in this volume.

2. Leviticus 24:10.

3. Lear, *Open Minded,* 186.

4. Lear, *Open Minded,* 181.

5. This is the question of Rabbenu Bachya: "It would have been better to censor it, for the honor of God."

6. See Ha'amek Davar to Leviticus 24:11.

7. See Rashi on Leviticus 24:12: Both cases happened in the same period, but the two accused are not housed in the same cell (despite the similar phrasing) because the uncertainty in the case of the wood gatherer is only about the *manner* of his execution.

8. See B.Sanhedrin 60a.

9. See, for example, Shakespearean expletives.

10. Zohar, 313.

11. Tanchuma Emor, 24.

12. See note 5.

13. Some such clues linking the two narratives are: the use of *vayetzei* ("he went forth") of both the blasphemer and Moses; the anonymity of the Egyptian man and the Hebrew/Israelite man in both stories; the opening scene of violence; the destructive blows (*makkeh*) of the Egyptian, which are met by Moses's equally violent *va-yach*—which in turn is revealed to have been a violent act of speech—with its parallel in the blasphemer story; and the unusual word for fighting (*nitzim*) that appears in both stories.

14. Seforno to Leviticus 24:16.

15. See the Gaon to Isaiah 8:21.

16. The euphemism *barech*—bless—is used in place of *curse,* to emphasize the horror of the act.

17. Job is recorded as sacrificing annually, "lest my children have sinned by blessing (a euphemism for cursing) God *in their hearts.*" At the beginning of *Job,* this repressed emotional state is a live possibility.

18. Freud, "Instincts and Other Vicissitudes," 1915c, 136.

19. See Rashbam, who makes the connection.
20. See William Blake, "The Poison Tree."
21. *B.Arachin* 16b.
22. Seforno to Genesis 27:29.
23. Rashbam to Exodus 22:27.
24. Bettelheim notes that in German the child is called *das Kind* in the neuter form—the *child thing*, the embodiment of impulse.
25. Robert Cover, *Narrative, Violence, and the Law: The Essays of Robert Cover* (Ann Arbor: University of Michigan Press, 1992), 208.
26. Cover, *Narrative, Violence, and the Law*, 213.
27. See *B.Sanhedrin* 42b. Some read this as a reference to the sins of blasphemy and idolatry, which are, in effect, the only offenses that are punishable by hanging.
28. See *B.Sanhedrin* 46a: "One official climbs up and hangs the prisoner and another climbs up and immediately brings him down and buries him before sunset."
29. A *chalal* is a corpse, empty of life. *Me-cholel* is to engender, to generate.
30. Rashi notes that where the euphemism "he *blessed*" is used, it refers to a less weighty divine Name than the ineffable Name, which is almost never to be made explicit. The stark curse *va-yikalel* refers to *the* Name itself—the ultimate sacrilege.
31. Cf. Genesis 30:28: Laban rehires Jacob, "Name (*Nokva*) your salary!" The word *vayikov* means literally to *make a hole, to pierce*. To make a hole beside an object is to draw particular attention to it, like naming it.
32. *Torat Kohanim* 14:1. There is one view that his Israelite status is compromised, since he has no place in the camp or in the inheritance of the Land. He is, in fact, nameless. See Ramban to Leviticus 24:10.
33. See Numbers 20:12.
34. An extraordinary midrash reads, "Even Moses our Teacher does not know the place of his (own) burial!" (*B.Sotah* 14a).
35. See Rashi to Deuteronomy 24:11.
36. See Elizabeth Hardwick, "Seduction and Betrayal II," *New York Review of Books*, June 14, 1973.
37. *B.Baba Metzia* 58b.
38. Eric L. Santner, *On the Psychotheology of Everyday Life: Reflections on Freud and Rosenzweig* (Chicago: Chicago University Press, 2001), 82.
39. See Maimonides, *Laws of Repentance*, 7:8.
40. See Exodus 10:1–2.
41. Rashi has a possible wordplay on *meitzar/mitzrayim*—grief/Egypt—to suggest the depth of his identification: his grief has an Egyptian coloration.
42. Execution by stoning involves at least the symbolic participation of the community.
43. Kafka in a letter to Oskar Pollak (January 27, 1904).

44. Rashi offers this etymology of *achzar* in his commentary on Job. Job's erstwhile friends have become alienated from him; their behavior is now callous, unkind.
45. *Vayikra Rabbah* 32:7.
46. See Ha'amek Davar to Leviticus 24:14.
47. The placing of hands on the head of the goat in the central ritual of the Day of Atonement conveys a similar desire to project outward inner guilt. Here, the blasphemer is not innocent but nevertheless perhaps he can be recognized as holding a "scapegoat" function for the unconscious violence in the community.
48. Roland Barthes, *Camera Lucida: Reflections on Photography* (Vintage: 2000), 27.
49. *Sefer Ha-Chinuch*, Commandment 70.
50. Jonathan Lear, *Happiness, Death, and the Remainder of Life* (Cambridge, MA: Harvard University Press, 2000), 92–93.
51. Lear, *Happiness, Death, and the Remainder of Life*, 93–94.
52. See Lear, *Happiness, Death, and the Remainder of Life*, 95–96: "Freud's deepest insight, I suspect, is that, appearances to the contrary, life can never be lived without remainder."
53. Lear, *Happiness, Death, and the Remainder of Life*, 93.
54. D. W. Winnicott, *Home Is Where We Start From: Essays by a Psychoanalyst* (New York: Norton, 1986), 82.
55. Winnicott, *Home Is Where We Start From*, 85.
56. Winnicott, *Home Is Where We Start From*, 87.
57. See Rashi and *B.Brachot* 54a.
58. *B.Yoma* 69b.
59. Lear, *Happiness, Death, and the Remainder of Life*, 94–95.
60. Genesis 9:6.
61. *B.Sanhedrin* 58a.
62. *B.Niddah* 30b.
63. Maharal, *Gevurot Ha-Shem*, 28.
64. *Shir Ha-Shirim Rabbah* 1:15.
65. *Mei Ha-Shilo'ach* 1: *Emor*.
66. The showbread stayed fresh for a whole week.
67. George Steiner, *Real Presences* (Chicago: University of Chicago Press, 1989), 55–57.
68. Octavio Paz, *Alternating Current* (New York: Viking Press, 1973), 68.
69. *Mei Ha-Shilo'ach* 1: *Tissa*.
70. The Calf, the *Egel*, is associated with the idea of immediacy, of instant and total understanding.
71. *Mei Ha-Shilo'ach* 1: *Emor*.
72. *Mei Ha-Shilo'ach* 1: *Emor*.
73. *B.Avodah Zarah* 3a.

74. Lear, *Happiness, Death, and the Remainder of Life*, 93–94.
75. *Mei Ha-Shilo'ach* 1: *Lech lecha.*
76. *Bereshit Rabbah* 39:1. There is an alternative reading of the Hebrew words *bira doleket*—a castle *brightly illumined.* It is not entirely clear which reading Mei Ha-Shilo'ach is using.
77. See Isaiah 40:26. This verse serves as the opening proof text of the Zohar.

7. BEHAR/BECHUKOTAI

1. See Seforno to Leviticus 25:1.
2. In Exodus 23:11–12, the laws of the Sabbath and the *Shmittah* are framed in terms of social and ethical value.
3. *B.Kiddushin* 20a. See also Rashi to Leviticus 26:1 for a briefer version of this passage.
4. *Torat Kohanim.*
5. Cf. Leviticus 25:42.
6. *B.Kiddushin* 22b.
7. *J.Kiddushin* 1:2.
8. See Seforno to Leviticus 25:42.
9. Sefat Emet, *Shemot*, 121.
10. Cited in Ernest Becker, *The Denial of Death* (New York: Free Press, 1973), 156.
11. Becker, *The Denial of Death*, 127.
12. Becker, *The Denial of Death*, 157.
13. *Difficile Liberté* is the title of Emmanuel Levinas's collection of essays on Jewish thought.
14. Deuteronomy 15:1–2.
15. See *B.Kiddushin* 22a.
16. Section 327.
17. *B.Rosh Hashanah* 8a.
18. *B.Rosh Hashanah* 9b.
19. See Ecclesiastes 5:8: "Even the king is subject to the field."
20. See Ha'amek Davar to 25:3.
21. See Leviticus 25:10, Genesis 2:3.
22. Rashi cites a psychological reading of *"all* your work": "When Shabbat begins, you should feel as though *all* your work has been completed, so that you will not mull over it."
23. Mechilta d'Rabbi Shimeon bar Yochai cited in *Torah Shelemah Yitro*, 242.
24. See *Torah Shelemah Yitro*, Appendix 14 (p. 243). "One may set sail on the eve of the Sabbath for the sake of fulfilling a commandment." Another example that *Torah Shelemah* discusses is the halachic issue of crossing the international date line. It is problematic not only to fail to keep Shabbat but also to fail to work on a "workday."
25. Pesikta Rabbati.

26. *Torah Shelemah Yitro,* Appendix 15.

27. Every city is required to support ten *batlanim*—unemployed, idle people. These are scholars who simply sit and study. The word *batel* carries ambivalent associations of laziness and availability for alternative, more spiritual uses of one's time.

28. John Keats, *Letters* (New York: Oxford University Press, 1954), 80. Letter 48, February 1818.

29. See chapter 3 in this volume.

30. Georges Bataille, *Theory of Religion* (New York: Zone Books, 1989), 52.

31. Bataille, *Theory of Religion,* 51.

32. Bataille, *Theory of Religion,* 48.

33. Bataille, *Theory of Religion,* 49.

34. See Bachya to Leviticus 25:2.

35. *Pirkei Avot* 5:12.

36. Leviticus 25:10. Bachya distinguishes *Shemittah* from the Jubilee in this regard.

37. *B.Shabbat* 33b.

38. Quoted from Elias Canetti, *Kafka's Other Trial: The Letters to Felice* (New York: Penguin, 1982), 67.

39. Canetti, *Kafka's Other Trial,* 68.

40. Rashi to Leviticus 26:33.

41. This is translated in the JPS edition as "a place of screeching monsters and ostriches."

42. It is striking that this line is written into the text, rather than in the stage directions—as though the animal sound becomes a part of inhuman/human language.

43. See Metzudot David. The *yelalah* is also the mode in which, according to several midrashic sources, Sarah reacts to the satanic news that her son Isaac has *almost* been slaughtered. Sarah becomes the voice of the void; she is lost in the wailing and dies.

44. In fact, doubled verbs abound in this section: see 15:4, 5, 10, 14. This feature, together with synonyms and parallelisms, conveys a sense of expressing the inexpressible, as in poetic diction.

45. *Likkutei Moharan* II: 4:1–2.

46. See Yishai Mevorach, *Ha-yehudi shel Ha-katzeh* (in Hebrew) (Tel Aviv: Resling, 2018), 55–62.

47. Louise Glück, *Proofs and Theories: Essays on Poetry* (Hopewell, NJ: Ecco Press, 1994), 133–34.

BIBLIOGRAPHY

Agamben, Giorgio. *Remnants of Auschwitz: The Witness and the Archive.* New York: Zone Books, 1999.

Assmann, Jan. *Moses the Egyptian: The Memory of Egypt in Western Monotheism.* Cambridge, MA: Harvard University Press, 1997.

Austin, J. L. *How to Do Things with Words.* Edited by J. O. Urmson and Marina Sbisà. Cambridge, MA: Harvard University Press, 1975.

Bachelard, Gaston. *Air and Dreams: An Essay on the Imagination of Movement.* Dallas, TX: Dallas Institute Publications, 1988.

———. *On Poetic Imagination and Reverie; Selections from the Works of Gaston Bachelard.* Translated, with an introduction by Colette Gaudin. Indianapolis, IN: Bobbs-Merrill, 1971.

Barthes, Roland. *Camera Lucida: Reflections on Photography.* Vintage, 2000.

Bataille, Georges. *Theory of Religion.* New York: Zone Books, 1989.

Becker, Ernest. *The Denial of Death.* New York: Free Press, 1973.

Bollas, Christopher. *The Shadow of the Object: Psychoanalysis of the Unthought Known.* Free Association Books, 1991.

Borges, Jorge Luis. "Funes the Memorious." In *Labyrinths,* edited by Donald A. Yates and James E. Irby, 87–95. Harmondsworth, Middlesex, UK: Penguin Books, 1970.

———. *Selected Non-Fictions.* New York: Viking, 1999.

Burke, Kenneth. *Language as Symbolic Action; Essays on Life, Literature, and Method.* Berkeley: University of California Press, 1966.

Callard, Agnes. *Aspiration: The Agency of Becoming.* New York: Oxford University Press, 2018.

Canetti, Elias. *Kafka's Other Trial: The Letters to Felice.* New York: Penguin, 1982.

Clément, Catherine. *Syncope: The Philosophy of Rapture.* Minneapolis: University of Minnesota Press, 1994.

Cover, Robert. *Narrative, Violence, and the Law: The Essays of Robert Cover.* Ann Arbor: University of Michigan Press, 1992.

Dickinson, Emily. *The Poems of Emily Dickinson.* Edited by R. W. Franklin. Cambridge, MA: Belknap Press of Harvard University Press, 1999.

Douglas, Mary. *Purity and Danger: An Analysis of Concepts of Pollution and Taboo.* London: Routledge & Kegan Paul, 1966.

Eigen, Michael. *Flames from the Unconscious: Trauma, Madness, and Faith.* London: Karnac Books, 2009.

Eliot, George. *Daniel Deronda.* New York: Penguin Classics, 1995.

———. *Middlemarch.* New York: Bantam Classics, 1985.

Felman, Shoshana. *Writing and Madness.* Ithaca, NY: Cornell University Press, 1985.

Foucault, Michel. *The Order of Things: An Archaeology of the Human Sciences.* New York: Pantheon Books, 1971.

Freud, Sigmund. *Civilization and Its Discontents.* New York: Penguin Books, 2002.

Frosh, Stephen. *Hauntings: Psychoanalysis and Ghostly Transmissions.* London: Palgrave Macmillan, 2013.

Fuller, Lon. *The Morality of Law.* New Haven, CT: Yale University Press, 1969.

Girard, René. *Oedipus Unbound: Selected Writings on Rivalry and Desire.* Palo Alto, CA: Stanford University Press, 2004.

Gladwell, Malcolm. *Outliers: The Story of Success.* New York: Little, Brown, 2008.

Glatzer, Nahum N. *Franz Rosenzweig: His Life and Work.* New York: Schocken Books, 1953.

Glück, Louise. *Proofs and Theories: Essays on Poetry.* Hopewell, NJ: Ecco Press, 1994.

Greenstein, Edward. "Deconstruction and Biblical Narrative." In *Interpreting Judaism in a Postmodern Age,* edited by Steven Kepnes, 21–54. New York: New York University Press, 1996.

Hardwick, Elizabeth. *Seduction and Betrayal: Women and Literature.* New York: New York Review of Books, 1973.

James, William. *The Varieties of Religious Experience: A Study in Human Nature.* New York: Fontana Library, 1960.

Kristeva, Julia. *Black Sun: Depression and Melancholia.* New York: Columbia University Press, 1989.

Kundera, Milan. *The Book of Laughter and Forgetting.* New York: Penguin Books, 1981.

Lear, Jonathan. *A Case for Irony.* Cambridge, MA: Harvard University Press, 2011.

———. *Happiness, Death, and the Remainder of Life.* Cambridge, MA: Harvard University Press, 2000.

———. Introduction to Hans W. Loewald, *The Essential Loewald: Collected Papers and Monographs.* Hagerstown, MD: University Publishing Group, 2000.

————. *Love and Its Place in Nature: A Philosophical Interpretation of Freudian Psychoanalysis.* New Haven, CT: Yale University Press, 1998.

————. *Open Minded: Working Out the Logic of the Soul.* Cambridge, MA: Harvard University Press, 1998.

Leibowitz, Nehama. *Studies in Vayikra (Leviticus).* Jerusalem: World Zionist Organization, 1980.

Levi, Primo. *The Periodic Table.* New York: Schocken Books, 1984.

Levinas, Emmanuel. *The Levinas Reader.* Edited by Seán Hand. Cambridge, MA: B. Blackwell, 1989.

————. "A Religion for Adults." In *Difficult Freedom: Essays on Judaism,* trans. Seán Hand, XXX–XXX. Baltimore: Johns Hopkins University Press, 1997.

Lichtenstein, Aaron. "Does Jewish Tradition Recognize an Ethic Independent of Halakha?" In *Modern Jewish Ethics,* edited by Marvin Fox, 62–88. Columbus: Ohio State University Press, 1975.

Luban, David. "Natural Law as Professional Ethics: A Reading of Fuller." *Social Philosophy and Policy* 18 (2000): 176–205. In *Georgetown Law Faculty Publications and Other Works.*

Mayer, Elizabeth Lloyd. *Extraordinary Knowing: Science, Skepticism, and the Inexplicable Powers of the Human Mind.* New York: Bantam Books, 2007.

McGilchrist, Iain. *The Master and His Emissary: The Divided Brain and the Making of the Western World.* New Haven, CT: Yale University Press, 2009.

Mevorach, Yishai. *Ha-yehudi shel Ha-katzeh.* In Hebrew. *The Jew of the Edge: Towards Inextricable Theology.* Tel Aviv: Resling, 2018.

Milgrom, Jacob. *Leviticus 17–22: A New Translation with Introduction and Commentary.* New York: Doubleday, 2000.

Paz, Octavio. *Alternating Current.* New York: Viking Press, 1973.

Phillips, Adam. *The Beast in the Nursery.* London: Faber and Faber, 1998.

————. *On Kissing, Tickling, and Being Bored: Psychoanalytic Essays on the Unexamined Life.* Cambridge, MA: Harvard University Press, 1993.

Powers, Richard. *The Overstory: A Novel.* London: William Heinemann, 2018.

Ricoeur, Paul. *History and Truth.* Evanston, IL: Northwestern University Press, 1965.

————. *Interpretation Theory: Discourse and the Surplus of Meaning.* Fort Worth: Texas Christian University Press, 1976.

Rosenzweig, Franz. *The Star of Redemption.* Notre Dame, IN: University of Notre Dame Press, 1985.

Santner, Eric L. *On the Psychotheology of Everyday Life: Reflections on Freud and Rosenzweig.* Chicago: University of Chicago Press, 2001.

Sebald, W. G. *Austerlitz.* Translated by Anthea Bell. New York: Random House, 2001.

Steiner, George. *Real Presences.* Chicago: University of Chicago Press, 1989.

Stern, David. "Midrash and the Language of Exegesis: A Study of Vayikra

Rabba." In *Midrash and Literature,* edited by Geoffrey H. Hartman and Sanford Budick, 122. New Haven, CT: Yale University Press, 1986.

Turner, Victor. "Metaphors of Anti-structure in Religious Culture." In *Dramas, Fields, and Metaphors: Symbolic Action in Human Society,* 272–99. Ithaca, NY: Cornell University Press, 1974.

Winnicott, D. W. "Fear of Breakdown." In *Psycho-Analytic Explorations,* edited by Clare Winnicott, Ray Shepherd, and Madeleine Davis, 92. Cambridge, MA: Harvard University Press, 1989.

———. *Home Is Where We Start From: Essays by a Psychoanalyst.* New York: Norton, 1986.

———. *Human Nature.* London: Free Association Books, 1988.

Zornberg, Avivah Gottlieb. *Genesis: The Beginning of Desire.* Philadelphia: Jewish Publication Society, 1995.

———. *The Murmuring Deep: Reflections on the Biblical Unconscious.* New York: Schocken Books, 2009.

INDEX

A NOTE ON THE TEXT

This book is set in Reminga, a font designed for the type foundry FontFont in 2001 by the award-winning French type designer Xavier Dupré (1977). It is one of the most robust and versatile typefaces available with multiple weights and a complete range of figure sets. The Pro version of Reminga can support multiple language options.

After earning his degree in applied arts, Xavier Dupré moved to Paris to study type design and calligraphy, and this training shows in the elegant calligraphic italics in this font.

Typeset by Scribe, Philadelphia, Pennsylvania

Printed and bound by Berryville Graphics, Berryville, Virginia

Designed by Betty Lew